SUPPORTING EARLY CHILDHOOD PRACTICE THROUGH DIFFICULT TIMES

Supporting Early Childhood Practice Through Difficult Times encourages early childhood students and practitioners to take stock of current practices and pedagogies in light of challenges like the COVID-19 pandemic, ecological concerns, and regulatory pressures.

The contributions from various scholars and practitioners present a range of theoretical concepts as well as innovative practice examples, inviting deep reflection on your own beliefs and attitudes. They examine and envisage different ways of working with and for young children, their families and communities for a better future. Chapters in this timely book include experts from around the globe examining key issues in early childhood education. The first section questions the increasing digitalisation in nurseries and pre-schools and its impact on staff members, parents and children. The second section focuses on workforce development, management systems and the role of parents in policymaking. The third section showcases innovative pedagogical approaches looking beyond widely accepted early learning goals, assessments and curricula to develop inclusive environments that foster all children's development and learning. Lastly, the fourth section steps back from day-to-day practice and considers what concern for the environment, social justice and posthumanism means for early childhood education and pedagogy.

This book will be a key resource for early childhood education and care practitioners, graduate students, policymakers and researchers facilitating the step from the here-and-now to revised future practice and policy that will enable all children to flourish.

Ute Ward is a former Senior Lecturer at the University of Hertfordshire, UK.

Towards an Ethical Praxis in Early Childhood
Written in association with the European Early Childhood Education Research Association (EECERA), titles in this series will reflect the latest developments and most current research and practice in early childhood education on a global level. Feeding into and supporting the further development of the discipline as an exciting and urgent field of research and high academic endeavour, the series carries a particular focus on knowledge and reflection, which has huge relevance and topicality for those at the front line of decision making and professional practice.

Rather than following a linear approach of research to practice, this series offers a unique fusion of research, theoretical, conceptual and philosophical perspectives, values and ethics, and professional practice, which has been termed 'Ethical Praxis'.

Other titles published in association with the European Early Childhood Education Research Association (EECERA):

Science, Technology, Engineering, Arts and Mathematics (STEAM) Education in the Early Years
Achieving the Sustainable Development Goals
Edited by Weipeng Yang, Sarika Kewalramani and Jyoti Senthil

Resilience and Wellbeing in Young Children, their Families and Communities
Exploring Diverse Contexts, Circumstances and Populations
Edited by Zoi Nikiforidou, Babs Anderson and Wilma Robles-Melendez

Supporting Early Childhood Practice Through Difficult Times
Looking Towards a Better Future
Edited by Ute Ward

For more information about this series, please visit: www.routledge.com/education/series/EECERA

SUPPORTING EARLY CHILDHOOD PRACTICE THROUGH DIFFICULT TIMES

Looking Towards a Better Future

Edited by Ute Ward

LONDON AND NEW YORK

Designed cover image: Christopher Ward

First published 2025
by Routledge
4 Park Square, Milton Park, Abingdon, Oxon OX14 4RN

and by Routledge
605 Third Avenue, New York, NY 10158

Routledge is an imprint of the Taylor & Francis Group, an informa business

© 2025 selection and editorial matter, Ute Ward; individual chapters, the contributors

The right of Ute Ward to be identified as the author of the editorial material, and of the authors for their individual chapters, has been asserted in accordance with sections 77 and 78 of the Copyright, Designs and Patents Act 1988.

All rights reserved. No part of this book may be reprinted or reproduced or utilised in any form or by any electronic, mechanical, or other means, now known or hereafter invented, including photocopying and recording, or in any information storage or retrieval system, without permission in writing from the publishers.

Trademark notice: Product or corporate names may be trademarks or registered trademarks, and are used only for identification and explanation without intent to infringe.

British Library Cataloguing-in-Publication Data
A catalogue record for this book is available from the British Library

ISBN: 978-1-032-74841-2 (hbk)
ISBN: 978-1-032-74840-5 (pbk)
ISBN: 978-1-003-47117-2 (ebk)

DOI: 10.4324/9781003471172

Typeset in Galliard
by SPi Technologies India Pvt Ltd (Straive)

CONTENTS

List of Contributors	*ix*
Series Editor Foreword	*xx*

1	Early Childhood Practice in Difficult Times *Ute Ward*	1

PART I
The Impact of Digitalisation   **7**

2	The Mixed Blessing of Digital Tools *Ute Ward*	9
3	'Big sister' is watching: A feminist critical discourse analysis of texts supporting the use of live stream video feed technology *Brooke Richardson and Joanne Lehrer*	13
4	Using the European Framework for the Digital Competence of Educators to develop didactic Tools on AI for Early Childhood Settings *Ulrike Stadler-Altmann*	26

vi Contents

5 Narratives of Crisis: Raising children in digital times 39
Naomi Hodgson and Stefan Ramaekers

PART II
Early Childhood Workforce and Management Issues **51**

6 Enhancing the Development of Practitioners and Settings 53
Ute Ward

7 Professional development of Croation early childhood
teachers in a virtual world – opportunity or obstacle? 57
Adrijana Višnjić-Jevtić and Antonija Vukašinović

8 Impact of neoliberal-inspired policies on educators'
professional identity in five countries: Visions for
a better future 70
*Marg Rogers, Fabio Dovigo, Laura K. Doan, Khatuna
Dolidze and Astrid Mus Rasmussen*

9 Fostering practice-based philosophy in early childhood
educators: Reflections on developing a pedagogic creed 83
Lewis Stockwell and Michael Young

10 The LEYF Model: A sustainable ECEC model that
addresses the disadvantage gap 95
June O'Sullivan

11 Involving families: Lessons from updating Australia's
approved learning framework 108
*Fay Hadley, Linda Harrison, Leanne Lavina,
Lennie Barblett, Susan Irvine, Francis Bobongie-Harris,
and Jennifer Cartmel*

PART III
Alternative Pedagogies and Practices **123**

12 Embracing Diversity and Inclusion 125
Ute Ward

Contents **vii**

13 The quiddity of inclusion: Knowing what matters in early childhood settings 129
Sharon Skehill

14 Promoting inclusivity through embedding art into daily practice 140
Silvia Blanch-Gelabert and Gemma París-Romia

15 Imagination: The missing element of Early Childhood Education? 157
Sue Nimmo

16 Education at the crossfire: A human right-based approach to support children with disabilities in disasters 169
Mabel Giraldo

17 'Children reading to their parents' – From Australia to Israel – Implementation and Challenges 182
Sigal Tish, Sivan Shatil Carmon, and Clodie Tal

PART IV
More than Education and Care: Philosophical Perspectives on Early Childhood Practice **197**

18 The need for different ways of thinking 199
Ute Ward

19 Learning in and from nature: Supporting Children's Development 203
Mehmet Mart

20 A Posthuman Perspective: Learning Entanglements Among a Child, Family Members, and the Material World 216
Sally Brown

21 The Need for Dialogue: bell hooks, Paulo Freire, and the English Early Years Sector 230
Poppie Ephgrave

viii Contents

22 Nurturing the spiritual in children – enacting a spiritual
pedagogy to develop children's sense of self   241
Elizabeth Rouse

23 Towards a better future   253
Ute Ward

Index   *262*

LIST OF CONTRIBUTORS

Lennie Barblett is a Professor at Edith Cowan University, Australia and has research interests in quality early childhood curriculum and practices, play-based pedagogies, leadership, effective environments and children's wellbeing. She has been invited to contribute to the work of numerous state and national committees and working parties focusing on curriculum reform, ethics and teaching standards. She is a co-writer of the ECA Code of Ethics and has recently worked with the team on the updates of the Early Years Learning Framework and the My Time, Our Place framework.

Dra. Sílvia Blanch Gelabert (PhD in Clinical Psychology and MA Educational Psychology) is Associate Professor at the Basic, Developmental and Educational Psychology Department. She has held different faculty roles, like Internship Vicedean and Director of the Early Childhood Degree of the Educational Science Faculty of the Universitat Autònoma de Barcelona (UAB). She is EECERA Country Coordinator and has been Co-convenor of the Special Interest Group Working with Parents and Family. She is Co-director of the ERIFE research team (Childhood, family, and education); member of the SINTE Team, trainer of trainers at the UAB ICE and co-founder of the BES team; training of trainers in early childhood, family counselling; Early Childhood Educational network coordinator and participating in several educational projects, such as Interstice, where she was codirector. Her work and publications are linked to early childhood education and family, also to innovative methodologies such as Portfolio, Cooperative Learning, Service-Learning and more recently Challenge Based Learning.

x List of Contributors

Francis Bobongie-Harris is a Senior Lecturer and Researcher with the School of Early Childhood and Inclusive Education at Queensland University of Technology, Australia. She is Specialist Area Coordinator (Indigenous Education) teaching pre-service teachers' strategies to embed Aboriginal and Torres Strait Islander Perspectives into their teaching and learning programs. Recent projects include updates to the Approved Learning Frameworks (ALFs) and Victorian Education Leadership Program (VELP).

Sally Brown is a Professor of Literacy Education at Georgia Southern University. She earned a Ph.D. in Language and Literacy from the University of South Carolina. Before working at university level, she taught in South Carolina public schools for 13 years. Sally teaches graduate reading classes and is the former co-editor of *Talking Points*, a National Council of Teachers of English journal. Her research focuses on the multiple ways that emergent bilinguals make sense of their world through multiliteracies and translanguaging. Sally is interested in the ways that technology facilitates early literacy practices and posthuman perspectives on young children. Her recent research has been published in the *Journal of Early Childhood Literacy, Reading & Writing Quarterly, Language Arts*, and *The Reading Teacher*.

Jennifer Cartmel is Associate Professor at Griffith University, Queensland, Australia. Her research interests include workforce development, children's social and emotional learning, intergenerational practice and the many facets of outside school hours care service delivery. Jennifer was a Chief Investigator on the team that updated the Australian Approved Learning Frameworks. Jennifer is an executive member for the World Education Research Association Task Force for Global Research on Extended Education.

Laura K. Doan is an Associate Professor in the School of Education at Thompson Rivers University in Kamloops, British Columbia, Canada. Laura is the lead researcher in the Peer Mentoring Program for Early Childhood Educators in British Columbia. This program of support for early childhood educators involves peer mentoring through communities of practice (CoP) and is a partnership with the Early Childhood Educators of BC (ECEBC), the professional association representing early childhood educators. Currently, there are 25 Peer Mentoring CoPs across the province of BC, with close to 200 early childhood educators. The purpose of this program is to support the ongoing professional development needs of beginning and experienced early childhood educators (ECEs).

Khatuna Dolidze (PhD) is associate professor and the program director of the early education BA program at Ilia State University, Georgia. She has initiated an innovative program dedicated to assisting children facing health challenges.

Her work primarily revolves around addressing the diverse needs of vulnerable and marginalized children, particularly in the fields of health and education. She has been involved in the development of university and post-graduate training programs for early educators, as well as supporting their professional development after entering the profession.

Fabio Dovigo (PhD) is a Professor of Education at the SWECW Department at Northumbria University, UK. His research interests are in the area of Early Childhood Education and Care and Inclusive Education. He is the holder of the UNESCO Chair "Supporting Early Years Care and Education" and a member (Networks' Representative) of the European Education Research Association Executive Board. Recently, he authored the *UNESCO Global Thematic Report* on "Early Childhood Care and Education teaching staff and educators: Challenges and Opportunities".

Poppie Ephgrave has worked in the Early Childhood and Education sector for eight years. She holds a BA in Early Childhood Education and achieved her MA in Early Childhood Education in September 2023 from the University of Hertfordshire. She is currently a degree lecturer at the London Institute of Early Years working alongside the University of Wolverhampton. She is passionate about play-based learning and pedagogies that centre around children's wellbeing whilst challenging social injustices. Her research interests include: critical pedagogy, social justice within the early years, and mental health education for children, with a specialism in philosophy.

Mabel Giraldo is PhD and Researcher (Rtd-A) in Didactics and Special Pedagogy at the Department of Human and Social Sciences, University of Bergamo, and co-founding member of the research group IperDEA (Inclusion for Disability Empowerment and Accessibility). Since 2012 she has carried out teaching activities for Bachelor's degree courses in Educational Sciences and Physical & Sports Sciences at the University of Bergamo and at international doctoral courses: the PhD School, Disability: inclusion or marginalization (Norwegian University of Science and Technology (NTNU), Department of Social Work, 2023) and the PhD School, Special Education (Stockholm University, Department of Special Education, 2021). Furthermore, she had some visiting periods abroad, in Norway (NTNU, Trondheim; 2023), Sweden (Stockholm University, 2021), and in the United States (New York University, 2012). Her main research interests concern: theatre and its use within educational contexts, including youth and children with disabilities; the historical, cultural, social and pedagogical debate on disability (at school and in the society) at Italian and international level; the construct of self-determination and related design and evaluation models to promote and support it for persons with disabilities across the life span.

xii List of Contributors

Fay Hadley is a Professor of Early Childhood in the School of Education, Macquarie University, and Deputy Director, Centre for Research in Early Childhood Education (CRECE). Fay's primary areas of research examine leadership in early childhood education and family partnerships. She is especially interested in the socio-political environment and how this affects early childhood teachers' work. Fay was the lead Chief Investigator (CI) on the recent Approved Learning Frameworks (ALFs) Update project and CI on the National Quality Improvement project. Fay is currently a CI on the UNICEF-funded project: Study on the Effectiveness of School Readiness Programme – Timor Leste.

Linda Harrison is a Professorial Research Fellow in Early Childhood Education at Macquarie University, Sydney and Adjunct Professor at Charles Sturt University, Bathurst, NSW. Linda has a long-standing interest in the design and use of innovative research methods to better understand the relationships and conditions that support high-quality practice and promote children's learning, development and well-being in education and care contexts. A key feature of her work has been to form or contribute to collaborative partnerships, including with Commonwealth, State and Local governments, providers of early education and care, and other stakeholders.

Naomi Hodgson is Reader in Education at Edge Hill University, UK, and Visiting Professor at KU Leuven, Belgium. Her research focuses on upbringing, culture, governance, and subjectivity, drawing particularly on Foucault and Cavell. Her publications include *Philosophical Presentations of Raising Children: the grammar of upbringing* (with Prof. Stefan Ramaekers, 2019), *Manifesto for a Post-Critical Pedagogy* (with Profs Joris Vlieghe and Piotr Zamojski, 2018), and *Philosophy and Theory in Educational Research: writing in the margin* (2016). She is currently writing a monograph on power. She is co-convenor of the BERA Philosophy of Education SIG and Assistant Editor of the journal *Ethics & Education*.

Susan Irvine is a Professor and Head of the School of Early Childhood and Inclusive Education at Queensland University of Technology, Australia. She maintains a longstanding interest in ECEC policy, curriculum and quality standards, and has undertaken multiple research projects focusing on the ECEC workforce. Recent projects include: the National Quality Improvement project, the Approved Learning Frameworks (ALFs) Update project and the in-progress ORICL project – Observe, Reflect, Improve Children's Learning.

Leanne Lavina is an Instructor and Research Associate with the School of Education at ECU and Adjunct Research Associate with Macquarie University.

Using arts-informed approaches, Leanne's research explores the relational, policy and place-based influences impacting the quality of learning and teaching in early childhood environments. Recent Team projects include updates to the Approved Learning Frameworks (ALFS) and the Goodstart Digital Technology Use Project.

Joanne Lehrer is Associate Professor in the Department of Education at *Université du Québec en Outaouais* in Gatineau, Quebec, Canada. She studies educational contexts for preschool-aged children, transitions in early childhood, relationships with families, and child perspectives on their educational contexts. She is particularly interested in the intersection between people's experiences and perspectives and societal discourses or metanarratives that shape those experiences and perspectives. She has experience as a kindergarten teacher and early childhood pedagogical consultant and is a member of the research team, *Qualité des contextes éducatifs de la petite enfance* (quality of early childhood educational contexts).

Mehmet Mart is an Assistant Professor in Ahmet Kelesoglu Faculty of Education, Department of Preschool Teachers' Training at Necmettin Erbakan University. Mehmet gained his MA degree at the University of Reading, and his PhD degree at the University of Plymouth with a scholarship from his government to get qualifications abroad. His research focus for his dissertation and thesis were outdoor activities. After the completion of his degrees, he started working in Türkiye, but is still collaborating with colleagues from different countries. Between 2021 and 2022, he worked as a post-doctoral researcher at the University of Plymouth with funding from his government to research 'maths in outdoor activities'. Mehmet is an editorial board member of Journal of Childhood, Education and Society, and is a co-convenor of EECERA Outdoor Play and Learning SIG. As a part of the SIG activity, he run a special issue in Journal of Childhood Education and Society with the theme: 'Children's experiences outdoors: Education and community contexts'. He still works on some international book projects on outdoors. His research interests include outdoor activities, professional development, and math in early years. He has publications on outdoor activities, maths in early years, comparative research, etc.

Sue Nimmo is Senior Lecturer at the University of Hertfordshire teaching on the MA in Education and the BA (Hons.) Early Childhood Education. She came into higher education after working for over thirty years in early years settings in Oxford, Newcastle, Bedfordshire and Hertfordshire. She is an advocate for educationalists to see children as unique and individual; she firmly believes in the right for children to have a voice and champions the need for children to play. Her areas of interest are the promotion of imagination in early years, as well as developing the understanding of how to scaffold mathematics, literacy and emotional intelligence in children's development. She is currently studying at Oxford Brookes University for a Doctor of Education. She is a thesis stage student and is researching the importance of imagination in all areas of young children's development. This is through a narrative enquiry into exploring early years educators' perceptions of children's imaginative thinking in everyday practice.

June O'Sullivan is the CEO and creator of the UK's leading childcare social enterprise and continues to break new ground in the development of LEYF's scalable social business model. She is a tireless campaigner, looking for new ways to influence policy and make society a better place for all children and families. June developed the LEYF Pedagogy for Social Justice and champions community-based, multi-generational early years education as the basis for greater social and cultural capital to deliver long-term social impact. She advises Governments as well as a range of organisations, academics and services at home and overseas about how best to implement a social enterprise vision for Early Years. June is a fellow of the Royal Society of Arts, Trustee of The Book Trust, and her local library, Upper Norwood Library Trust. She is currently a member of the London Mayor's Advisory Group on Child Healthy Weight and the Mayor's Skills Partnership Board. June was awarded an MBE in the Queen's Birthday Honours in 2013 for her services to London's children, and on 29 September 2023, she received an OBE by His Majesty the King for her services to Education.

Dra. Gemma París Romia (PhD in Painting at the University of Barcelona) is an artist and an Associate Professor at the Educational Science Faculty of the Universitat Autònoma de Barcelona (UAB), Barcelona. She has developed artistic projects that have been exhibited in galleries, artistic centres and museums around the world (Barcelona, Madrid, París, Milano, Argentina, among others). She has developed innovative and research projects such as espai c. Artist residencies in primary schools (ICUB, Barcelona Education Consortium and UAB). She has also led the European project Interstice which promotes encounters between artists, children, and educators (Erasmus+). She coordinates the artistic residency project at the Santa Mònica Arts Centre, Barcelona and is member of the Center for Research and Studies for Organizational Development (CRiEDO-UAB). Her work and publications are linked to Arts and Education; Artistic based Research; Artists on residence; Art thinking; Cooperative Learning.

Stefan Ramaekers is professor at the Laboratory for Education and Society (Faculty Psychology and Educational Sciences, KU Leuven, Belgium). His research is situated in the field of educational philosophy, at the intersection of the Anglo-Saxon and Continental philosophical traditions, and finds inspiration in the work of (among others) Friedrich Nietzsche, Ludwig Wittgenstein, Stanley Cavell, and Franco Berardi. Taking issue with (neuro) psychological and sociological accounts of parenting, his research critically investigates today's discourse of parenting/upbringing and aims at developing a contemporary pedagogical theory of upbringing, one that offers a richer understanding of the experience of being a parent. He has written about the instrumentalization, scientization, and (neuro)psychologization of upbringing; the pedagogical meaning of initiation; the pedagogical role of parents; and the meaning of digital technologies (such as parenting apps) in raising children. He published two books on these matters, *The Claims of Parenting. Reasons, responsibility, and society* (Springer, 2012), together with Judith Suissa of the Institute of Education (University College London, UK), and *Philosophical presentations of raising children: The grammar of upbringing* (Palgrave, 2019), together with Naomi Hodgson (Edge Hill University, UK). He has also written about the pedagogical stakes of film, multicultural education, postmodernism and scepticism, and the nature of educational research.

Astrid Mus Rasmussen (PhD) is a postdoctoral research fellow and lecturer within the School of Communication and Culture, Department of German and Romance Languages at Aarhus University, Denmark. She researches in various areas, including education, pedagogy and differentiated instruction.

Brooke Richardson, PhD, is an Assistant Professor in Child and Youth Studies at Mount Saint Vincent University (Halifax, Canada). She has published and presented nationally and internationally embracing a feminist care ethics lens in relation to child care and child protection policy and activism. She has recently published two edited volumes: *Feminisms and the Early Childhood Educator: Critical Conversations* (Bloomsbury) and *Mothering on the Edge: A Critical Examination of Mothering within Child Protection Systems* (Demeter Press) and is working on a third: *Disrupting Developmentalism in Canadian Early Years Teacher Education for Social Justice: Bringing Marginalized Knowledge to the Centre* (Canadian Scholars Press).

Dr Marg Rogers is a senior lecturer of early childhood education at the University of New England. Marg researches marginalised voices within families and education especially in regional, rural and remote communities. Specifically, she researches ways to support the wellbeing of military, first responder and remote worker families and early childhood educators. She is part of the Educator Peer Support Program project to support educator's work and wellbeing in Queensland 'childcare desert' areas by piloting the British Columbian model. Marg is a Postdoctoral Fellow with the Commonwealth Government funded Manna Institute.

xvi List of Contributors

Elizabeth Rouse has a long career in early years education, as a teacher, an academic and a researcher. She is currently an Associate Professor in Education (Early Childhood) at Deakin University, Australia, working in Initial Teacher Education. Her teaching focus in on curriculum, assessment and pedagogy in the early years, framing this through the lens of children's wellbeing, holistic teaching and relational pedagogy. Her research work has been in the area of educator professional practice, especially in relation to play pedagogies, children's spirituality and wellbeing, infants and toddlers, and partnerships. She has published a number of books and journal articles in these areas.

Dr Sharon Skehill is an Early Years Educator and Researcher at her outdoor service in Galway, Ireland, working with babies, toddlers and young children. She holds a PhD in Education and has worked for several years as a Lecturer in Early Childhood Studies. Sharon also works with the National Council for Curriculum and Assessment (NCCA) in Ireland as an Education Officer working on the updating of *Aistear, the early childhood curriculum framework*. Sharon has extensive experience developing curriculum content for undergraduate Early Childhood and Primary Education programmes, as well as postgraduate MA Educational programmes at university level. She has published work relating to early childhood education, sustainability, leadership, inclusion, outdoor learning and nature-pedagogy.

Sivan Shatil Carmon is a lecturer, pedagogical-mentor and researcher in the Early Childhood Education program at the Levinsky Wingate Academic Center in Tel-Aviv. Sivan Shatil Carmon has a Ph.D. from Bar Ilan University in Tel-Aviv awarded for research on Developmental dyslexia: 'Automation in skill learning: practice in regular reading and mirror reading among readers with developmental dyslexia compared to skilled readers'. She also holds an M.A. degree in Early Childhood educational consultation from Tel Aviv University. Her main areas of interest and research are: Early childhood education, literacy development in early childhood, reading and writing acquisition, reading disabilities, Integration and inclusion in early childhood education, multicultural education, emergent curriculum, and more. In the last 6 years Sivan Shatil Carmon has led and developed the implementation of the program 'Children reading to their parents' in the Israeli education system. The program promotes the reading quality of children in their first year of schooling, their sense of competence and motivation to read, and parents' involvement in their children's learning.

Ulrike Stadler-Altmann, Prof Dr, is an educational scientist and Head of the Chair of School Education at Humboldt University in Berlin. Prior to this, she worked for eight years as a full professor of general didactics at the Free University of Bozen-Bolzano in Italy. There she reconceptualised and scientifically managed the EduSpace Lernwerkstatt (learning workshop) at the Faculty of Education on the Brixen-Bressanone campus. Her research focuses on school and teaching development, teacher professionalism, knowledge transfer processes, pupil self-concept and gender in educational science, as can be seen from her publications (https://hu-berlin.academia.edu/UlrikeStadlerAltmann or https://www.researchgate.net/profile/Ulrike_Stadler-Altmann). She is a proven expert in the pedagogical design of analogue and digital teaching and learning spaces. In particular, she is interested in social practices in space, the empirical recording of teaching-learning actions and participatory design processes, such as in the CoReD project. (www.ncl.ac.uk/cored/). The culture of digitality and digital media are playing an increasingly important role in her research activities and Ulrike Stadler-Altmann, as chairwoman of the NeHle network (https://lernwerkstatt.info/international-network-hochschullernwerkst-nehle-ev), is responsible for the design of digital learning workshops.

Lewis Stockwell MSc, PgCert, BA(Hons), SFHEA is principal lecturer in philosophy of education and outdoor environmental education at the University of Hertfordshire in the UK where he leads postgraduate taught education programmes. His teaching and research areas are broad and topic based. He often explores philosophical concepts and ethical problems in the lived practice of educators. In recent years Lewis has worked with a range of early years practitioners to explore philosophy of education in the early years settings, which has culminated in undergraduate and postgraduate teaching focussing on pedagogic creeds, social justice and social change in education, and outdoor learning for socio-ecological justice. More recently Lewis has been published in areas on student-staff partnership in higher education, and aesthetic interpretations of professionalism in outdoor learning. Lewis is currently undertaking his PhD at Moray House School of Education and Sport, University of Edinburgh. There he is developing a philosophy of Education thesis on aesthetic education canoe journeying.

Clodie Tal is a developmental psychologist who has been involved throughout her professional life in Early Childhood Education (ECE). The preparation and in-service 'training' of caregivers and teachers working with young children are perceived as an ongoing preventive intervention; as means of improving the conditions of life of young children coming from diverse backgrounds and for improving the odds for those coming from unprivileged backgrounds to build meaningful lives. Clodie Tal has a PhD in Psychology from Bar-Ilan University, Israel and a Master's degree in Clinical Psychology from California State University, Fullerton. She served as the Head of the Master's degree in Early Childhood Education at Levinsky College of Teachers' Education, Tel Aviv, Israel. Before that she headed the Bachelor's degree in early childhood education and care at Levinsky College of Education and has been involved in extensive in-service training in communities throughout Israel. She is currently teaching in the ECE preparation program at Hemdat Academy and at the Levinsky-Wingate Academic centre in the ECE graduate program. Her main areas of interest which are also the focus of her research are teacher–child, teacher–parent relationships, teachers' values, promoting children's social competence and coping with behaviour problems, classroom management and teacher–children dialogic discourse in general and as focused on children picture-books in particular.

Sigal Tish is a researcher, lecturer and pedagogical-mentor in the Early Childhood Education program at the Levinsky Wingate Academic Center in Tel-Aviv. Sigal Tish has a Ph.D. from the University of South Australia awarded for international comparative research focused on the roles of parents in the literacy development of young children beginning school in South Australia and Israel. She also holds M.Ed. degree in literacy and language education from the University of South Australia. Her main areas of interest, teaching and research include Early childhood education, literacy development in early childhood, parent–teacher relationships, multicultural education, emergent curriculum, and outdoor learning. In the last 6 years Sigal Tish has initiated and led the translation, development and implementation of the program 'Children reading to their parents' in the Israeli education system. The program promotes the reading quality of children in their first year of schooling, their sense of competence and motivation to read, and parents' involvement in their children's learning.

Adrijana Višnjić-Jevtić, PhD, is an associate professor at the University of Zagreb. Areas of scientific interest include early childhood education, teachers' professional development, and collaboration with families. She authored over 70 scientific and professional publications and participates in numerous (inter) national conferences. She participates in national and international scientific projects as a member of the research team and supervisory board. In renowned international ECEC journals she serves as a reviewer and member of editorial boards. She is a member of the organizational and scientific committees of international conferences in Croatia and worldwide. She is visiting professor at North University (Croatia) and Maria Grzegorzewska University (Poland). Adrijana is the founder of a teachers' professional association 'Krijesnice', and the Croatian National Committee of the World Organization for Early Childhood Education (OMEP). She is a member of OMEP and EECERA. Currently, she is the vice-president of the OMEP in charge of the European region.

Antonija Vukašinović is a PhD Candidate of Post Graduate Study of Pedagogic and Contemporary School, Faculty of Humanities and Social Sciences in

Osijek. She is also an ECEC teacher. During her pedagogical work, she systematically worked on partnership relations with parents, and this is both her narrower area of interest and the topic of her doctoral dissertation. She has written several scientific papers in the field of ECEC, participated in the organising committees of scientific professional conferences, and reviewed papers for scientific conferences in Croatia and abroad. She is a member of the editorial board of the proceedings of the international scientific conference Global Competences for the 21st Century and participated in numerous domestic and foreign scientific conferences in the field of education. She is the founder of the association of educators, Loris, and was the president of the association for a period of three years. She is a member of OMEP and EECERA.

Ute Ward has been involved in the English early childhood sector for more than 25 years in a range of different roles and contexts. She started as a parent, volunteer and staff member in her local pre-school. Recognising the vital role parents play in a child's life she moved to working more directly with adults and later became children's centre manager. Through the National Professional Qualification in Integrated Centre Leadership and her Masters in Education she developed a strong interest in supporting the practitioners who work with children and their families. In October 2011 Ute became Senior Lecturer in Early Years at the University of Hertfordshire, UK, where she taught for 11 years on undergraduate and postgraduate programmes supporting the development of pre-service and in-service practitioners. In 2020 her doctoral thesis explored parents' perceptions and expectations in their interactions with their children's educators.

Michael Young (MEd, PG Cert Academic Practice (PCAP), PGCE Primary with QTS, BA (Hons.) English, FHEA) is a Senior Lecturer and Module Leader on both the BA (Hons.) Early Childhood Education and MA Education degree programmes at the University of Hertfordshire in the UK. Having initially taught in early years and primary school settings throughout North London, Hertfordshire and Essex, Michael moved onto learning support and curriculum management in Further Education alongside working for a children's charity and running his own private tuition business. He has taught and contributed to programme development at a number of Higher Education institutions (principally The Open University) since 2007. Michael's research interests have included evaluating the accessibility of written assignment feedback provided to multi-cultural undergraduates and developing the use of technology-enhanced learning with mature university students. He remains a staunch advocate of raising the profile of men in the early years workforce and is currently undertaking his doctorate (EdD) focusing on the impact of male practitioners on young children's personal, social and emotional development.

SERIES EDITOR FOREWORD

Tony Bertram and Chris Pascal

Reflections on the focus

Many of us are living through a series of global crises which include increasing war and conflict around the globe, dramatic environmental changes, pandemics, rising poverty, diminishing health and mental wellbeing, mass population movements through war and climate breakdown, changing and increasingly diverse family structures, the creation of digital childhoods and the growth of AI, increasing surveillance and privacy intrusion and the dominance of metrics and big data. Regrettably but importantly, we are now realizing sharply the negative impact of these global crises on children and childhoods. These changes have shifted the nature of childhood and family life and the evidence is that they have impacted more heavily on the young than any other section of society. Reflecting on the current state of children's early lives and the conditions and experiences which now shape it causes us to deeply reflect on our priorities for early childhood education and care (ECEC).

This scholarly and reflective book entitled *'Supporting Early Childhood Practice through Difficult Times: Looking Towards a Better Future'* edited by Ute Ward provides the thirteenth book in the EECERA Ethical Praxis book series and offers a timely and very important agenda for our re-thinking. Its focus on how ECEC addresses *'the unprecedented challenges…ranging from global warming and climate change to war, financial uncertainty, inflation and energy poverty'*. As this book points out, ECEC has been at the forefront in supporting children and families as these issues impact but this is often overlooked in the discourse. This book aims to address this gap and provide a reflective space for those with an interest in ECEC to consider future possibilities and actions. We agree with the urgency of this focus for informing our thinking about policy and practice, with contributions from theory, recent research and innovative practice. The book also aims to address issues of social justice, equality and inclusion within this agenda and this is especially welcome and in tune with EECERA's mission.

The editor writes optimistically '*I firmly believe that even small changes can make a difference and in the long-run build considerable change.... This is the spirit which drives this book, and two questions are at its core: What is the current state in which we find early childhood education and care?, and What can we learn from recent events, crises and developments to work towards a better future and to be prepared for further challenges when they come?*' These are two vital questions for our time and this collection of research informed chapters on a diverse range of contemporary topics from an internationally diverse group of scholars and locations addresses them directly. The solution focused approach in the book is heartening, with the authors '*raising many issues that need addressing but also identifying positive initiatives and actions that are already part of practice in some countries and could provide solutions for others further afield*'. Collectively, the contributions of each chapter provide an excellent fusion of theory, research and practice which lives out the intent of the EECERA Praxis Series and should stimulate critical and deep reflections and actions to transform and improve current ECEC policy and practice as we move forward to an uncertain future.

Underpinning aspirations

The EECERA Book Series entitled '*Towards an Ethical Praxis in Early Childhood*' offers an innovative and exemplary vehicle for the international early childhood sector to develop transformative pedagogy which demonstrates effective integrated praxis. The EECERA Book Series is designed to complement and link with the European Early Childhood Education Research Journal (EECERJ), which is primarily a worldwide academic platform for publishing research according to the highest international standards of scholarship. The EECERA **Ethical Praxis** Book Series aims to highlight pedagogic praxis in order to demonstrate how this knowledge can be used to develop and improve the quality of early education and care services to young children and their families.

Pedagogic approach

The approach taken in the book series is not a linear one, but rather a praxeological one focused on praxis, meaning a focus on pedagogic action impregnated in theory and supported by a belief system. It is this fusion of practice, theoretical perspectives, ethics and research which we term '**Ethical Praxis**'. This fusion is embodied in all EECERA research and development activity, but we anticipate the book series will have a stronger focus on the development of pedagogic praxis and policy. In addition to offering a forum for plural, integrated pedagogic praxis, the series will offer a strong model of praxeological processes that will secure deep improvements in the educational experience of children and families, of professionals and researchers across international early childhood services.

The book series acknowledges pedagogy as a branch of professional/practical knowledge which is constructed in situated action in dialogue with theories and research and with beliefs (values) and principles. Pedagogy is seen as an 'ambiguous' space, not of one-between-two (theory and practice) but as one-between-three (actions, theories and beliefs) in an interactive, constantly renewed triangulation. Convening beliefs, values and principles, analysing practises and dialoguing with several branches of knowledge (philosophy, history, anthropology, psychology, sociology amongst others) constitutes the triangular movement of the creation of pedagogy. Pedagogy is thus based on praxis, in other words, action based on theory and sustained by belief systems. Contrary to other branches of knowledge which are identified by the definition of areas with well-defined frontiers, the pedagogical branch of knowledge is created in the ambiguity of a space which is aware of the frontiers but does not delimit them because its essence is in integration.

Praxeological intentions

There is a growing body of practitioner and practice focused research which is reflected in the push at national and international levels to integrate research and analysis skills into the professional skill set of all early childhood practitioners. This is a reflection of the growing professionalism of the early childhood sector and its increased status internationally. The development of higher-order professional standards and increased accountability are reflective of these international trends as the status and importance of early education in the success of educational systems is acknowledged.

Each book in the series is designed to have the following praxeological features:

- strongly and transparently positioned in the socio-cultural context of the authors
- practice or policy in dialogue with research, ethics and with conceptual/theoretical perspectives
- topical and timely, focusing on key issues and new knowledge
- provocative, ground breaking, innovative
- critical, dialogic, reflexive
- euro-centric, giving voice to Europe's traditions and innovations but open to global contributions

- open, polyphonic, prismatic
- plural, multi-disciplinary, multi-method
- praxeological, with a concern for power, values and ethics, praxis and a focus on action research, the learning community and reflexive practitioners
- views early childhood pedagogy as a field in itself, not as applied psychology
- concerned with social justice, equity, diversity and transformation
- concerned with professionalism and quality improvement
- working for a social science of the social
- NOT designed as a textbook for practice but as a text for professional and practice/policy development

This thirteenth book in the series exemplifies these underpinning philosophies, pedagogical ethics and scholarly intentions beautifully. We believe it is topical and timely, focusing on key issues and new knowledge, and also provocative and critical, encouraging and opening polyphonic dialogue about our thinking and actions in developing high-quality early childhood services internationally.

1

EARLY CHILDHOOD PRACTICE IN DIFFICULT TIMES

Ute Ward

In 2022 I attended the first face-to-face conference of the European Early Childhood Research Association in Glasgow after two difficult years of COVID-19, lockdowns and online meetings. It was a delight to talk to and be with others who feel equally passionate about early childhood education and care (ECEC). What struck me during the conference was the immense hope and optimism delegates brought to the symposia, discussions and keynote speeches in spite of the difficult times we find ourselves in. In particular, Michel Vandenbroeck's comments towards the end of his symposium have stayed with me: He agreed that the context in which we find early childhood practice is not an easy one. Nonetheless, he was looking forward – the time may not be right for big changes now but the right time will come, and we need to be ready for it. In addition, I firmly believe that even small changes can make a difference and in the long run build considerable change, for example, when we offer children more outdoor play or when we shift our language to be more inclusive. This is the spirit which drives this book, and two questions are at its core: What is the current state in which we find early childhood education and care, and what can we learn from recent events, crises and developments to work towards a better future and to be prepared for further challenges when they come?

To understand fully the context ECEC finds itself in, we need to look beyond the boundaries of individual pre-schools, kindergartens and nurseries and consider wider economic, societal and political issues. Globally education and society in general have been facing unprecedented challenges over the last few years ranging from global warming and climate change to war, financial uncertainty, inflation and energy poverty, to name but a few of the issues.

DOI: 10.4324/9781003471172-1

Some of these are not new, but many were unexpected and took everybody by surprise, like the spread of COVID-19 and the ensuing lockdowns. The ECEC sector is not immune to these challenges; in fact, it often appears to be at the forefront of dealing with crises and supporting children and their families through difficult times. The COVID-19 pandemic led to wide-ranging closures of nurseries and schools, which meant early childhood educators had to become experts at supporting children and parents in their own homes and communicating with them predominantly through digital tools. When nurseries reopened, working practices had to be adapted drastically to meet new hygiene rules and to ensure the safety of both children and educators. Since the health threat eased, the consequences for children's development, learning and well-being have become more apparent (Watts and Pattnaik, 2022).

Shortly after the pandemic eased its grip, armed conflict in Ukraine led to increased numbers of refugees in neighbouring countries. At the same time old and new conflicts flare up, for example, in Sudan and Gaza, bringing misery to many and heightening the fears that unrest may spread well beyond the immediate conflict zones and swell the number of families embarking on perilous and at times deadly journeys seeking a better future for themselves and their children (UNICEF, 2023). The ongoing turmoil has increased the price of oil at a time when many countries were still trying to overcome the economic costs of lockdowns and heightened demand for health services. The ensuing price rises and inflation mean that child poverty is increasing in many countries (for example, Child Poverty Action Group, 2023).

These current challenges play out against a backdrop of concerns for the environment and a growing awareness that persisting with anthropocentric practices will endanger the future of the following generations (Chomsky, 2021). Consequently, there is much fear about growing digitalisation and the increasing use of artificial intelligence (AI). Some proponents of AI go as far as predicting that it will replace all jobs, which raises concerns for employees worldwide (BBC, 2023). Some robotic technology is already trialled in the care of the elderly (Savage, 2022) but ethical and well-being issues are yet to be discussed in detail.

In light of these multiple challenges, we need to step back and reflect on recent events, take stock of the current situation, re-negotiate values and purposes of our work and plan for a better future for children, families and EC settings. To help you with these reflections and the re-thinking needed at this point, you will find a broad range of topics addressed in this book. The chapters are grouped into four sections, each prefaced by a brief introduction to the issues and topics covered. The opening section explores how the increasing digitalisation is impacting practitioners, parents and children. The next section looks in more detail at workforce and management issues with some examples of staff development, value-based higher education programmes and different approaches to leadership and management. This is followed by a

Early Childhood Practice   **3**

section which focuses on some aspects of pedagogy, in particular in relation to inclusive practice. The last section steps back from day-to-day practice and introduces a consideration of practice through a philosophical lens. The final chapter offers a summary of the insights, and the suggestions from the different contributions will serve as the basis for a discussion of the changes required to overcome current crises and build a better future.

The authors of the individual chapters are based in a number of different countries offering insights into ECEC contexts in, for example, Australia, Canada, Ireland and Croatia. Many of the authors are academics at universities across the globe, ranging from the University of Hertfordshire in the UK to Georgia Southern in the USA and Deakin University in Australia. You will therefore find many chapters which present recent research. This will enable you to gain insights into new knowledge as well as into research methods and approaches in the field of ECEC. Other authors present reflections on their professional and practice-based experience of many years in a range of different roles. The common thread through all the chapters is the authors' commitment to ECEC and their firm belief that we can – and must – make a difference in children's lives.

In addition to the authors' shared commitment and belief, four themes are repeatedly evident across the different chapters. The first one represents the overall tenant of this book: How can we overcome crises and prepare for future challenges? Included here are health and economic crises as well as war, conflict and increasing numbers of refugees. The latter in particular is a growing problem worldwide. UNICEF (2023) estimated that in 2022 there were about 17.5 million child refugees and asylum seekers and 25.8 million children displaced within their own countries. Authors explore the potential impacts of varying crises on children, families and staff members and try to envisage effective services which do not impede but foster children's well-being and help individuals and societies to recover after challenging or traumatic events. The reflective questions for you to ask should explore your own context on a personal, professional, regional and national level and should consider the ensuing priorities and possibilities for you to contribute to change.

The second recurring theme focuses on the inclusion of all children and families to increase social justice. Research confirms that in more unequal societies poor and disadvantaged children learn less well, are less happy and attain less well-being in their lives (UNICEF, 2018; Wilkinson and Pickett, 2010). Equity and equal access to a wide range of resources for all children and families are therefore crucial. This is firstly a topic of particular interest in the third section of this book where authors examine how changes to pedagogical approaches could broaden access to learning and ensure more children have a voice. This could greatly enhance children's sense of belonging helping them overcome disadvantage and trauma (Einarsdottir, 2023). Social justice is also a key consideration in Chapter 10 introducing a social enterprise model for

ECEC and Chapter 11 showcasing parental participation in policy-making. The questions accompanying your reading, beyond ascertaining similarities and differences to your own context, should focus on your personal attitudes and professional actions – up to which extent do you already promote social justice and inclusion, and how could you improve your practice further so that it offers truly equitable services for all children?

In all sections of the book, you will find an engagement with neoliberalism, the pervading approach to local, national and international policy-making and economic management. Peter Moss has urged ECEC practitioners for many years to resist neoliberal pressures and plan for more ethical and just services (Moss, 2010). As he is hopeful that we are nearing the end of neoliberal dominance (Moss, 2023), it is timely to consider the current influence of neoliberalism and new managerialism, for example, on educators' identity (Chapter 8), to discuss how we can work towards changes and improvements for the children and families we work with. You may want to reflect on how you and ECEC services should respond to or resist neoliberal performativity and accountability demands. What is your scope to enhance supportive ethical ECEC practice beyond narrow outcomes, constant assessment and persistent top-down pressures?

The fourth theme, which is vital at this particular point in human development, arises from the devastating effect that much of our activities have on the natural world and non-human beings. Chomsky (2021) is just one of many voices warning that we are heading for the abyss if we do not reverse some of the damage we have done and fundamentally change the way we define our own position in this world. Posthumanist thinking offers some ways forward demonstrating how a different conceptualisation of human beings, greater attention to non-humans and a re-assessment of the values underpinning our world views can help us resist and at least partially reverse current trends, which could ensure a stronger and healthier planet for our children. In addition to reflecting on ECEC practice and national policy, two questions need consideration: What can you do in your private and professional sphere to contribute to environmentally sustainable practices? And how can you work with children to help them become aware of our responsibility towards non-human beings and the planet as a whole?

The four section introductions in this book proffer an overview of the chapters in the section as well as a brief discussion of the key problems or issues in the specific topic area. Additionally, they contain an indication as to which chapters address the different themes. The final chapter presents some answers to the questions raised above, provides a summary of the range of suggestions the contributors have made for improvements in practice and helps you envisage and prepare for changes to local practice and national policy.

References

BBC (2023). *'There will come a point when no job is needed' says Elon Musk.* Retrieved from: https://www.bbc.co.uk/news/av/technology-67304427

Child Poverty Action Group (2023). *Families will be substantially worse off than 5 years ago if benefits rise below inflation.* Retrieved from: https://orcid.org/0000-0003-0264-390X

Chomsky, N (2021). *The Precipice.* Great Britain: Penguin Books.

Einarsdottir, J (2023). Children's belonging in early childhood practice. *Keynote speech:* European Early Childhood Research Association Conference. Cascais, Portugal, 2nd November 2023.

Moss, P (2010). We cannot continue as we are: The educator in an education for survival. *Contemporary Issues in Early Childhood, 11*(1), 8–19. https://doi.org/10.2304/ciec.2010.11.1.8

Moss, P (2023). Introduction: From the politically impossible to the politically inevitable. In M Vandenbroeck, J Lehrer, & L Mitchell (eds) *The Decommodification of Early Childhood Education and Care: Resisting Neoliberalism,* pp. 1–14.

Savage, N (2022). *Robots rise to meet the challenge of caring for old people.* Retrieved from: https://www.nature.com/articles/d41586-022-00072-z

UNICEF (2018). *An unfair start: Inequality in children's education in rich countries.* Retrieved from: https://www.unicef.org.uk/wp-content/uploads/2018/10/UN0245008.pdf20European%20Union%20(EU)

UNICEF (2023). *Child displacement.* Retrieved from: Child Displacement and Refugees - UNICEF DATA

Watts, R & Pattnaik, J (2022). Perspectives of parents and teachers on the impact of the COVID-19 pandemic on children's socio-emotional well-being. *Early Childhood Education Journal, 51,* 1541–1552.

Wilkinson, R & Pickett, K (2010). *The Spirit Level: Why Equality is Better for Everyone.* Penguin.

PART I

The Impact of Digitalisation

2

THE MIXED BLESSING OF DIGITAL TOOLS

Ute Ward

This brief chapter will introduce you to some of the issues addressed in this section of the book and the topics that are examined in the three following chapters. The focus here is the increasing digitalisation we are confronted with in many areas of our lives. The use of websites, social media, apps and other digital tools is widespread now across the globe and had already become a permanent feature of ECEC services before the COVID-19 pandemic started early in 2020 (Stratigos & Fenech, 2021). Two different types of digitalisation can be distinguished: the digitalisation of the communication between educators and parents, and the digitalisation of education itself, which became prevalent during lockdowns and restricted access to nurseries and schools. Using emails, WhatsApp groups or Facebook pages to stay in touch with parents has been a core part of the practitioner role. However, these are not always effective avenues to engage parents in their children's learning and to involve parents in the nursery community. Erdreich (2021) points out that practitioners and teachers often shape digital communication with parents and, therefore, are able to control and restrict the interactions. The inherent power imbalance can reduce parents to passive recipients of information rather than as active participants in a dialogue between setting and home.

During lockdown, the digitalisation of education and, in our particular field of interest, online learning for the youngest children was not very successful (Levickis et al., 2022). Much depended on parents' scope to get involved in their children's activities, and digitalisation does not allow for a strong play-based approach to learning. More broadly, there are conflicting views about the use of digital media: On the one hand, we have all experienced how helpful and beneficial online education and communication were during the pandemic; on

DOI: 10.4324/9781003471172-3

the other hand, there are concerns about the amount of children's screen time and their safety online. Research findings detailing that screen time does not harm children's brains are reported in the media alongside articles trying to advise parents on how to reduce the time their children spend gaming online (Lay, 2023; Maxted, 2023). This leaves many parents and practitioners uncertain about the best approach to take. In addition, a much wider issue looms regarding the use of Artificial Intelligence (AI). Elon Musk recently suggested that in the not-too-distant future, AI would eradicate the need for work (BBC, 2023). Although this may be a tempting idea in the areas of manufacturing, what would this mean regarding caring professions or education? Tronto (2013) reminds us that caring is not a simple or simplistic activity. She distinguishes between caring about, for and with – these describe more than the act of physical care and focus on interrelational and interpersonal connections between people. This deep human connectedness is not something that AI could substitute. Does this mean AI is not a good idea? Bergheim and Wehrheim (2021) suggest that it is not the digital tools themselves that constitute the problem, but it is the use we decide to make of them that can turn them into beneficial devices or a problematic issue and safety concern.

Some of the complex issues arising from increasing digitalisation are addressed in the three chapters in this section. Chapter 3, entitled 'Big Sister is Watching', explores the use of life-streaming in Canadian nursery settings. This is still a fairly new practice but one that receives more and more attention – and one which is heavily marketed by the companies offering the relevant hardware and software tools needed. The concept of remote parenting is not new (Vuorinen, 2018) but cameras in the nursery or pre-school room seem to drive this to a new level, enabling parents to check on their children every minute of the day. This raises issues around the commodification of ECEC and the positioning of children as objects to be observed and checked up on any time a parent wishes, and, of course, parents will be able to see all children in the nursery room, not just their own. This surveillance appears to reinforce the neoliberal demand for accountability while also undermining children's and practitioners' rights as they are not asked for their consent to be observed throughout the day. Brooke Richardson and Joanne Lehrer use feminist critical discourse analysis to gain a deeper insight into the assumptions and underlying beliefs which companies use to shape this particular aspect of digitalisation and to market it to nursery managers under the guise of enhancing quality.

The next chapter turns our attention to practitioners and educators. Based on a substantial research project involving several countries in the European Union, Ulrike Stadler-Altmann follows up on the lack of IT skills that many teachers and nursery staff struggled with when their work changed from classroom to virtual environment (for example, Aizenberg & Zilka, 2022). She introduces us to the European Framework for the Digital Competence of Educators (DigComEdu), a tool that could help practitioners, managers and policymakers to structure the enhancement of digital skills. This could act as a cornerstone in greater preparedness for the next pandemic, which is bound to come. However, her chapter goes beyond introducing a set of competencies and also tackles the practicalities of introducing AI to young children. In light of the mixed feelings and views on AI, this may appear questionable but for the children growing up now, AI will form part of their daily lives. It therefore seems crucial to introduce children not simply to the technology but also to the moral and ethical dilemmas arising from AI. The tool kit introduced in this chapter offers themed boxes like 'How can we recognise a robot?' and 'Can a robot be my friend?', enabling practitioners to extend children's as well as their own knowledge regarding AI.

The final chapter in this section turns to parents and the challenges arising for them through increased digitalisation. Naomi Hodgson and Stefan Ramaekers discuss parenting and the parent–child relationship in digital times. They argue that much parenting advice takes an instrumental approach (Do this and your child will ....), which is firmly grounded in neoliberal thinking. However, raising children is much more complex, and purely framing it as scientific findings applied to practice leaves out the important component of culture and parenting as the transmission of culture. This places parents in the role of mediators between their children and culture, technology and the wider world. The crisis the authors hold needs addressing is not a crisis of technology but a crisis of judgement – that is to say, the decisions parents need to make daily when they are living with and bringing up their children.

After these three chapters presenting dilemmas and issues arising in digital times, the next section in this book considers workforce-related matters including training as well as management and leadership issues.

References

Aizenberg, M & Zilka, G (2022). Preservice kindergarten teachers' distance teaching practices during the COVID-19 lockdown period. *Journal of Early Childhood Teacher Education.* https://doi.org/10.1080/10901027.2022.2075813

BBC (2023, November 2). *'There will come a point when no job is needed,' says Elon Musk.* Retrieved from: https://www.bbc.co.uk/news/av/technology-67304427

Berg, S & Wehrheim, J (2021). Parental Control Technologies und die Überwachung kindlicher Mobilität. In Sub/urban, Band 9, Heft 3/4, Seiten 105-121.

Erdreich, L (2021). Managing parent capital: Parent-teacher digital communication among early childhood educators. *Italian Journal of Sociology of Education, 13*(1), 135–159. https://doi.org/10.14658/pupj-ijse-2021-1-6

Lay, K (2023, November). Children's brains 'not harmed by more screen time'. *The Times.* p. 31.

Levickis, P, Murray, L, Lee-Pang, L, Eadie, P, Page, J, Yi Lee, W & Hill, G (2022). Parents' perspectives of family engagement with early childhood education and care during the COVID-19 pandemic. *Early Childhood Education Journal,* Downloaded from: https://doi.org/10.1007/s10643-022-01376-5

Maxted, A (2023, November 18). Gaming and addiction – what parents need to know. *The Times; Weekend*. p. 8.

Stratigos, T and Fenech, M (2021). Early childhood education and care in the app generation: Digital documentation, assessment for learning and parent communication. *Australian Journal of Early Childhood*, 46(1), 19–31.

Tronto, J (2013). *Caring Democracy: Markets, Equality and Justice*. New York and London: New York University Press.

Vuorinen, T (2018). "Remote parenting": Parents perspectives on, and experiences of, home and preschool collaboration. *European Early Childhood Education Research Journal*, 26(2), 201–211.

3

'BIG SISTER' IS WATCHING

A feminist critical discourse analysis of texts supporting the use of live stream video feed technology

Brooke Richardson and Joanne Lehrer

Introduction

The use of digital technologies in childcare[1] programs is not a new phenomenon. Digitizing records, documenting children's learning, and communicating by phone, text, or email with parents are part of daily practice in many childcare programs in wealthy nations. This project raises urgent ethical concerns about a less visible, burgeoning use of technology that has largely flown under the radar in Canada: live-stream video. We begin by contextualizing our research in the contemporary Canadian political and organizational childcare context. Jurisdictionally, we focus on the provinces of Ontario and Alberta, as the growth of live-stream technologies has paralleled the pronounced corporatization of childcare in these provinces over the past decade. Next, we embed the project within a feminist political economy (FPE) and feminist care ethics (FCE) theoretical framework. We then turn to feminist critical discourse analysis (FCDA) as a methodological tool to analyze public messaging by childcare programs and the companies who provide the technology supporting the use of video streaming technologies. Our results raise critical concerns about live-stream video technologies rupturing, rather than strengthening, relationships between children, educators, mothers, fathers, and families, and prioritizing surveillance and productivity over consent, engagement, and learning.

The Canadian childcare context

Like other English-speaking, wealthy Western nations, the provision of childcare in Canada is primarily determined through the 'free' market. A fee-for-service model determines (grossly) inequitable access, while it is (erroneously)

DOI: 10.4324/9781003471172-4

assumed that supply will meet demand and the invisible hand of the market will ensure 'quality' childcare programs. Childcare falls under provincial jurisdiction, making access, quality, and cost of services 'consistently inconsistent' across the country (Richardson & Langford, 2018). Outside of Quebec,[2] childcare fees are often one of families-with-young-children's greatest expenses (Macdonald & Friendly, 2021).[3]

Licensed, centre-based childcare programs are offered through public, non-profit (NP), for-profit (FP), and corporate models (childcare 'chains'). Public childcare programs, where a government body not only funds but also administers and delivers care, are increasingly rare. Almost all licensed, centre-based childcare in Canada is offered through privately-run, non-profit (NP), and for-profit (FP) childcare organizations. In most provinces, both NP and FP childcare organizations receive some public funding, either through direct operational grants ('supply-side') or indirectly through fee subsidies paid to parents ('demand-side') (Cleveland and Krashinsky, 2004). The key differences between NP and FP programs are that NP must be run by a community-based board of directors, including parents and staff, and that the centre is legally required to re-invest any surplus revenues back into the program. FP programs are typically run by an owner, and key decisions are made by a single person rather than a committee that represents community interests. FP childcare revenues and expenditures are not overseen or managed by any public body.

It is also important to distinguish between one-off FP childcare programs – a single program run by an owner, and corporate childcare chains – where a single owner operates several childcare programs at different locations. Writing about the Alberta context, Langford (2011) defined corporate childcare chains as FP childcare programs with more than five locations. At that time, corporate childcare was a relatively new phenomenon in Canada – there were only a handful of childcare chains with more than five locations, mostly in Alberta and Ontario. Since then, corporate childcare chains have expanded in Canada and internationally. Richardson (2017) built on Langford's definition, noting these companies' 'financial backing by related and/or unrelated industries (usually real estate), diverse business interests (such as linked companies and/ or ancillary services), the operation of at least twenty centres, and its potential to be publicly traded on the stock exchange' (p. 120). Vandenbroeck, Lehrer & Mitchell (2023) take this one step further, suggesting that the corporatization of care occurs when 'major multinational corporate businesses take over large parts of the childcare market, often by acquiring pre-existing smaller businesses or private services' (p. 17). Distinguishing between corporate and other FP is useful in this study because it appears that live-stream video feeds are emphasized as an additional feature on corporate childcare providers' websites (Richardson & Worotynec, 2023).

Interestingly, one of the largest corporate providers in Canada, Brightpath Inc. (87 centres in 3 provinces), stopped using live-stream video technologies in their centres in the past few years (moving instead to a real-time communication app). It is worth noting that this shift away from live-stream video feeds occurred shortly after it was bought out by UK-based childcare conglomerate, Busy Bees, in 2017 (BrightPath Early Learning Inc., 2017).

Theoretical grounding

The motivation for this project is rooted in Feminist Care Ethics (FCE). Central to FCE is the conceptualization of human beings as both caregivers and care-receivers, throughout the lifespan and in any given moment. FCE recognizes that needs are not only inevitable but a key mechanism for living a meaningful life. The neoliberal story has tried to convince us that we can and should pursue a path of transcendent independence whereby 'success' is equated with production in the formal market economy. In stark contrast, FCE understands humans as 'inevitably dependent and inextricably interdependent' (Kittay, 2015, p. 51). To try to live any other way creates divisions between ourselves and each other, and between our minds and bodies, in a futile effort to separate our existence from the material and environmental realities in which we exist. A FCE perspective suggests that these separations are fundamentally harmful in that they break us, as individuals and as a collective, into pieces.

FCE provides a framework for identifying when relations may be considered. These are 1) caring *about* (noticing need), 2) caring *for* (taking responsibility for care), 3) caregiving (the actual acts involved in meeting needs), 4) care *receiving* (ensuring those whose needs are being met have an opportunity to respond to the care act), and 5) caring *with* (ensuring both those being cared for and those doing the caregiving are part of the broader democratic process of allocating care resources) (Tronto, 2013). Caring relations may occur at an individual, interpersonal, community, national, or international level. Each of the phases of care are deeply political and ethical, though the last phase (caring *with*) invites focused attention on the distribution of care at the macro, political, and socioeconomic levels.

The allocation of material resources necessary for social reproduction is the focus of Feminist Political Economy (FPE). FPE theorists have demonstrated that formal market economies rely on exploitative social reproductive labour (paid and unpaid) disproportionately carried out by women (Arat-Koç, 2006; Luxton, 2006). Women who are racialized, have dependents, or are otherwise marginalized, are at a distinct disadvantage as they struggle to compete in a market designed for white, unattached, able-bodied, cis-gendered men, the classic homo economicus. Women's social reproductive responsibilities mean that they face social and economic exclusion due to: 1) inability to participate full-time in the paid market economy, 2) exploitation as (poorly) paid caregivers, or 3) some combination of the two.

FPE brings attention to how a market model of childcare positions educators and mothers *in opposition to* each other. Privately-run childcare programs (NP and FP) are reliant on parent fees to operate. The cost of care falls to parents, whereby the fees are often comparable to a low/middle-income mother's earnings (particularly if more than one child attends) (Macdonald & Friendly, 2021). This arrangement does not work for either group: mothers are paying far too much *for* care and educators are paid far too little *to* care. Furthermore, there are regulated childcare places for only about a quarter of children requiring care in Canada. Mothers who are both paid and unpaid caregivers are particularly vulnerable, as they do not earn enough to pay for the care they require to work.

Because social reproductive labour is systematically undervalued and rendered invisible,[4] women are stressed, tired, and constantly overwhelmed in meeting their own and their family's daily needs. FCE illustrates how and why women (mothers and caregivers/educators) in these material positions are unable to take the time and energy required to care *about, for*, and *with* others. As Held (2006) asserts, it is *possible* that women can care well amidst horrendously oppressive conditions. History illustrates this. But it is not plausible, let alone sustainable on a widespread level. The social reproductive labour will get done, because it has to, but whether it is *caring* is another question entirely.

Methodology

We use feminist critical discourse analysis (FCDA) to illuminate hegemonic power relations that continue to misconstrue and undervalue gendered care labour (Lazar, 2005, 2007). Discourse itself is understood as the textual representation of what is or could be accepted as 'true' or 'real' (Fairclough, 2003; Fairclough & Wodak, 1997). Lazar (2005, 2007) argued that FCDA can 'show the complex, subtle, and sometimes not so subtle, ways in which frequently taken-for-granted gendered assumptions and hegemonic power relations are discursively produced, sustained, negotiated, and challenged in different contexts and communities' (p. 142). We understand FCDA as a mechanism of making visible and thereby interrupting hegemonic, gendered power relations that continue to deny women full participation in social, economic, and political life. Indeed, Lazar (2007) refers to FCDA as 'analytical activism' (p. 145).

Our data includes publicly available, online texts produced by corporate childcare companies that use video surveillance technology (Kids & Company, Willowbrae, AllAboutKids Inc.) and the companies that sell the technologies

(SecureDaycare, DaycareWebwatch, and Watch Me Grow). Together, these six corporations appear to be spurring the growth of video streaming technologies in childcare programs in Alberta and Ontario's largest cities. All text related to the use of webcams (the colloquial term used to refer to live-stream video streaming technologies) by these companies was copied and pasted into a Word document for analysis. We then read and re-read the texts to explore the representations of the technology in relation to childcare programs, parents, children, and educators. We were particularly interested in how the discourses in the texts reinforced or resisted a hegemonic, commodified conceptualization of childcare.

Findings

'Daycare' as a market commodity

Interestingly, 'daycare', not 'childcare', 'early childhood education' or 'early learning' was the term preferred by producers of the technology. Consistent with a neoliberal, marketized lens, daycare is a colloquial term that 'reflect[s] a basic, custodial care approach to caring for children whereby the main goal is keeping children physically safe in their parent's absence' (Lehrer, Richardson, Vandenbroeck & Mitchell, 2022, p. 39). 'Daycare' is a static commodity rather than an active process, obscuring the idea of caring for/with children, and of rich pedagogical relationships and learning. This choice of term implies that the audience for these texts consists of potential consumers – childcare owners/entrepreneurs, who typically do not have a background in ECE.

Even more concerningly, these websites further conceptualize 'daycare' as a 'business' in a growing 'industry':

> Our easy-to-use software was created specifically for the business of childcare. It makes running your business easier and more profitable [...] By offering premium services not available at other daycare centers [webcams], yours will stand apart and become the daycare of choice for parents in the vicinity and beyond - driving enrollment higher.
>
> *(DaycareWebwatch, 2024)*

The underlying assumption here is that the presence of live-stream video feeds will be the deciding factor in whether parents 'choose' one childcare centre over another. WatchMeGrow similarly notes, 'the comfort of checking on their child online is one of the most compelling reasons [for parents] to choose your school'. Again, the priority here is selling a commodity rather than ensuring meaningful education or care experiences for children, educators, and families.

A schoolification discourse

A schoolification discourse emerged in texts of childcare programs that used the software. For example, the quickly growing corporate childcare chain, Willowbrae Inc., refer to themselves as an 'academy' in their communications. In the Canadian context, where public schools are accepted as a public good to which all citizens have a right to access, 'academy' is a term embraced by the elitist private school sector. Private 'academies' purport to go above and beyond what public schools can offer, for a price. Again, it is hard to understand this discursive approach as anything other than a marketing strategy, capitalizing on parents' anxieties about their child's future academic potential. Willowbrae also refers to educators as 'teachers' and WatchMeGrow uses the terms 'school' and 'classroom' to refer to childcare centres and playrooms. These terms are part of a larger discourse that reduces children's experiences in childcare to preparation for primary school.

Webcams as a marker of 'quality'

Live-stream video feed technologies are often framed as a marker of 'quality' in and of itself. For example, texts read: 'If the day care centre goes so far as to have webcams in its facility, parents can have confidence in it' (SecureDaycare, 2024); 'Our technology allows us to meet and far exceed licensing standards, so we can provide services to parents that are second to none' (Willowbrae, 2024); and '[the use of webcams illustrates] a priority on quality care and education' (WatchMeGrow, 2023). To assume that the presence of webcams is itself an indicator of 'quality' is troubling as it completely overlooks the decontextualization and thus objectification of the humans (children and adults) being monitored. Indeed, an argument could be made that the presence of webcams is indicative of *poor* quality, since these webcams act as a smokescreen to finding out what is actually going on in childcare programs.

The 'magic' of making up for lost time

The idea that webcams compensate for parent's 'lost' time with their child was heavily prevalent throughout the texts. One webcam technology producer states: 'SecureDaycare gives working parents and distant relatives the opportunity to be a part of their child's life *even* [emphasis added] while the child is in daycare'. This producer goes on to position its technology as a 'solution' to the purported problem that 'parents are often too busy with their careers that they miss the glory of parenthood' (SecureDaycare, 2024). Here 'daycare' is positioned as a necessary evil – something that is not really wanted, but required because 'parents' (a gender-neutral term though care work is overwhelmingly done by mothers) must work outside the home.

One childcare company goes as far as referring to live stream video feeds as 'magic': 'Parents can view our video stream on their mobile phones. To see this magic, try browsing this site on your mobile device' (Willowbrae, 2024). In using the word 'magic', the company implies that the streams defy the natural world, allowing parents to be in two places at once. SecureDaycare (2024) draws on such magical thinking when they suggest that the live-feed allows parents to 'talk with their child about what they did at day care *as if it was done as a family*' (emphasis added). The 'magic' in this case is altering an event where they were not present to one they were included in. The reality is that parents are not, and cannot, be in two places at once, nor can the past be changed through technology.

Finally, there appears to be an assumption throughout the texts that watching the video stream allows parents to actively be part of care experiences/interactions. Phrases used include: 'staying connected' (DaycareWebwatch, 2024), and 'complete family engagement' (DaycareWebwatch, 2024). It is false to assume that watching a video stream can be categorized as a way of 'engaging' or 'connecting' *with* families. Watching a video stream is an entirely unidirectional action – often taking place without children's awareness or consent. At best it could be said that watching a video feed reflects a parent's care *about* their child, but video feeds do not include the other phases required for good, complete, care.

Increasing parent's workplace productivity

Another interesting finding, which contradicts the making up for 'lost' time discourse, is that the live stream video feeds increase parents' productivity at work. Consider this highly romanticized vignette on a technology producer's website:

> Imagine it's 3:00 o'clock in the afternoon and you've been in meetings all day. Too tired to tackle a new assignment you look out the window and see children playing in the park across the road. Your thoughts drift away to your child. You get on the Internet, log on to SecureDaycare.com, type in your private user ID code and there she is, painting a picture of a house with colourful flowers, green trees and a bright yellow sun. For a few moments, you are taken into her world at day care, sharing in her creativity and imagination. You smile and sign off. Somehow, the meetings don't seem quite as bothersome as they did a few minutes ago. In fact, you tackle your workload with a renewed sense of enthusiasm. After all, you just reminded yourself what it's all about.
>
> *(SecureDaycare, 2024)*

The parent begins 'too tired' to 'tackle' a task. By simply seeing their child and their 'sunny pictures' they instantly have the 'enthusiasm' to pursue their 'bothersome' work.

Less dramatically, Kids and Co. uses the same argument, suggesting that the videos will help parents be more productive:

> It's hard to stay focused at work when you are thinking about your children. That's why Kids & Company locations are equipped with web-enabled cameras. This gives you the ability to check in on your child from anywhere in the world over the Internet.
>
> *(Kids & Co., 2024)*

It is ironic that parents must take time away from work to watch the feeds. These companies do not acknowledge that most working parents have access to photos of their child(ren), which could provide the same inspirational impact as the live feeds, if the feeds inspire them to work more productively.

Building trust

Another idea that emerges in these texts is that the video feeds build 'trust' and relationships with families and that webcams allow parents to be 'informed and involved and are better prepared to support daycare staff and management' (DaycareWebwatch, 2024). One software producer asserts: 'WatchMeGrow builds instant trust with families' (WatchMeGrow, 2023). Ironically, webcams thrive in a context of little or no trust between families and caregivers/educators. An atmosphere of constant surveillance is only necessary when families do not believe their children can be entrusted to educators/caregivers.

Similarly, webcams are marketed as a mechanism of 'open communication'. For example, Watchmegrow (2023) states:

> When parents and teachers work together and form a positive, open line of communication, children will receive the finest childcare possible... All of our classrooms and outdoor playgrounds are equipped with secure, live, highdefinition cameras.

While we agree that open communication between educators, parents, and children is an essential component of building trust and providing good care, we do not believe that live-stream video feeds provide this. Again, they are a unidirectional mechanism of communication which do not require children's awareness or consent. Caregivers/educators may be aware of their use, but they have little agency to challenge the practice: the people choosing to install and use the cameras are the same people paying their wages. Furthermore, resistance to the use of the cameras by staff could be interpreted as proof they have something to hide. So, while caregivers/educators could theoretically resist the use of these technologies, doing so may put their employment, and livelihood, on the line.

Children and educators

The needs and interests of children and educators are largely absent in these texts. SecureDaycare (2024) explicitly positions their needs as subordinate to those of parents and providers: 'we have proceeded to create an online environment that places the needs of parents as well as day care providers at the forefront' (SecureDaycare, 2024). Consistent with a neoliberal conceptualization of the family, children are positioned as the purview of their parents, the purchasers (but not direct consumers) of childcare 'services'. There is also no consideration given to how the cameras may impact the children or educator's lived experiences nor their consent sought to participate in this social experiment. For educators, lack of voice and/or participation in how and when they are used undermines their professional autonomy and privacy. The potential harms of constant surveillance are unacknowledged.

Discussion and conclusion

Live-stream video feeds are becoming an increasingly common phenomena in multi-site, corporate childcare programs in Canada (Richardson & Worotynec, 2023), indicating that hyper-individualized neoliberal, market-based thinking is driving their use. The texts we analyzed further entrench the commodification of care in ways that exacerbate existing hegemonic power relations and occlude the needs of children.

There was no mention in any of these texts of caring for children as a dynamic, inherently relational process that is fundamentally incongruent with the commodification of care. 'Daycare' was the base product, while the technology was an upgrade, or perk – more accurately a mechanism to increase profits. Even more problematic was the assumption that the feeds are an indicator of childcare quality. Surveillance, and the transparency it purports to offer, does not inherently make anything better or of higher 'quality'. That childcare programs are looking for a quality 'quick-fix' is troubling and likely indicative of poor quality. Furthermore, framing webcams as an indicator of 'quality' completely dismisses the very real harms to children and educators/caregivers that may come from the use of feeds (i.e., an invasion of privacy, the decontextualization of information). And perhaps most harmful is the fact that such thinking reflects and perpetuates caring for children as a static, market-based commodity. Instead of ensuring childcare programs have the necessary resources to create enjoyable, meaningful, nuanced, relational, and dynamic learning/care environments for young children, educators, and families, webcams purport to bypass all this in the name of 'transparency' and surveillance. Ultimately, the children, families, and highly gendered workforce pay the price.

Ironically, while 'daycare' is conveniently reduced to a commodity, the feeds themselves are positioned as relational. They are framed as allowing parents to be a 'part of their child's day even when they are not there' (SecureDaycare,

2024). One company claims them to be 'magic', allowing parents to stay 'connected' and 'engaged' with the children and educators while not physically present themselves. As noted above, 'watching' an event from afar is not the same as being an active participant in a consensual, reciprocal care interaction. And the surveillance is not consensual for children or educators. It is parents and employers who decide if, when, and how the feeds will be used.

Even more far-fetched is the idea that the feeds 'build trust': instead, they capitalize on the lack of trust between providers and parents. And the idea that increasing a parent's productivity at work is a worthwhile reason to subject children and educators to the harms of technology is extremely troubling. Aside from the fact that parents must take time away from work to view the feeds, that what they view will not necessarily be reassuring/inspiring, this prioritizes the market production of parents/workers over the lived experiences of children and educators.

Noted briefly above is the fact that the gender-neutral language of 'parents' was overwhelmingly present in these texts ('mother' never appeared). We wanted to understand how the feeds perpetuate, or interrupt, mothers as the primary person responsible for a child's care. In using the more 'inclusive' term 'parents', the fact that caring about, for, and with children continues to be borne by mothers is not acknowledged. Indeed, the feeds require *more* from parents/mothers as they are now 'required' to oversee their child's care when they are at work, adding 'big sister' to their long list of home and work responsibilities. While using gender-neutral language does imply that fathers are involved in care labour (and therefore this discourse has the potential to socially shape a more egalitarian Canadian society), it renders invisible the disproportionate care labour mothers are already doing.

The increasing use of live-stream video technologies is deeply troubling from both an FPE and FCE perspective. The technology cements childcare's position as a commodifiable market product, conveniently overlooking the nuances and complexities of caring relations. The 'magic' the feeds claim to offer is an illusion: no one can be actively involved in a caring interaction in two different places at once. And the harms the feeds instantiate – particularly given the lack of agency and consent of children and educators with regards to their use – are conveniently overlooked. If access to and the experience of good care are a priority for parents, families, and societies, surveilling the over-extended childcare programs that currently exist (and using the existence of the technology as a market indicator of 'quality') is not the way to go. It is truly a care*less* step in the wrong direction.

We remain hopeful, at this critical moment in Canadian childcare policy development, that the social infrastructure required to ensure good care *about*, *for*, and *with* children, educators, and families is prioritized in the rolling out of a national childcare system. We call urgent attention to an overall lack of emphasis on creating decent working conditions for educators/caregivers in these programs. There are no quick fixes to quality in the ECEC sector. We hope this analysis will contribute to further research and political action that resists the idea of care as a market commodity. We also hope that educators and students reading this are equipped with arguments against implementing live-stream video technology, should they be consulted on its use.

Acknowledgement

We wish to acknowledge unceded territories on which we live and work. Brooke created this chapter on the unceded lands of the Anishinaabe, Chippewa, the Wendant and Mississaugas of the Credit. This land is colonially known as 'Toronto, Canada'. Joanne is on the unceded territory of the Anishanaabe Omàmiwininiwak, colonially known as 'Gatineau, Quebec'. We pay respect to the knowledge embedded in the custodians of the lands and waters and to the Elders, past, present, and future.

We also wish to thank Zonia Foster (formerly Worotynec) and Alexandra Paquette who assisted with background research for this paper.

Notes

1 The most commonly used term to refer to all education/care programs for young children internationally is 'Early Childhood Education and Care' (ECEC). We use the term 'childcare' because we are interested in programs for children offered in the private sector (i.e., not publicly financed or administered like kindergarten or preschool programs) that serve children/families younger than school-age (typically age 4 or 5 in Canada). ECEC is does not necessarily make this distinction. We also consider care and education to be one and the same in the early years, thus challenging the positioning of care as subordinate to (and therefore always referred to after) education.

2 Quebec is the only province to deviate significantly from this model. Quebec has embraced a 'supply-side' funding approach where programs are funded directly, reducing the fees charged to all parents since 1997. As a result, out-of-pocket costs for parents in Quebec are much lower than in other provinces.

3 This was the case before the pandemic but became even more pronounced throughout the pandemic when childcare programs struggled to remain operational due to low enrollments and additionally required (expensive) operating procedures.

4 Ironically, we are often the victims of our own success here. In many ways, working mothers (ourselves included) have managed increased social and economic reproductive responsibilities *too* well over the past several decades, deeply struggling to manage it all while making it look effortless.

References

Arat-Koç, S (2006). Whose social reproduction?: Transnational motherhood and challenges to feminist political economy. In K. Bezanson & M. Luxont (Eds.), *Social Reproduction: Feminist Political Economy Challenges Neo-Liberalism* (pp. 75–92). McGill-Queens University Press.

BrightPath Early Learning Inc. (2017, July 28). *Brightpath Completes Arrangement with Busy Bees*. Retrieved from https://www.newswire.ca/news-releases/brightpath-completes-arrangement-with-busy-bees-637151603.html

Cleveland, G, & Krashinsky, M (2004). *Financing Early Learning and Child Care in Canada. Child Care for a Change: Shaping the 21st Century*, Winnipeg, November 12–14, 2004. Retrieved from http://www.childcarecanada.org/documents/research-policy-practice/04/11/financing-early-learning-and-child-care-canada

DaycareWebwatch (2024, January 3). *Daycare Webwatch*. Retrieved from: https://www.daycarewebwatch.com/index/home

Fairclough, N (2003). *Analyzing Discourse: Textual Analysis for Social Research*. Routledge.

Fairclough, N & Wodak, R (1997). Critical discourse analysis. In T.A. van Dijk (Ed.), *Discourse Studies. A Multidisciplinary Introduction* (Vol. 2, pp. 258–284). Sage.

Held, V (2006). *The Ethics of Care: Personal, Political and Global*. Oxford University Press.

Kids & Company (2024, January 3). *Welcome to Kids & Company*. Retrieved from: https://kidsandcompany.com/

Kittay, E (2015). A theory of justice as fair terms of social life given our inevitable dependency and our inextricable interdependency. In D. Engster & M. Hamington (Eds.), *Care Ethics and Political Theory* (pp. 51–71). Oxford.

Langford, T. (2011). *Alberta's daycare controversy: from 1908 to 2009 and beyond*. Athabasca University Press.

Lazar, M (Ed.). (2005). *Feminist Critical Discourse Analysis: Gender, Power and Ideology in Discourse*. Palgrave Macmillan.

Lazar, M (2007). Feminist critical discourse analysis: Articulating a feminist discourse Praxis. *Critical Discourse Studies*, 4(2), 141–164. https://doi.org/10.1080/17405900701464816

Lehrer, J. Richardson, B. Vandenbroeck, M. & Mitchell, L. (2022). Resisting children as human capital. In M. Vandenbroeck, J. Lehrer, L. Mitchell (Eds.). *The Decommodification of Early Childhood Education: Resisting Neoliberalism*. Routledge.

Luxton, M (2006). Feminist political economy in Canada and the politics of social reproduction. In M. Luxton & K. Bezanson (Eds.), *Social Reproduction: Feminist Political Economy Challenges Neo-liberalism* (pp. 11–44). McGill-Queens University Press.

Macdonald, D & Friendly, M (2021). *Sounding the Aarm: COVID-19's Impact on Canada's Precarious Child Care Sector*. Retrieved from https://www.policy alternatives.ca/sites/default/files/uploads/publications/National%20Office/2021/03/Sounding%20the%20alarm.pdf

Richardson, B (2017). Taking stock of corporate childcare in Alberta: Licensing inspection data in not-for-profit and corporate childcare centres. In R. Langford, S. Prentice, & P. Albaense (Eds.), *Caring for Children: Social Movements and Public Policy in Canada* (pp. 119–140). University of British Columbia Press.

Richardson, B & Langford, R (2018). Early childhood education and care in Canada: Consistently inconsistent childcare policy. In G. Richards, S. Phillipson, & H. Harju-Luukkainen (Eds.), *International Perspectives on Early Childhood Education and Care* (Vol. 1, pp. 20–33). Routledge.

Richardson, B & Worotynec, S (2023). The corproate creep: Enviornment scan of live stream video feeds in Ontario and Alberta. *Transforming Care Conference*. University Sheffield, UK, 2023, June 26–28.

SecureDaycare (2024, January 3). *Home*. Retrieved from: https://securedaycare.ca/

Tronto, J. (2013). *Caring Democracy: Markets, Equality and Justice*. New York and London: New York University Press.

Vandenbroeck, M, Lehrer, J, & Mitchell, L (2023). *The Decommodification of Early Childhood Educatin and Care: Resisting Neoliberlaism*. Routledge.

WatchMeGrow (2023). *Introducing WatchMeGrow*. Retrieved from https://www.youtube.com/watch?v=flIbLIz1NVw&t=4s

Willowbrae Academy (2024, January 3). *Braeview® Communication Software*. Retrieved from: https://willowbraechildcare.com/braeview

4

USING THE EUROPEAN FRAMEWORK FOR THE DIGITAL COMPETENCE OF EDUCATORS TO DEVELOP DIDACTIC TOOLS ON AI FOR EARLY CHILDHOOD SETTINGS

Ulrike Stadler-Altmann

Introduction

As educators, we cannot ignore the ongoing discourse around artificial intelligence (AI) and digital technology. These advances, and our attitudes towards them, will undoubtedly shape our world. As teachers, we have a responsibility to prepare children for a future that is uncertain, even for us. It is therefore vital that we actively engage with significant societal changes and integrate them into our educational practice. This presents us with the challenge of understanding our own relationship with digital media and how we can improve our skills in this area. The COVID-19 pandemic has highlighted the difficulties of being an educator in a digital age, such as creating online educational programmes for children. As a result, it is imperative to consider the intersection of digital technology, AI and pedagogy and strive to find effective solutions in our teaching practices.

When examining the state of early childhood education (ECE) across Europe, we observe a similarity in research findings and approaches at political, governmental and practical levels (Alexiadou & Stadler-Altmann, 2020). At the European level, the European Framework for the Digital Competence of Educators (DigCompEdu) (Redecker & Punie, 2017) serves as a guiding framework that can be used at the national level. This framework provides direction for the development of additional training programmes in the field of digitalisation in ECE.

As part of the European project 'I'm not a robot', a survey was conducted to gather insights from educators in four European regions. These insights have served as a basis for the development of didactic and pedagogical materials which will be described in this chapter. The main focus is to address the

DOI: 10.4324/9781003471172-5

needs of educators in using digital media in their daily work. The analysis results and ideas for ECE materials will be aligned with the DigCompEdu framework to provide practical suggestions for the effective use of digital media. These findings will then be used to create comprehensive toolboxes around the themes of digitalisation, robotics and AI. These toolboxes serve as the core of the project, providing educators with concrete implementation strategies for integrating complex technical topics such as AI into their kindergarten curriculum. The toolboxes are developed with a child-centred approach, using children's questions in the field of robotics and AI as a starting point, ensuring that children's perspectives remain at the forefront of pedagogical considerations (Borowski, Diethelm & Wilken, 2016).

Childhood in a digital world

According to Stalder (2018), our society is already deeply immersed in a culture of digitality. Digital media has become ubiquitous in almost every aspect of our daily lives. Therefore, it is not surprising that children have access to and engage with digital media. Von Carlsburg and Möller (2022) have shown that children are exposed to digital media at a young age and quickly become skilled users. As a result, there is an increasing number of programmes and apps designed for children, including some targeted at infants and toddlers (Heider & Jalongo, 2015). In ECE settings, this requires the recognition of digital media as an integral part of a child's world, not only for entertainment purposes, but also to facilitate their understanding and engagement with these relatively new technologies. Media pedagogy therefore has a responsibility to look more closely at the use of digital media in kindergarten settings. It is advantageous for educators to incorporate digital media into their own lives, consciously or unconsciously, as smartphones, for example, have become commonplace and almost every educator has their own device. In a cross-cultural study of technology use in ECE, Slutsky et al. (2021) show that educators' personal use of digital media significantly influences their pedagogical practices. Nieding and Klaudy (2020) found that teachers' familiarity with digital devices and their understanding of how digital media are used in everyday life play a crucial role. This finding can also be extended to educators, as emphasised by Wilmers, Anda, Keller and Rittberger (2020a). Attitudes towards digitisation and digital media are key predictors of how educators incorporate digital media into their teaching practices (Wilmers, Anda, Keller, Kerres and Getto, 2020b).

European comparison concerning the role of educators in the use of digital media in kindergarten

In addition to the aforementioned studies, empirical research conducted by Friedrichs-Liesenkötter (2016) and Knauf (2019) has shed light on pedagogical professionals' attitudes towards digital media in kindergarten settings. The findings suggest that educational professionals tend to align themselves with either a preservationist pedagogical approach or a lifeworld approach when it comes to incorporating digital media into their pedagogical practices. It is therefore not surprising that the use of digital media in kindergartens is often inconsistent and infrequent. This can be attributed to a lack of meaningful integration of digital media into pedagogy. However, in order to successfully implement digital media for pedagogical purposes, it is crucial to gain a detailed understanding of educators' motivations and behaviours. From a European perspective, a country comparison involving Italy, Germany, Denmark and Lithuania (as shown in Figure 4.1) reveals similar attitudes among educators, as described by Friedrichs-Liesenkötter (2016). The survey sought to assess agreement with statements reflecting the preservationist pedagogical approach, such as 'digital media do not belong in kindergarten'.

Corresponding statements from the open-ended responses in the questionnaire support these findings:

- Children should deal with digital media because children encounter them in their everyday lives (response from Denmark)
- Overall, I don't really see myself at the point to engage media education (response from Lithuania)
- Media education is primarily a matter for the parents (response from Germany)
- I want to have more time work with the kids and do not waste time working with computers (response from Italy)

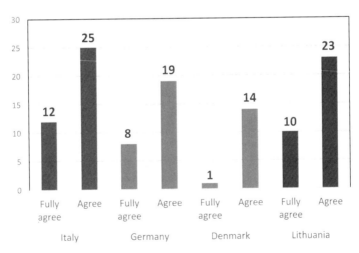

FIGURE 4.1 Teachers' Resistance to Digital media in pedagogical work (Stadler-Altmann et al., 2023); N = 752.

The study conducted by Stadler-Altmann et al. in 2023 included a total of 752 educators from Germany, Italy, Denmark and Lithuania. The data collected were subjected to hierarchical multiple regression analysis and clustering. Figure 4.1 illustrates notable differences between countries: Germany (27%), Italy (37%) and Lithuania (33%) showed relatively negative attitudes towards digital media. In contrast, only 15% of respondents in Denmark thought that digital media should not be used in kindergarten education. This clear contrast can be explained by the fact that the Danish educators in our sample have extensive experience in using digital media, which is an integral part of their training and daily work. Therefore, it is not only educators' attitudes that are important, but also their familiarity with digital media within their educational and professional contexts. At the European level, the European Framework for the Digital Competence of Educators (Redecker & Punie, 2017) recognises the importance of education and professional development to enhance digital media literacy.

European framework on digital competencies

The appropriate use of technology, media and especially digital media in preschool education is of growing interest in Europe. This can be seen in a large number of projects in the European countries themselves and at the European level (European Commission, 2023), as well as in projects on digital media in kindergartens. In this context, a look at the digital literacy of educators is essential. Like other transversal competences, digital competences are also referred to as cross-curricular competences (Kiper & Mischke, 2008) or transdisciplinary competences (as in Fröhlich-Gildhoff, Nentwig-Gesemann & Pietsch, 2011). It is clear that digital literacy is not only described for educators but that the development of children's digital literacy is also considered. In the General Competence Model of Fröhlich-Gildhoff et al. (2011), the complexity of a multidimensional dispositional structure – knowledge, situation perception, motivation, action potentials – is linked to action planning and readiness and subsequent action in a situation. Thus, increasing teachers' competence should also increase children's competence.

As a result of this general debate on competences and competence models for educators, several models have been developed at the European level for different competence areas. The European Framework for DigCompEdu is a comprehensive model for digital competence. The aforementioned debate on competence models in ECE, with the distinction between professional, personal and social competences, has been further developed and placed in the context of the pedagogical objective. In particular, a distinction is made between the professional competences of educators, the pedagogical competences of educators and the competences of learners. In this way, pedagogical competences are given a central importance and at the same time it becomes clear that pedagogical competences result from the respective professional, personal and social competences of the respective educators.

The model pays particular attention to the pedagogical competences of educators. These include 'using digital resources', 'teaching and learning', 'assessment' and 'empowering learners'. Two further competence groups, namely, professional engagement and facilitating learners' digital competence will be discussed later. In order for educators to be able to integrate digitality into their everyday pedagogical work, it is essential that they first familiarise themselves with the topic and become aware of their own attitudes and skills in this area. As explained earlier, educators consciously or unconsciously use digital tools in their private environment and this use influences their pedagogical work. This link is particularly emphasised in DigCompEdu. Therefore, in addition to this model, an online tool 'Selfie for Teachers' is offered, with which you can quickly assess your own convictions about digitality and your own skills in dealing with digital media. This is also one of the competence areas of the model 'Using digital resources'. The second competence area 'Teaching and learning' first describes the general principles of learning and teaching and then focuses on the specifics when digitality is the learning topic. Questions about how to approach digitality and technological foundations and what competences are needed are addressed here. For example, teachers should have an idea of what binary coding is, i.e. the translation of reality into a computer-readable language of ones and zeros, and why algorithms are necessary. Only if the content is understood by the educators themselves can it be taught well. The third area of competence, assessment, emphasises that digital media must also be accessible, i.e. educational work on digitality only makes sense if digital media are available and play a role in the children's world. Accordingly, educators should find out which digital media children use, which digital media are available to children and what kindergarten children already know about digital media. All three areas of competence described earlier are important prerequisites for the fourth area of competence, 'empowering learners'. The ultimate aim is to enable children to use digital media in an independent and self-determined way. For this to be successful, educators need to be aware of children's learning processes, be able to observe how children use digital media and be able to continually redirect learning through dialogue and feedback.

From the perspective of general didactics, the DigCompEdu model is a detailed description of competences for educators and teachers that can be applied to all pedagogical activities. Digital competences are embedded in general pedagogical and didactical competences. It should therefore not be too difficult for educators who care about children's learning and development to familiarise themselves with this model. After all, it is about giving children perspectives and opportunities to act with digital media. The child is always at the centre of the considerations. Consequently, the competence development of educators has a clear goal: the competence development of learners, and digital media are simply a tool, just like other learning aids and toys.

However, DigCompEdu (Redecker & Punie, 2017) is a theoretical framework model that describes in detail the individual components of digital literacy at the European level. For the concrete implementation to promote digital literacy, it refers to the European countries and their respective education or support plans. It remains to be seen how the promotion of digital literacy will be implemented in everyday pedagogical practice.

Fostering digital competencies in everyday pedagogical work

In theory, and in the frame of reference mentioned above, it seems easy to promote digital literacy among educators and, as a consequence, digital literacy among children. However, the implementation into pedagogical practice is quite different. Media pedagogy offers a variety of approaches that can be used to promote digital literacy in ECE. The use of digital media is only one aspect of media education, but it is currently receiving particular attention. Knauf (2019) points out that many educators are open to new technologies and enjoy pedagogical work with digital media. However, her study (Knauf 2019), like our survey (Stadler-Altmann et al., 2023), shows that there are two conflicting opinions about the use of digital media in particular: On the one hand, the computer and digital media are seen as part of the children's lifeworld and it is therefore the task of the childcare centre to deal with digital media. On the other hand, the daycare centre is seen as a place where children should be protected from digital devices.

Against this background and under the Erasmus+ project 'I'm not a robot. Working with AI in Early Childhood Education' (I'm not a robot n.d.), we set ourselves the task of getting educators excited about the topic of digitality, digital media and artificial intelligence by showing them how these complex topics can be integrated into everyday educational activities with children. The target group of the project was therefore educators and their digital literacy.

Based on the notion that training in early childhood education is particularly successful when it is of direct benefit to educators (Strecker et al., 2022), we worked in a multi-professional and multinational team to develop topic boxes. Our aim was to design these topic boxes in such a way that they could be used in kindergartens with as little effort as possible. Priority should be given to using materials already available in the kindergarten. The team of the EduSpace learning workshop of the Free University of Bozen/Bolzano at the Campus Brixen/Bressanone was responsible for the development of the theme boxes. The pedagogical workshop approach was combined with a democratic and participatory development process (Stadler-Altmann, 2024). The aim was to bring together the project participants with their different professional backgrounds in an equal working community and to avoid hierarchical differences between representatives of universities and pedagogical practice, an approach that is particularly successful in pedagogical workshops (Stadler-Altmann, 2024).

The development process, which lasted three years, was divided into five phases: conceptualising, designing, experimenting, testing and finalising.

Conceptualising

The first phase focused on the conceptual development of the theme boxes. To this end, the different levels of knowledge and experience of the project participants were gathered and the initial direction for the structure and content of the boxes was set. The consensus of the working group, consisting of educators, kindergarten directors, researchers and professors, was to look at the big issues of digitality and digital media from the children's point of view. The challenge was to find a point of reference from children's interests to make the topic boxes particularly interesting for children and educators. One topic that fascinates children between the ages of about two and seven is the robot. This is why the robot became the central element of the theme boxes and also the overall theme of the project. Even though robots don't seem to have much to do with AI at first glance, the topic is meant to open the door to the subject of digitality and its technical and social foundations. As a starting point, children's questions about robots were chosen, an approach that according to Borowski et al. (2016) is connectable and promising.

Accordingly, questions and considerations that children have about robots were chosen as the titles of the theme boxes. In order to keep the topic manageable and not too long, the number of boxes was limited to twelve. These twelve boxes, which were renamed toolboxes, covered relevant areas of the topic in a pedagogical way and at the same time found attractive headings for the individual activities in the boxes, as can be seen in Table 4.1.

Designing

In the design phase, all project participants were asked to think about the individual boxes and develop concrete ideas for implementation and games for everyday teaching. The results of this work were compiled and it was discussed how each box should be structured, built and filled with content. It was decided that each box should contain a short introduction to the theme of the box, a link to the expected level of knowledge of the children, a description of the objective and instructions for playing.

TABLE 4.1 Theme boxes, titles and contents

No.	Title	Content
1	Let's start!	Introduction to the project, explanation of the topics robotics, digitality and digital media – Target group: Educators
2	Who can recognize a robot/AI?	Identify robots in everyday life, identify and visualize differences between robots and humans – Target group: Educators & children.
3	Let us play robots!	Robots as a play stimulus, children transform themselves into robots and learn about the first modes of operation of a robot – Target group: Educators & children
4	How does a robot think?	Basic functioning of a robot, Computorial Thinking, Deep Learning, Programming – Target group: Educators & children.
5	How clever is a robot?	Mathematics and language as the basis of programming, speech and face recognition through AI in everyday life – Target group: Educators & children.
6	What does a robot eat?	Basics of electricity and data, electricity generation and use; collecting and processing data – Target group: Educators & children.
7	How does a robot talk?	Communication and symbols for communication, programming language and commands – Target group: Educators & children.
8	Does a robot have feelings?	Emotions and their expression in humans in contrast to robots – Target group: educators & children
9	Can a robot be my friend?	Basics on robot ethics, ethical and moral questions about technology and AI – Target group: Educators & children.
10	How can a robot help me?	Technical facilitation in everyday life, e.g. voice control and autonomous driving, limits of technology and AI as support systems – Target group: Educators & children.
11	Where does a robot come from?	Insight into the development of robots, building of robots – Target group: Educators & children.
12	Let's create a robot!	Playful and creative approach to the topic of robotics and AI, can be used as a project conclusion or as a project kick-off – Target group: Educators & children

It was also agreed that the game ideas (exercises) should be described in such a way that they could be easily implemented. Therefore, each box lists the materials needed, outlines what educators need to prepare and what the core idea of the game is. In addition, possible variations are offered for those new to the subject and for educators and children with previous knowledge.

34 Ulrike Stadler-Altmann

Experimenting and testing

Following the development of the toolboxes in four developer groups, the boxes were first tested by the project partners themselves. This showed that some good ideas still needed to be specified and expressed in an easy-to-understand language in the actual implementation. One challenge was the different languages used in the project. During the joint design, testing and trial phases, most of the work, discussion and writing was done in English. The test version of the boxes was also initially developed in English. However, in order to try out and test the toolboxes in kindergartens in the partner countries themselves, the boxes had to be translated into the respective national languages.

After a year of conception and design, the toolboxes were tested in the pedagogical field. In order to obtain structured feedback on the toolboxes, a feedback form was designed, asking in particular about the impressions and experiences of the pedagogical staff regarding contents and game ideas. In addition to general information about the implementation of the game, explicit questions were asked about the structure, the explanation of the content and the design of the pedagogical activities that were to be worked on in a way that matched the individual toolboxes. To gain feedback from the children, educators were asked to note down the children's statements verbatim and to describe the children's engagement during the game.

The toolboxes were tested between September 2022 and January 2023 in the partner countries Italy, Denmark, Lithuania and Germany in the respective cooperating institutions of the partners. For the researchers this was problematic in terms of the comparability of the test results, but it was also very helpful for the improvement and further development of the toolboxes, as the diversity of feedback also introduced a variety of new game ideas for the toolboxes.

Overall, the toolboxes were well received by the different test groups. It was emphasised that the kits were ready to use, that no special knowledge was required on the part of the educators and that the children found the game ideas interesting and enriching. The educators reported that the explanations on robotics, digital media and AI helped them during the implementation and increased their own knowledge on these topics.

Finalising

In a final step, the toolboxes were revised by the developer groups and feedback from the testing of the toolboxes was incorporated. It was important to prepare the explanations and guidance on robotics, digital media and AI in a way that would enable educators to assess and develop their own digital literacy. In Toolbox One, for example, not only was the DigCompEdu framework used as a matrix for pedagogical work with digital media, but educators were explicitly asked to use the online DigCompEdu self-reflection tool or SELFIEforTeachers from the EU Science Hub before working with the toolboxes. This helps educators to understand the dimensions of digital literacy and to reflect on their own competence and pedagogical work with digital media. Accordingly, further guidance on how to improve digital literacy for educators and children has been included in all toolboxes.

After final editing, professional translation into the project languages and graphic revision, the toolboxes are now available online on the project website (www.im-not-a-robot.eu). In addition, an e-learning platform is available for anyone interested in learning more about the topic and understanding the contents of the toolboxes. All this is available in the project languages of English, German, Danish, Italian and Lithuanian.

DigCompEdu and pedagogical work in kindergarten

DigCompEdu and the findings of the above-mentioned studies on the key role of educators in dealing with digital media in kindergartens (Nieding & Klaudy 2020; Knauf 2019), as well as the results of our own survey on the attitudes and beliefs of educators towards digital media in kindergartens (Stadler-Altmann et al. 2023), were used as the theoretical basis for this project. The results of our survey have been directly incorporated into the design of the toolboxes by strongly emphasising the lifeworld reference. At the same time, the fears expressed by educators in the open-ended responses that digital media in kindergartens would replace all other play opportunities and that children would lose touch with their living environment were taken up in the explanatory texts of the toolkits. As described above, the educators were particularly convinced during the test phase that basic aspects of robotics, digital and AI could be worked on by children using simple, familiar play materials, for example, Montessori or Fröbel materials.

In general terms, principles can now be derived as to how the digital competences of educators can be challenged and promoted in a project. For this purpose, the theoretical model from DigCompEdu (Redecker & Punie, 2017) has been supplemented with aspects from the project work that are particularly relevant for the success of the project and the promotion of competences.

As described above, the individual aspects of competence in DigCompEdu are grouped into three broad areas: educators' professional competences, educators' pedagogical competences and learners' competences. Within these three areas, a total of six competence aspects are described. All six areas of DigCompEdu have to work together to promote the development of competences through a specific project. Therefore, in the 'I'm not a robot' project, for each of the sub-areas defined in the framework model – Professional Engagement, Digital Resources, Teaching and Learning, Assessment, Empowering Learners, Facilitating Learners' Digital Competence – corresponding links have been developed.

Professional engagement is supported by information on digitisation, robotics and AI, as well as suggestions for further exploration of these topics. To this end, each of the twelve toolboxes contains explanatory texts, examples and further links and references. The digital resources area has been illustrated with tested digital media. At the same time, the toolboxes also use everyday material to explain digital. This shows that kindergartens do not always need the latest digital equipment to be able to explain digital contexts and technical developments. In the area of teaching and learning, the toolboxes provide very concrete suggestions for playing and learning. These are easy to implement in everyday teaching and stimulate the understanding and learning of kindergarten children. In addition, the learning of the educators is also stimulated by didactic hints.

The aim of the theoretical considerations in the DigComEdu framework is to strengthen learners' digital competence. This is to be made possible by empowering learners and facilitating learners' digital competence. These aims are also pursued in the tool boxes. In order to support learners, the toolboxes have been designed from the children's point of view. On the one hand, the perspective of the children and their learning is strengthened and on the other hand, the educators are enabled to reflect on their own learning based on the children's learning. This approach is also reflected in the play and learning activities in the toolboxes, which are designed according to prior knowledge. Ultimately, the toolboxes make it easier for children to get started and deal with the complex issues of digitality, robotics and AI. This strengthens the digital skills of kindergarten children and educators.

Looking back on the 'I'm not a robot' project, it is clear that listening to educators and paying attention to their concerns is a key element for the success of the project as well as for improving educators' competences. Educators play an essential role in kindergarten learning. Their openness to new topics, their willingness to deal with topics that are not in their personal sphere of interest are crucial. Therefore, it is important to acknowledge the attitudes of educators, and to include them in project development, as was done in the presented project. However, this cannot work without a theoretical basis. Therefore, the inclusion of DigCompEdu was an essential step in the project design to strengthen the digital competence of educators and children.

References

Alexiadou, N, & Stadler-Altmann, U (2020) (eds.). *Early Childhood Education Research in Europe*. Special Issue Education Inquiry, http://www.tandfonline.com/loi/zedu20/current

Borowski, C, Diethelm, I, & Wilken, H (2016). What children ask about computers, the internet, robots, mobiles, games etc. WiPSCE'16, October 13–15, 2016, Münster, Germany: ACM. ISBN 978-1-4503-4223-0/16/10. DOI:http://dx.doi.org/10.1145/2978249.2978259

European Commission (2023, November 7). *The Digital Europe Programme*. Retrieved from: https://digital-strategy.ec.europa.eu/en/activities/digital-programme

Friedrichs-Liesenkötter, H (2016). Media-educational habitus of future educators in the context of education in day-care centers, *Journal of Media Literacy Education*, 7(1), 18–34.

Fröhlich-Gildhoff, K, Nentwig-Gesemann, I, & Pietsch, S (2011). *Kompetenzorientierung in der Qualifizierung frühpädagogischer Fachkräfte*. München: DJI.

Heider, KL & Jalongo, MR (2015). Young children and families in the information age. *Applications of Technology in Early Childhood*. Springer, DOI:10.1007/978-94-017-9184-7

I'm not a robot (n.d.) Retrieved from https://www.im-not-a-robot.eu/en

Kiper, H & Mischke, W (2008). *Selbstreguliertes Lernen – Kooperation – Soziale Kompetenz Fächerübergreifendes Lernen in der Schule*. Stuttgart: Kohlhammer.

Knauf, H (2019). *Digitalisierung in Kindertageseinrichtungen. Ergebnisse einer Fragebogenerhebung zum aktuellen Stand der Nutzung digitaler Medien*. Bielefeld, urn:nbn:de:0111-pedocs-179992

Nieding, I & Klaudy, EK (2020). 'Digitalisierung in der frühen Bildung. Der Umgang mit digitalen Medien im Spannungsfeld zwischen Schutzraum und Schlüsselkompetenz', in A. Wilmers, C. Anda, C. Keller, & M. Rittberger (Hrsg.), *Bildung im digitalen Wandel. Die Bedeutung für das pädagogische Personal und für die Aus- und Fortbildung*, Waxmann, S. 31–56.

Redecker, G & Punie, Y (2017). *European Framework for the Digital Competence of Educators (DigCompEdu)*. Luxembourg: Publications Office of the European Union. Retrieved from https://joint-research-centre.ec.europa.eu/digcompedu_en

Slutsky, R, Kragh-Müller, G, Rentzou, K, Tuul, M, Gol Guven, M, Foerch, D, & Paz-Albo, J (2021). A cross-cultural study on technology use in preschool classrooms: early childhood teacher's preferences, time-use, impact and association with children's play, *Early Child Development and Care*, 191:5, 713–725, DOI: 10.1080/03004430.2019.1645135

Stadler-Altmann, U (2024). 'Demokratische und partizipative Erarbeitung von didaktischen Materialien. Pädagogische Arbeit in einer Hochschulwerkstatt als Schlüssel zum Erfolg eines internationalen Projektes', in: E-K Franz (Hrsg.), *Demokratie und Partizipation in Hochschullernwerkstätten*. Bad Heilbrunn: Klinkhardt. (in press).

Stadler-Altmann, U, Tandzegolskiene-Bielaglove, I, Knauf, H, Kaminskienė, L, Monkevičienė, O, & Lang, A (2023). Digitalization and digitality from the perspective of educators: Which impact have personal beliefs on the pedagogical work? Presented at *ECER 2023, 06 SES 04A, 08-23-2023*.

Stalder, F (2018). *The Digital Condition*, trans. Valentine Pakis, Cambridge, UK: Polity Press.

Strecker, A, Becker, J, Buchhaupt, F, Katzenbach, D, Lutz, D, & Urban, M (2022). *Qualifizierung für Inklusion. Elementarbereich*. Münster, New York: Waxmann. URN: urn:nbn:de:0111-pedocs-245911. DOI:10.25656/01:24591

von Carlsburg, GB & Möller, M (2022). Social-emotional conceptualizations: Online learning innovations and prototypical interfaces. In GB von Carlsburg, & G Kvieskienė, (Eds.) *Prototype Modelling in Social-Emotional Education. At the Example of a COVID-19 Online Learning Environment. New Approaches in Educational and Social Sciences*, vol. 39, Berlin: Peter Lang.

Wilmers, A, Anda, C, Keller, C, & Rittberger, M (2020a) (Hrsg.). *Bildung im digitalen Wandel. Die Bedeutung für das pädagogische Personal und für die Aus- und Fortbildung.* Münster: Waxmann.

Wilmers, A, Anda, C, Keller, C, Kerres, M, & Getto, B (2020b). Reviews zur Bildung im digitalen Wandel: Eine Einführung in Kontext und Methodik. In A. Wilmers, C. Anda, C. Keller, & M. Rittberger, (Hrsg.), *Bildung im digitalen Wandel. Die Bedeutung für das pädagogische Personal und für die Aus- und Fortbildung,* Waxmann, S. 7–29.

5

NARRATIVES OF CRISIS

Raising children in digital times

Naomi Hodgson and Stefan Ramaekers

Introduction: raising children in digital times

The ubiquity of digital technology today raises an abundance of questions for parents and carers. When do I allow my children to have a smartphone? What's the appropriate age for them to use social media, such as TikTok and Instagram? Should I enable 'parental controls' on my children's phones? Or limit their access to the Internet? How do I get them off their screens and get them to play outside? Should I worry about my child being contacted by individuals who have bad intentions? How do I prevent my child from becoming a victim of cyberbullying? How do I protect my child from the many idealised images that they see online? What games can I allow my child to use, and at what age? How do I deal with the fact that my daughter is sharing semi-erotic pictures on Snapchat? Will my child become addicted to social media? Will my child start acting violently because they are playing video-games?

It is little wonder that parents are anxious about their children's access to and use of the internet and apps via digital technology. Aside from some very real dangers, part of this anxiety may stem from the different relationship the older generation tend to have with such technology as compared with their children. We, the older generation, are so-called digital migrants, for whom mobile, personal digital technology has entered our lives anew, gradually. The younger generation, however, are digital natives, born into a world already digitised. Hence, our responsibility for making judgements about introducing our children to such technology begs the question: How do we as the older generation introduce the younger generation to something we do not fully understand?

DOI: 10.4324/9781003471172-6

In this chapter we consider the way in which the crisis of childhood is currently understood in academic and popular literature, and the role attributed to digital media in this. We show how this is also reflected in advice for parents and the particular form this advice takes. Namely, we argue, the framing of the issue and the means to overcome it are indicative of the reframing of raising children as 'parenting'. By turning attention to inherent, existential aspects of raising children, we draw out a different sense of crisis in relation to digital technology: one relating to our judgement in taking responsibility for that which is largely unknown and unknowable.

Crisis

The extended periods spent on screens necessitated by the pandemic have only exacerbated the long-standing sense of the crisis of childhood. In a 2006 letter to the *Telegraph*, 110 signatory academics, writers and medical experts 'asserted that children have been 'tainted' by over-exposure to electronic media, lack of space to play and an over-emphasis on academic testing in schools' (Kehily, 2010, p. 172). Similarly, Sue Palmer in her 2006 book *Toxic Childhood*, cites technological change, consumerism, 'the denigration of play and places to play, and the stress of exams' as constituting a 'toxic cocktail' that is damaging children's experience of childhood (p. 173). For Frank Furedi (2008), the very discourse of the crisis of childhood that abounds in parenting literature undermines parents' confidence in their ability to raise their children (ibid.). Reports in recent years that rank the UK poorly against other European countries in terms of children's happiness and wellbeing, and a succession of cases that have led to a strengthening of safeguarding legislation, also contribute to the sense that, collectively, we are not doing the best for our children.

Digital technology seems at once to represent both the problem and the solution: a source of essential skills for educational attainment and future employment, a key form of literacy, a means to access inclusive, personalised learning, and yet a danger to children's social development and their face-to-face interactions that places them at risk of misinformation, radicalisation, bullying, and abuse. As parents we navigate these benefits and risks often with little confidence, only getting to grips with the technology being used and the sites being accessed as the questions – Can I have a phone? Can I get Snapchat? – and issues arise.

Research literature increasingly reports on the risks related to social media use and online activity. For example, the implications of posting self-sexualised images and the risk of engaging in sexting and other risk behaviours have been identified (e.g. Van Ouytsel, Walrave, Ojeda, Del Rey & Ponnet, 2020). Prolonged use of social media is reported to have negative effects on children's mental wellbeing (Gray, Lancy & Bjorklund, 2023; Pilkington, 2023). Our response, as parents, to the questions that arise for us will more generally be shaped by media coverage of this, which is often focused on its negative effects, and by popular literature.

In terms of crises, none seems more widely felt and discussed than the crisis in the mental health and wellbeing of children and young people, of which digital technology and living life online is seen to be a significant contributor. Jonathan Haidt's 2024 book *The Anxious Generation: How the Great Rewiring of Childhood Caused an Epidemic of Mental Illness*, for example, is described as follows:

> It's about what we've done to Gen Z, and how to stop doing it and restore healthy childhood. The primary prescription: 1) more unsupervised time to play and explore (before puberty), in order to learn to become self-governing; and 2) less and later access (after puberty) to social media and the screen-based life.
>
> *(Haidt, 2023)*

The book offers 'a path forward for parents, teachers, friends, and relatives who want to help improve the mental health of children and adolescents. Change is possible, if we can act together' (ibid.). The book suggests at once both an overprotection of children by their parents in the real world and a failure to protect them in the online world.

Such calls to action can also, ironically, be heard from those who share their expertise via platforms such as Instagram. Dr Shefali Tsabary, a conscious parenting expert endorsed by Oprah Winfrey, writes in one post, entitled 'How to break your kids [sic] screen addiction':

> Screen addictions are becoming the #1 problem parents (and all humans) face.
>
> Are fights around screens one of your biggest problems with your kids?
>
> If you are having stress around screens and disrespectful behavior or a lack of motivation on part of your kids, then I can help you.
>
> I will be teaching parents to become more conscious at EVOLVE.
>
> You will walk away with key strategies to become the best parent you can be!
>
> *(Tsabary, 2023)*

We can see in Dr Shefali's post how issues relating to our children's use of digital technology are framed in particular ways: our use of screens and the issues they raise for us in relation to our children are immediately framed as problems; these problems are described in psychological and behavioural terms; it is suggested that with the right strategies you can become more successful at being a parent. This way of speaking about raising children is not

42 Naomi Hodgson and Stefan Ramaekers

specific to the discussion of digital technology, however, but is indicative of the wider recasting of raising children as 'parenting'.

The 'parenting' account of raising children

In recent decades, the word 'parent' has shifted from being something that we are, or are not, to something that we do. In Western contexts at least, there has been a concerted policy focus on parents, and a proliferation of sources of information, advice, and guidance on how to 'parent'. This spans policy interventions focused on reaching 'at risk' families, to a focus on parental engagement by schools, to an abundance of popular literature on different parenting styles, supported by a marketplace of classes, products, mass and social media, such that it has been characterised as a 'parenting culture' (Lee, Bristow, Faircloth, and Macvarish, 2014).

In Anglophone contexts the word 'parenting' and the use of the word 'parent' as a verb are now embedded in our day-to-day vocabulary and, for the most part, used unquestioningly. 'Parenting' is, however, a relatively recent coinage (cf. e.g. Smith, 2010; Furedi, 2008). Although there is no direct equivalent for the word 'parenting' in countries such as Germany, The Netherlands, and Flanders (the north part of Belgium), and the 'old' terminology remains in use (*opvoeden, grootbrengen, erziehen*), what these terms are taken to refer to has shifted – or, perhaps, narrowed – to 'parenting' as a particular framing of what it means to raise children (see Hodgson and Ramaekers, 2019, chapter 2).

The term 'parenting' provides a more inclusive language than might be presupposed by 'old' ways of discussing childrearing, upbringing, or raising children, which perhaps brings with it traditional assumptions about who raises children and in what familial context. Today, it is no longer assumed that a child is being raised by two biological parents in a co-habiting, probably married, heterosexual relationship, and therefore reference to what we do rather than who is doing it seems appropriate. Critical accounts of the turn to 'parenting', however, draw our attention to the qualitative difference in what is referred to by the term parenting that is not necessarily entailed in the language of childrearing, upbringing, or raising children. As in many areas of educational and social life, the move towards evidence-based practice also extends to raising children. The framing of what parents ought to do predominantly in the language of developmental psychology and positive psychology presents parenting as a set of skills and a repertoire of expertise; each daily challenge of life with children is a parenting problem to be solved with the right strategy; each choice we make about how we raise our children is seen to have a causal link to future educational and life outcomes. Constituted as 'parenting', raising children is 'confined to what can be located in behavioural terms in the one-to-one-interactions between parent and child – interactions, that is, for which causal links can be shown' (Ramaekers, 2018, pp. 1005-1006). Many of the sources of parenting advice imply: 'Do this, and your child will …'.

The 'parenting culture' has therefore been characterised in critical sociological and educational literature in terms of scientisation, psychologisation, instrumentalisation, and politicisation. Scientisation refers to the ways in which the parenting account of raising children narrows how we understand the parent-child relationship to the application of a set of evidence-based principles that are presented as having a causal link to our children's educational and social outcomes (Faircloth, 2010; Ramaekers and Suissa, 2010). The discourse of the First 1000 Days is a good and well-known example of this (see e.g. Cusick and Georgieff, 2013). Psychologisation (De Vos, 2012) broadly refers to the way in which the various fields of psychology have come to provide the dominant explanatory schemes with which we think about ourselves and others. As the 1000 Days example indicates, however, this has intensified in recent years to a more specific focus on the brain and brain development as a focus of parenting activity, shaped by the development of neuroscientific understandings of child development and life outcomes (see Macvarish, 2016).

The causal relationship between what we do – how we 'parent' – and educational and social outcomes instrumentalises the role of the parent, reflective of the broader shift in our educational discourse in recent decades, such that what we do is only held to have value if it leads to, and ideally improves, particular outcomes (see e.g. Westerling and Juhl, 2021). This instrumentalisation has been referred to more specifically as a politicisation, as educational practices – including those of parents – are seen to be in service of wider policy aims (see e.g. Richter and Andresen, 2012), e.g. better educational outcomes for a better economy, happy, resilient children for a happy, resilient future workforce able to withstand the challenges of an uncertain and globally competitive economy.

These critiques do not seek to deny the importance of our upbringing for who we become, nor do they discredit the various fields of scientific and psychological research that underpin many of the claims made about the impact of what parents do. What they do find to be problematic, however, is the extent to which the terms we have at our disposal to talk about what we do when we raise children are narrowed by the causal, scientific framing of raising children as parenting, and the translation of scientific findings into such causal claims. These critiques also draw attention to the way the parent is positioned in relation to their child by the parenting account of raising children. The parent is asked to take the position of the expert, an external, third-person perspective from which they see their child as the expert sees them: as a set of milestones to be reached, a series of problems to be overcome, in a manner that optimises outcomes (cf. Ramaekers and Suissa, 2012). This is not to suggest that there is something wrong with wanting what is best for our children and those in our care, of course. Rather, it is to question the implication in much parenting literature that 'best' could ever be fully determined, that it might look the same for all individuals, all families, all cultures, that all that we say and do, and the effects that it has, can ever be fully captured or determined.

The parenting account of raising children, therefore, is a very specific way of speaking and enacting what it means to raise children, one that narrows down the terms in which we express what it means to be a parent and directs our attention in particular ways in relation to the day-to-day challenges this can present. In the next section we set out how we understand the idea of raising children as a human practice with particular characteristics and unavoidable existential dimensions.

Raising children as an intergenerational relationship

There are three key aspects to the human experience of raising children that risk being left out of the picture if we limit our understanding to the 'parenting' account:

1   Raising children is always 'essentially' about inheritance and thus involves, in specific ways, forms of taking care of the world, of maintaining the practices of ordinary life, of maintaining an order of the day vis-à-vis the new generation. There cannot be any 'parenting' if not conditioned by such consideration of inheritance.
2   Parents do not have control over the meaning of the world into which they introduce their children.
3   Raising children is always already a collective, political responsibility.

(Hodgson and Ramaekers, 2019, pp. 46–47)

Raising children doesn't take place in a vacuum in which the parent and child are isolated, and the words, actions, and desires of the parent are passed seamlessly from parent to child. Raising children takes place in a cultural and historical context and is shaped by that context and the values and beliefs of parents, family, and community. The parent, then, is representative of that culture. Not in the sense that they actively, explicitly advocate for it, but in their day-to-day sayings and doings, they initiate their child into that culture, into a shared language, a set of morals and values, a set of daily practices and important rituals (cf. Noens, 2017; Cavell, 1979). The younger generation in this sense inherits the world from the older generation who, in this representational role, pass on what is of value and the practices that maintain a collective form of life. The parent is positioned between child and world, continually making judgements on which aspects of the world it is appropriate for our children to be initiated into and how.

In this taking care of the world there is, then, a great deal at stake. Not least because parents do not have control over the meaning of what they pass on, the world to which they introduce the new generation. That is, there are no guarantees that our children will accept what we pass on as we intend it, no certainty that our values will be their values. In the framing of parenting as a skill and set of strategies that we as individuals can work on and improve, the political, collective aspect of raising children is overlooked. If as parents we are representatives of a culture, initiating our children into a common world they will inherit, we speak not only for ourselves and our personal interests and preferences but for those shared practices that collectively constitute a culture, a society (cf. Arendt, 2006; Cavell, 1979).

Given what is at stake in raising children, then, the anxiety we experience, the sense of helplessness we feel in the face of present and future crises is understandable. So, too, then is our instinct to seek solutions, means to mitigate risk, and protect our children from, or at least prepare them for, uncertainty. There is a substantial marketplace that responds to (and arguably in part constitutes) our need for answers, of which Haidt's book and Dr Shefali's content are representative examples. The approach we see here, however, can be contrasted with the research about and with parents and children. In the next section we discuss recent research that was undertaken with parents and is about their experience of life with children and their navigation of the digital as part of this.

Digital technology and the constitution of our lives with children

The account offered by Livingstone and Blum-Ross (2020) provides a more nuanced picture of the complexities of navigating the current context, and what they refer to as 'digital parenting', than the 'parenting' account suggests. Their concern is not with what parents ought, or ought not to do, in order to achieve optimal outcomes in the future, but with what parents *do* in the present. They write:

> … we identify three distinct genres for "digital parenting". By genres we mean clusters of practices made meaningful by particular values, beliefs, and imaginaries (social, digital and future), in ways that are not always conscious or coherent.
>
> *(Livingstone and Blum-Ross, 2020, p. 11)*

These three genres are: embrace, balance, and resist, which they define as follows:

- *embrace*, in which parents seek out digital technologies for themselves or their children to ease family life or to gain valued professional skills or, for some, 'future ready' identities and lifestyles;

- *balance*, in which parents try to hedge their bets by encouraging some digital practices and not others, often *ad hoc*, weighing opportunities and risks salient in the present or future;
- *resist*, in which parents articulate their efforts as attempting, at least some of the time, to stem the seemingly unstoppable incursion of digital technology into family life.

(p. 11)

These genres do not correlate to particular types of families or to particular parenting styles; they 'refer to culturally shared constellations of practices, values and imaginaries rather than the neat classification of individuals or families' (p. 13). Livingstone and Blum-Ross do *not* see these genres as ways of 'categorising' parents; their tripartite set is not meant as a tool for 'diagnosing' parents' 'style' of dealing with digital media in relation to raising their children. No normative *claim* is made either; for example, they do not suggest that *embracing* is 'better' than *resisting* the use of social media. (There is a danger here, we suspect, that in the wrong hands, these genres do become categories with which to assess parents' ways of dealing with digital media.) Rather, through their empirical research they show how parents navigate concerns and questions raised by digital media and the judgments this requires, and thus capture an existential truth of raising children: the inherent uncertainty of the experience. They show that what parents do will depend on the specific questions and needs they have, at that time, in that context.

Livingstone and Blum-Ross (2020) do also identify, however, that these genres of practices and judgments are embedded in a wider normative gaze:

Insofar as parenting practices are constantly judged as being in advance of, lagging behind, or settling at what appears to be the emerging norm, these genres embedded a normative gaze that can isolate parents from each other, as each watches and evaluates the other before determining her own approach.

(p. 13)

Through their empirical research with parents, the authors identify that, whichever approach they are taking in that moment is accompanied by an anxiety 'as parents ask themselves: Did I get it right? Will it pay off? [...] Is this right? How can I tell?' (p. 13). This questioning seems to reflect the extent to which the 'parenting' account of raising children has become embedded: the parent-child relationship has been constituted by a specific discourse of 'parenting', which is infused, as discussed in the critical literature referred to earlier, with a causal logic, which creates the sense that we ought to be clear on the outcome of our action, that we might be able to determine this fully in advance, and that a pay-off, some added values ought to come of our decisions. The more telling question parents seem to raise here, though, is 'How can I tell?'.

The findings reported above from Livingstone and Blum-Ross's research remind us that raising children is not as straightforwardly linear as the parenting discourse suggests. Not only do they not make any normative claims about the genres they identify, but also, and more importantly, they show that parents ask questions (question themselves) irrespective of what they are doing (embracing, balancing, resisting). These questions relate to matters of worth; they relate to what they find valuable (to pass on, to do, to cherish) and important (in relation to their children). To put the point differently, it is not about which genre is the most valuable, the most appropriate to adopt, but what the genres express about what parents find valuable and about the more complex, nuanced, indeterminate picture we gain when we see ourselves as *raising* our children.

Crisis?

As we have seen, the concern relating to the affordances and dangers of digital technology is often framed in terms of its impact on children, expressed in psychological terms, and how parents ought to take responsibility for maximising (e.g. learning outcomes, digital literacy) or limiting (e.g. screen time, social anxiety) these impacts. The arguably more pedagogically relevant question, however, relates to the role that digital technology has played in the lives of the older and younger generations and therefore, how the question of digital technology is constituted when we see the parent–child relationship as an intergenerational relationship. Put simply, how do digital migrants introduce digital technology to digital natives? How do we as the older generation introduce the younger generation to something we largely do not know or understand? This points us to a different sense of crisis than we saw above in the work of Palmer and Furedi; not an anxiety over the future impact of digital technology but crisis as in its Greek etymological sense, *krinein*, which means to judge or make a judgement, a distinction. It is a crisis of judgement precisely because a parent cannot *not* be 'in-between', child and world, past and future.

The sensitive and sometimes heated debate around children's use of digital technology and social media shows us something about the 'essence' of raising children: that parents are always in-between the world and their child, that they cannot evade the responsibilities inherent to their in-between-ness, and that as in-between figures they are always, necessarily, thinking, judging, as in the original sense of the world 'crisis'. We could say that the current anxiety and insecurity regarding social media is precisely about not knowing very well which lines to draw and where to draw them. So, it becomes a question of seeking certainty, turning to the experts, to solve the issue. Here, instead, we take this 'crisis' as a reminder that raising children necessarily always entails 'making distinctions' about what is valuable – in your own life, in your child's life; now, in the future – and what isn't – yet, or perhaps ever.

48 Naomi Hodgson and Stefan Ramaekers

A crisis cannot be solved by bringing in more data. Empirical findings alone do not tell us what to do. A crisis brings us back to the very core of the concept itself, *krinein*, to make distinctions. And these distinctions can only be made in context, in relation to the particular conditions in which they are called for. A crisis, in this sense, doesn't need statements such as 'when this, then that'; in a crisis we weigh up the elements that arise in the situation, perhaps having first made a judgement about which elements are relevant to 'factor in'. The account offered by Livingstone and Blum-Ross conveys this very message: whether parents engage in embracing, balancing, or resisting, what they always do is ask questions, make decisions, based on the criteria relevant for them in the particular situation they find themselves in with their children. The crisis of digital media is a reminder of the pedagogical, political nature of parental responsibility. To reaffirm this requires such reminders that we do, continually, make judgments, convey values, in our specificity as parents. The third-person perspective of the expert can provide essential guidance, information, clarity even, but no ultimate certainty.

This may have some far-reaching implications for practitioners and the way in which they are trained. As it stands, most are trained in a number of (usually psychological) models (or models based on psychological research), which provide a framework, a reference point, when they are interacting with and supporting parents in the context of practice, especially perhaps if they are still quite young (or at least younger than the parents). But these models are limited, as practitioners sometimes will concede themselves, because they cannot replace the necessity that it is parents who have to 'make distinctions' in the end. What seems to be needed in addition, we suggest, is (minimally) that practitioners develop a 'healthy distance' towards the models they are taught and to the extent to which such models form part of the picture of supporting parents. When these models fill the frame of what raising children consists in, there is little space to think beyond them. Developing such 'healthy distance' also implies being able to confront discomfort – e.g. in the form of not knowing 'the answer' – in relation to parents. To see parents only as 'parenters', that is, in instrumental, strictly causal terms in relation to their children, is to deny the complexity of who they are, the lives they lead, and the decisions they make in that context.

References

Arendt, H (2006). *Between Past and Future*. New York: Penguin.
Cavell, S (1979). *The Claim of Reason: Wittgenstein, Skepticism, Morality, and Tragedy*. New York: Oxford University Press.
Cusick, S & Georgieff, M (2013). *The First 1,000 Days of Life: The Brain's Window of Opportunity*. UNICEF. Retrieved from: https://www.unicef-irc.org/article/958-the-first-1000-days-of-life-the-brains-window-of-opportunity.html
De Vos, J (2012). *Psychologisation in Times of Globalisation*. London: Routledge.

Faircloth, C (2010). 'What Science Says is Best': Parenting practices, scientific authority and maternal identity. *Sociological Research Online, 15*(4), https://doi.org/10.5153/sro.2175

Furedi, F (2008). *Paranoid Parenting*. London: Bloomsbury.

Gray, P, Lancy, DF, & Bjorklund, DF (2023). Decline in independent activity as a cause of decline in children's mental well-being: Summary of the evidence, *The Journal of Pediatrics*. DOI: https://doi.org/10.1016/j.jpeds.2023.02.004

Haidt, J (2024). *The Anxious Generation: How the Great Rewiring of Childhood Caused an Epidemic of Mental Illness*. Penguin.

Haidt, J (2023). *The anxious generation*. Retrieved from: The Anxious Generation | Jonathan Haidt

Hodgson, N, & Ramaekers, S (2019). *Philosophical Presentations of Raising Children: The Grammar of Upbringing*. Palgrave.

Kehily, MJ (2010). Childhood in crisis? Tracing the contours of 'crisis' and its impact upon contemporary parenting practices. *Media, Culture & Society, 32*(2), 171–185. https://doi.org/10.1177/0163443709355605

Lee, E, Bristow, J, Faircloth, C, & Macvarish, J (2014). *Parenting Culture Studies*. Basingstoke: Palgrave.

Livingstone, S, & Blum-Ross, A (2020). *Parenting for a Digital Future*. Oxford University Press.

MacVarish, J (2016). *Neuroparenting: The Expert Invasion of Family Life*. Basingstoke: Palgrave.

Noens, P (2017). *Family 'matters': Re-'taking' Upbringing in a Culture of Parenting*. Unpublished PhD dissertation, KU Leuven.

Palmer, S (2006). *Toxic Childhood*. Orion.

Pilkington, E (2023). US surgeon general issues advisory on 'profound' risks of child social media use, *The Guardian*, 23 May 2023. https://www.theguardian.com/media/2023/may/23/social-media-warning-kids-mental-health

Ramaekers, S (2018). Childrearing, parenting, upbringing: Philosophy of education and the experience of raising a child. In P. Smeyers (Ed.), *International Handbook of Philosophy of Education*. Springer International Publishing AG.

Ramaekers, S, & Suissa, J (2010). The scientisation of the parent-child relationship. In L. Hopkins, M. Macleod, & W. Turgeon (Eds.), *Negotiating Childhoods*. Brill.

Ramaekers, S, & Suissa, J (2012). *The Claims of Parenting: Reasons, Responsibility, and Society*. Dordrecht: Springer.

Richter, M, & Andresen, S (Eds.). (2012). *The Politicization of Parenthood: Shifting Private and Public Responsibilities in Education and Child Rearing*. Dordrecht: Springer.

Smith, R (2010). Total parenting. *Educational Theory, 60*, 357–369.

Tsabary, S (2023 September 1). *How to break your kids screen addiction*. [Instagram post]. Retrieved from https://www.instagram.com/p/Cwp0l-_Po5J/

Van Ouytsel, J, Walrave, M, Ojeda, M, Del Rey, R, & Ponnet, K (2020). Adolescents' sexy self-presentation on Instagram: An investigation of their posting behavior using a prototype willingness model perspective. *International Journal of Environmental Research and Public Health, 17*, 8106. doi:10.3390/ijerph17218106

Westerling, A, & Juhl, P (2021). Collaborative instrumentalization of family life: How new learning agendas disrupt care chains in the Danish welfare state. *Nordic Psychology, 73*, 2.

PART II

Early Childhood Workforce and Management Issues

6

ENHANCING THE DEVELOPMENT OF PRACTITIONERS AND SETTINGS

Ute Ward

After the previous section on the increasing digitalisation of early childhood already examined some practice issues, this second section will look in more detail at workforce and management issues, touching on training and education of practitioners, management systems and parental involvement. You will find further references here to neoliberalism, its emphasis on top-down guidance, narrow curricula and accountability demands. These often combine to leave practitioners feeling powerless and unable to exercise professional autonomy and judgement (Osgood, 2010). During the pandemic, practitioners often felt their impression confirmed that their work was undervalued and poorly paid, which was not only the case in countries where the ECEC workforce holds a wide range of different qualifications but also in countries where higher education qualifications are required to work in the sector (for example, in Croatia; see Chapter 7). A further factor in the wellbeing of the workforce is the emotional labour required when working with young children and their families, leaving many practitioners experiencing emotional exhaustion and even burnout. The worrying aspect here is that exhaustion and burnout have a direct impact on how well practitioners can engage with children, and the quality of children's experience invariably drops when staff feel exhausted (Trauernicht, Anders, Oppermann & Klusmann, 2023).

In many countries the pandemic exacerbated the stresses and strains that already existed in the sector. For example, in England, there was little guidance for nurseries and pre-schools apart from having to stay open to care for key worker children. The ECEC workforce was split between those practitioners having to care for key worker children face-to-face and those who were sent home to support children and families online. Neither group could draw on

DOI: 10.4324/9781003471172-8

adequate preparation or resources, and support in general depended on individual managers and colleagues (Blanch Gelabert et al., 2023). The inherent shift in practitioners' work roles included developing online resources for children and psychological support for parents and children, which was often experienced as an increase in workload (Yildiz, Kilic & Acar, 2023).

The additional burden during the pandemic combined with the pre-existing poor conditions and status and increased staff turnover with many practitioners not simply leaving to work in another ECEC setting but often leaving the ECEC sector completely (Hardy et al., 2023). This raises questions about the economic sustainability of the sector, particularly in countries where governments are planning to increase ECEC entitlement or to cut funding.

The chapters in this section will present a range of different strategies and projects which can help to address some of these and related issues faced by ECEC practitioners and managers, starting with three contributions addressing practitioner training and development. Adrijana Višnjić-Jevtić and Antonija Vukašinović's chapter on professional development in Croatia connects this section to the previous one on digitalisation – a sign that the strict categorisation of chapters into sections in this book is somewhat artificial because of the interconnectedness and complexity of most issues in the ECEC sector. The authors present Croatian practitioners' experiences during the pandemic in relation to their continuous professional development (CPD). Their low status and their attitudes to online tools for CPD are explained. Interestingly, many practitioners persevered with CPD during the pandemic and found much support and new knowledge in online communities beyond the borders of their own country. The communities of practice they were able to access and participate in are evidence of the role and power practitioners can have in developing individually and collectively. This could potentially contribute to economically sustainable training and development initiatives.

The idea of mutual support from fellow practitioners is also mentioned in Chapter 8 by Marg Rogers and her colleagues. They specifically looked at how neoliberal pressures impact practitioners' professional identity in five different countries, and it is interesting to note that in spite of different national contexts, their experiences and perceptions of identity have many similarities. Like the participants in the Croatian study, practitioners here also valued mutual support and the deep understanding of complex lived experiences that colleagues and fellow practitioners can offer. This forms the basis for a peer mentoring programme set up in British Colombia, Canada, to support practitioners' professional identity and increase their self-efficacy. If you are particularly interested in CPD, Chapter 13 by Sharon Skehill in the next section addresses training for leadership in inclusion.

In Chapter 9 by Lewis Stockwell and Michael Young, the focus shifts from in-service support to pre-service training and an example of an early childhood degree programme at an English university. They reflect on the design and introduction of a final year module engaging students with philosophy of education and enabling them to develop and express their own values for early childhood education and for their work with children. The aim is to open students' eyes to practice beyond the implementation of standardised curricula, national assessment guidelines and ever more accountability, and includes discussions of Dewey, Aristotle, Mezirow and others. Although grounded in higher education, this chapter also gives valuable ideas for self-study or staff development.

After the exploration of workforce development, the next chapter turns to management and leadership issues in the ECEC sector. Together with other thinkers, Noam Chomsky (2021) sees increased citizen activism and stronger democracy as a way to overcome the neoliberal hold on modern society. In her chapter introducing the London Early Years Foundation (LEYF), June O'Sullivan describes how a social enterprise model can counteract top-down pressure and deliver quality care and education, in particular for children facing disadvantage. Her settings build on a commitment to social justice and inclusion for children, families and staff members. At the same time, economic, social and environmental sustainability form the cornerstones of LEYF, as does social leadership, showcasing a different relationship between managers and staff. In their teaching and learning, LEYF has adopted a social pedagogical approach which embraces ongoing change to adapt to the children's and their communities' lived experience.

The final chapter in this section extends the theme of greater democratisation and returns to parents and their perspectives, which were already discussed earlier regarding parenting in the digital age. Fay Hadley and her colleagues from Australia present their insights from a project seeking parents' views to update and improve their national early years framework. In many national curriculum frameworks, we find a commitment to parental involvement, for example, in the English Early Years Foundation Stage (Department for Education, 2023). However, it is rare that parents' views are sought in such a structured manner and at the point of national policy formation. It is often assumed that parents lack the necessary knowledge and are not interested in issues beyond the immediate care of their children although this was already challenged two decades ago (Knopf & Swick, 2007). Here, the authors have equally found that parents appreciate being asked to contribute to policy matters and are indeed insightful and knowledgeable. In addition to gaining an insight into how parents can be engaged in policy formation, this chapter reflects parents' views on assessment practices and on inclusion and cultural diversity, in particular regarding Aboriginal and Torres Strait Islander peoples.

This section already includes some exploration of social pedagogy in Chapter 10 introducing LEYF, and early childhood pedagogy also forms the focus of the third section in this book, with a particular emphasis of supporting inclusive practice. To extend your understanding of change management,

I would recommend reading Chapter 17 entitled 'Children reading to their parents' as it offers a valuable case study of how change can be planned and implemented.

References

Blanch Gelabert, S, Heland-Kurzak, K, Tal, C, Tal, P, Tish, S, Višnjić-Jevtić, A, & Ward, U (2023). Perceptions of parents and educators on their relationships during and after Covid-19 in five countries. *European Early Childhood Education Research Conference*, Cascais, Portugal, 2023 August 30–September 2.

Chomsky, N (2021). *The Precipice*. Great Britain: Penguin Books.

Department for Education (2023). *Statutory Framework for the Early Years Foundation Stage*. London: Crown Copyright. Retrieved from: https://assets.publishing.service.gov.uk/government/uploads/system/uploads/attachment_data/file/1170108/EYFS_framework_from_September_2023.pdf

Hardy, K, Stephens, L, Tomlinson, J, Valizade, D, Whittaker, X, Norman, H, & Moffat, R (2023). *Retention and return: Delivering the expansion of early years entitlement in England*. Retrieved from: https://static1.squarespace.com/static/646ca30371 a2ef6a657e9309/t/65482050ded6710668b8b62a/1699225681784/Retention+and+Return.pdf

Knopf, H, & Swick, K (2007). How parents feel about their child's teacher/school: Implications for early childhood professionals. *Early Childhood Education Journal*, *34*(4), 291–296.

Osgood, J (2010). Reconstructing professionalism in ECEC: The case for the 'critically reflective emotional professional'. *Early Years*, *30*(2), 119–133.

Trauernicht, M, Anders, Y, Oppermann, E, & Klusmann, U (2023). Early childhood educators' emotional exhaustion and the frequency of education activities in pre-school. *European Early Childhood Education Research Journal*, *31*(6), 1016–1032. https://doi.org/10.1080/1350293X.2023.2217485

Yildiz, S, Kilic, G, & Acar, I (2023). 'Early childhood education during the COVID-19 outbreak: The perceived changing roles of preschool administrators, teachers and parents. *Early Childhood Education Journal*, *51*, 743–753. https://doi.org/10.1007/s10643-022-01339-w

7

PROFESSIONAL DEVELOPMENT OF CROATIAN EARLY CHILDHOOD TEACHERS IN A VIRTUAL WORLD – OPPORTUNITY OR OBSTACLE?

Adrijana Višnjić-Jevtić and Antonija Vukašinović

Introduction

The current comprehension of professional competence reveals it to be an inherent aspect of development, indicating an ongoing learning journey. Certain scholars (Hindin & Mueller, 2016) highlight lifelong learning as a viable means to enhance acquired competencies. Therefore, it is rational to anticipate a need for continuous professional development among early childhood education (ECE) teachers. Evans (2002) defines teachers' professional development as a process of modifying professional attitudes and improving the performance of their professional acting. While experience can contribute to the development of teachers' professional competencies, only continuous educational processes within existing professional communities united by shared interests can lead to changes in the practices and theories of individuals.

In Carpenter's (2016) view on professional development, the transmission of knowledge and continuous change in existing practices aligns with a traditional approach that, despite practice changes, doesn't contribute to its development. The contemporary approach, contributing to real and enduring changes, always focuses on content linked to the curriculum of educational institutions and collective support. Some authors (for example, Carpenter, 2016; Svanbjörnsdóttir, Macdonald & Frímannsson, 2016) see professional development as a long-term, continuous process of knowledge acquisition built in collaboration with peers. Despite ECE teachers' professional responsibility towards the norms of their own profession, ECE teachers might have their own approach to development. Although occasional training activities do not lead to lasting changes in their own practice, they can influence an

DOI: 10.4324/9781003471172-9

individual's awareness of potential directions for professional development. Stewart (2014) sees professional development as a way to change ECE practices, but highlights professional learning activities as a form that leads to changes in theories and assumptions both in individuals and in professional communities.

Learning within one's own professional community (*in-service*) impacts the quality of relationships among all participants in the interaction and contributes to the development of teachers' competencies (Peeters & Vandenbroeck, 2011; Visković & Višnjić Jevtić, 2017). New insights arising from these processes alter established knowledge, thus requiring the development of fresh approaches to professional training that both steer and enhance professional advancement. Given the essential nature of continuous professional development for ECE teachers, exploring innovative approaches to such development becomes crucial. Hence, it is important to explore how ECE teachers engage with novel activities that enhance their professional growth, particularly focusing on virtual methods.

Cultivating Bright Futures: Early Childhood Education and Care in Croatia

Early childhood education represents the first tier within the Croatian education system. It involves structured programs providing care and education for children aged six months to school entry, focusing on children's personal, educational, and social well-being. While ECE is acknowledged as one level of institutional education in Croatia, mandatory participation for children only occurs a year before school entry, specifically through the Preschool Program, lasting 250 hours (MSES, 2014). The establishment and funding of kindergartens are contingent upon local administration, which allocate resources for kindergarten facilities including materials and professional development for ECE teachers (Eurydice, 2023).

In Croatia, the level of education required for ECE teachers is the university bachelor's degree in early childhood education with a specific focus on child development, learning theories, and pedagogical approaches tailored to young children. Although it is not mandatory, more and more ECE teachers decide to continue their education at Master's level. After completing their education, ECE teachers are required to work as interns for one year and then pass a state exam to be able to work independently as ECE teachers. Continuous professional development is also mandatory to stay up-to-date with the latest practices in the field.

The professional development of ECE teachers is primarily the personal professional accountability of the ECE teachers and, subsequently, the institution in which they work. In the Republic of Croatia, alongside these actors, the Education and Teacher Training Agency (ETTA) takes on the organization of activities that contribute to the professional development of ECE teachers. An analysis of the topics of professional meetings for ECE teachers available on the websites reveals the diversity of topics. However, topics are dependent on the region of ETTA's regional offices and are not standardized, meaning professional training on a specific topic is not available to all ECE teachers in Croatia.

While training organized by ETTA is recognized as *official* and mandatory, there are various activities that respond to ECE teachers' interests and intrinsic motivation (Lestari, Sumantri & Dhieni, 2022; Visković & Višnjić Jevtić, 2018; Višnjić Jevtić & Halavuk, 2021). Transformative activities and reflective research practices are defined as prerequisites for teachers' professional progress in the National Curriculum for Early and Preschool Education (MSES, 2015). As a result, ECE teachers should seek various forms of professional development and themes that match to their specific preferences.

During the COVID-19 pandemic, due to the impossibility of physical contact, ECE teachers' professional development shifted online (Jin, 2023). ECE teachers had the opportunity to participate virtually in various activities of professional development (Abduraxmanova & Jo'rayev, 2022) or engage in online learning communities (Avidov-Ungar, Merav & Cohen, 2023; Duran, 2021). ECE teachers' intrinsic motivation for professional development was rooted in professional accountability (Byun & Jeon, 2023) and the desire for social-professional interaction (Li & Luo, 2022) through virtual forms of professional development. Apart from the advantages that virtual professional development offered, numerous factors posed as obstacles. Even though ECE teachers in Croatia are educated to Bachelor and Master levels, society does not perceive them as professionals in their field but rather as caregivers. Equally, it seems that the educational system does not recognize them as equal to other teachers (in primary or secondary schools). Consequently, ECE teachers do not have an electronic identity that gives them access to a variety of content intended for educators. In pandemic times, this identity was the entrance ticket to various online programs aimed to contribute to the teachers' professional development.

Revolutionizing ECE Teacher Growth: Exploring the Virtual Frontier of Professional Development

This section discusses the advantages, challenges, and various aspects surrounding the virtual professional development of ECE teachers. Highlighting the nuances of this domain, it explores both the benefits and obstacles faced by teachers engaging in virtual learning, shedding light on the pivotal role of digital competencies and institutional support in this sphere. Advantages of ECE teachers' virtual professional development are evident in the reduction of material costs associated with travel, accommodation, and other expenses related to attending conferences and training. Furthermore, teachers have the convenience of participating in virtual forms of professional development from the comfort of their own homes, allowing them flexibility in organizing their free time, choosing education according to their interests, and deciding on the effectiveness of interactive participation (Hu, Yuan, Luo & Wang, 2021). Research results referred to by Roberts, LoCasale-Crouch, Hamre, and Jamil (2020) emphasize the importance of virtual professional development for teachers because this enables individual development at one's own pace and greater virtual mobility in participating in various courses within a short time frame.

However, the results of numerous studies (Abdul-Majied, Kinkead-Clark & Burns, 2023; Dahri, Vighio, Al-Rahmi & Alismaiel, 2022; Negrín-Medina, Bernárdez-Gómez, Portela-Pruaño & Marrero-Galván, 2022; Powell & Bodur, 2019) indicate barriers to virtual professional development for ECE teachers. Pölzl-Stefanec and Geißler (2022) stress the importance of systematic support for teachers in virtual professional development and environment. Research results highlight the inadequacy of technical and functional equipment available to teachers to participate in virtual professional development. Furthermore, ECE teachers point out that a lack of free time and personal space within the family circle reduces the effectiveness of attentive monitoring of virtual training and the possibility of relaxed interactive participation in training. In addition to technical difficulties mentioned as obstacles in the virtual professional development of teachers, Mystakidis, Fragkaki, and Filippousis (2021) believe that teachers' digital competencies are crucial for advancing in virtual professional development. Insufficiently developed digital competencies of teachers can contribute to frustration, insecurity, and a loss of confidence when participating in virtual training (Abdul-Majied et al., 2023).

Dahri et al. (2022) emphasize the need for a theoretical framework to make virtual learning an integral part of teachers' professional development. The authors believe that virtual professional development of teachers should be accessible to all regardless of socio-economic, cultural, socio-political, or other differences. Saxena and Chiu (2022) emphasize that systematic support and teamwork are necessary to motivate teachers for their professional development. They also found that training sessions aimed at enhancing teachers' digital competencies and literacy resulted in increased level of self-efficacy. Hooper, Potts, and Walton (2023) consider virtual professional development for teachers as a tool for implementing quality educational practice in kindergartens. Support for teachers in virtual professional development largely depends on the leadership of the institution and the headmaster's attitude towards the importance of virtual professional development. Zhou, Nakatsubo, Wu, and Liu (2022) point out that by using WeChat (a social media messaging app), teachers developed a connected learning community that helps them in their virtual professional development. A shared vision, the exchange of reflective practice, and mutual support of kindergarten staff motivated teachers for professional development through social media. Negrín-Medina et al. (2022) emphasize that the use of information and communication technology for the virtual professional development of teachers resulted in the European Union adopting the European Framework for the Digital Competence of Educators: DigCompEdu (Redecker & Punie, 2017). The teachers who participated in the abovementioned research support the development of online learning communities and the gamification of online content as motivation for virtual professional development.

Somolanji Tokić and Vukašinović (2020) highlighted that the non-compulsory nature of early childhood education and care in Croatia restricts ECE teachers from fully acquiring the competencies outlined in the European DigCompEdu Framework. Thus, the question arises as to how people with insufficient digital competence can be involved in virtual activities that should improve their professional development. To find the answer, research with ECE teachers was conducted about their experience of virtual activities that contribute to professional development.

Method

The aim of the research was to find out whether ECE teachers see virtual professional development as an opportunity to broaden their professional horizon or as an obstacle. Focus group research was conducted to explore the comprehension of virtual professional development among ECE teachers. While focus groups may not offer a comprehensive understanding of a specific issue, they significantly contribute to insights. Gawlik (2018) affirms that such a research approach facilitates mutual intellectual stimulation, culminating in the formulation of collective opinions. Hyman and Sierra (2016) note that when a synergy of opinions occurs, individuals are more inclined to express their views and beliefs within these groups, anticipating support from the collective expertise. The focus group was held on a digital communication platform to enable ECE teachers to join regardless of the place where they live. The eight participants differ by educational backgrounds, areas they live in, previous virtual learning experience, and self-perception of their ICT competences (see Table 7.1).

The process of knowledge creation within a consensus involves the amalgamation of diverse perspectives, beliefs, and experiences to form a shared understanding. It emerges through the collaborative efforts of a group, community, or society where individual insights coalesce to shape a collective wisdom (Kamberelis, Dimitriadis & Welker, 2017). This consensus-based knowledge-making is a dynamic interplay between various viewpoints, cultural nuances, and shared values. It necessitates open dialogue, critical analysis, and the reconciliation of differing ideas to reach a unified understanding. Within this

TABLE 7.1 Participants

Participant*	Education	Area	Virtual learning experience	ICT competences
Alma	Master's degree in education	Urban	Basic	Intermediate
Bela	Master's degree in ECE	Urban	Basic	Intermediate
Cvita	Bachelor's degree in ECE	Rural	None	Beginner
Dora	Bachelor's degree in ECE	Urban	Proficient	Advanced
Ema	Bachelor's degree in ECE	Urban	Proficient	Advanced
Fiona	Bachelor's degree in ECE	Urban	None	Beginner
Greta	Master's degree in education	Rural	Proficient	Advanced
Hana	Master's degree in ECE	Urban	Basic	Advanced

* To protect participants' identities, pseudonyms were used.

framework, new insights surface, evolving from the convergence of diverse thoughts and opinions, ultimately contributing to the broader pool of shared knowledge. The result of a focus group discussion is therefore a consensus and could possibly lead to creating new knowledge.

The research questions pertaining to community support during the COVID-19 period for teachers' professional development delve into multifaceted aspects. Firstly, they aim to explore how ECE teachers perceive the support received from their professional communities during this challenging time. This involves understanding the various forms of assistance, resources, and collaborative efforts extended by the community to facilitate teachers' professional growth amidst the pandemic. Secondly, the questions aim to investigate how ECE teachers managed to engage and participate in professional development opportunities during such tumultuous times. Understanding the strategies, platforms, and modes employed by ECE teachers to continue their professional growth becomes a pivotal aspect of this inquiry. Additionally, the research explores the challenges encountered by ECE teachers in this pursuit, seeking to unearth the obstacles, limitations, or difficulties they faced while navigating professional development amidst the pandemic. Lastly, the research aims to identify key takeaways—lessons, insights, and recommended practices—so that ECE teachers, communities, and educational institutions can adapt and better prepare for any future disruptions, ensuring more effective, adaptable, and resilient professional development strategies. This comprehensive exploration provides a holistic view of the dynamics between community support, professional development, challenges faced, and the essential learnings to be derived from this unique period.

Professional Development During COVID-19—Results and Discussion

The presentation below encompasses the comprehensive study conducted to explore the challenges confronting ECE teachers in their professional development amid the COVID-19 era. The presentation not only captures the resilience displayed by ECE teachers but also delivers vital insights and key learning essential for a more adaptable, informed, and prepared approach to future strategies for professional development. Embedded within these results are the narratives, approaches, difficulties, and successes of ECE teachers navigating the unexplored territories of learning within a pandemic-changed landscape.

Perceptions of support: insights of ECE teachers

Research participants had mixed thoughts about the support they received during the pandemic. They unanimously stated that they expected support from their institution, the Ministry of Science and Education, and the public. During the initial phase of the pandemic, they felt the necessity for support in their day-to-day professional tasks, prioritizing immediate needs over considerations for professional advancement. Research by Nadeem, Shernoff, Coccaro, and Stokes-Tyler (2022) also showed that teachers expected support from institutions in dealing with emotionally demanding situations. Nevertheless, Alma concludes:

> You know, the basic functioning, Viber groups and Zoom meetings. It was not for the purpose of development, but it contributed to my development. I learned to use new tools - and that is development.

The problem they repeatedly returned to was the lack of support from the ETTA. The participants point out that it was ETTA that should have provided support during the transition to virtual activities. Hana says:

> You know, they (ETTA, author's note) have to organize trainings. I kind of expected a workshop or at least a list of tools we can use.

Frequently, participants highlighted a prevailing perception that the educational system does not view them (ECE teachers) on a par with other educators, such as primary or secondary school teachers. Bela explained that ECE teachers lack a distinct electronic identity granting access to a wide array of educational resources. This absence of an essential digital identity restricts their access to various online programs intended for professional development, which is granted to their counterparts in primary school teaching. Bela became aware of the disparities in access privileges when she compared her own access to educational resources with that of a friend teaching at primary level. It appears that there were widespread similarities globally. Gomes et al. (2021) also highlighted the lack of government support for ECE teachers in, for example, Australia.

Jen, Mathijssen, and Hoogeveen (2022) provide a list of resources shared by UNESCO to enhance teachers' competence and their professional development. It is possible that the participants in the research did not research (perhaps due to a lack of experience in virtual sources) support outside the borders of Croatia. Only one participant mentioned that lists of various websites that could be used in virtual learning arose at some point. Other participants pointed out that it is still meant for higher education and is oriented at teaching, not at the work of ECE teachers. Reflecting on support, Greta states:

> We have real support in each other. But how can we support each other when we are not allowed to meet. We solved a lot of things over coffee. We had - coffee reflection!

Challenges and inequalities – ECE teachers' struggle with professional engagement

Participants identified "home" education as a formidable challenge due to the intricate balance required between their familial responsibilities and professional accountability. Alma expressed frustration, stating "It is not fair to have lectures in my free time!", which highlights the difficulty of managing work-related obligations during their personal hours. Additionally, some participants perceive online training as an opportunity for some teachers to abstain from active involvement, attributing their disengagement to insufficient equipment or internet connectivity. Moreover, participants acknowledged disparities stemming from uneven conditions, primarily attributed to foreign language and information and communication technology (ICT) competencies. These observations underscored the significant impact of family-professional life balance, challenges with timing, and varying competencies, signifying the complexity and inequities faced by educators in their remote teaching environments. Persistent gender-based inequities in how household work is divided, with women (and ECE is predominantly a women's profession) generally bearing the brunt of domestic labour, which contributed to the impossibility of harmonizing private and professional obligations (Nagasawa & Tarrant, 2020).

Cvita pointed out:

> I think the worst thing was that we didn't know where to start - do I need more work after being stressed all day. And then again, I know I have to get moving and work on myself.

The participants concur with this perspective, affirming that upon arriving home, their primary desire was to be in a secure environment and to take a respite from work. Among the issues they raise, the demand for additional devices within the household is highlighted. Simultaneously, Fiona contends that children require a computer for their classes, asserting that this takes precedence over their own pursuit of virtual training. Perry (2022) points out that *de-prioritization* of professional development was expected in times of pandemic. Insisting on additional work obligations could lead to an excessive burden even on already overburdened teachers.

Takeaways — *lessons learnt from crises*

The participants perceive the opportunity to engage in global professional communities as a distinct advantage. They see the ability to take part in online training events as a significant benefit. Cvita emphasized: "You may join at the time that fits in your schedule," highlighting the flexibility and convenience of such opportunities. Additionally, participants highlighted the advantage of choice, stating, "You may choose between many webinars," which affords them a diverse range of learning options. Ema mentioned: "I had the opportunity to hear different practices," indicating the richness of exposure to various methodologies and insights. Overall, participants appreciate the global reach of these opportunities, as they enable flexibility, choice, and exposure to diverse teaching practices. Although some other research (i.e. Eddy, Macdonald & Baer, 2021) highlighted saving time that was normally spent on traveling to the place where the activities, meetings, or training are held, none of the participants mentioned this as an advantage.

Participants reflect that despite the challenging period of the pandemic, it equipped them for upcoming crises and provided them with new tools and skills. Dora highlights:

> Covid compelled me to step out of my comfort zone; I refined my digital skills and re-engaged with speaking in English. It made me realize - the world is genuinely a global village. I can learn from someone located far away but who shares a similar mindset, as opposed to those I work closely with. I connected with educators who share common interests and challenges. This is crucial because it enables us to seek solutions together without any sense of guilt.

Virtual professional development enabled participants to join virtual learning communities, which connect not by workplace but by interests and mindset. Besides improving digital and language skills, networking with other professionals is the most valuable *takeaway*. Gomes et al. (2021) summarise the strengths of ECE teachers in the pandemic as *adaptability* and *responsiveness.* It is likely that the crisis precipitated by the pandemic spurred ECE teachers to adjust to the new circumstances and remain receptive to the challenges. Accountability was perceived through empowerment, inspiration, and motivation (Eddy et al., 2021). Consequently, fellow experts transformed into a mutual source of support and encouragement for each other.

Conclusion

The challenges faced by ECE teachers during the pandemic were numerous. The support they expected was often absent or focused solely on activities required for working with children. Considering the primary task of ensuring the well-being of children during those demanding times may have meant that the professionals themselves did not prioritize their own professional well-being. Since professional development is imperative for the well-being of ECE teachers, it is justified to contemplate the support that society should subsequently provide for these professionals. The conducted research shows that, according to the participants' opinions, support within the system was lacking. Simultaneously, support from peers emerged, leading to the formation of new professional communities.

The challenges encountered by the research participants were the same as those faced by professionals across the globe. Most often, the lack of support in the development of digital competencies and the absence of equipment were highlighted, along with the difficulty of balancing private and professional life. Despite the challenges, participants highlight the most significant takeaway as pushing their own boundaries, stepping out of their comfort zone, and enhancing their competencies.

Due to the nature of the research, the obtained data cannot be generalized and does not justify drawing conclusions that would apply to the entire population. What is indicative, though, is that participants feel unfairly excluded from national support systems, which affects their professional identity. The question arises as to whether ECE teachers are only nominally part of the education system. As stakeholders in the system, it is crucial for policy-makers and managers to provide ECE teachers with support and conditions similar to the support and conditions enjoyed by other teachers.

References

Abdul-Majied, S, Kinkead-Clark, Z, & Burns, SC (2023). Understanding Caribbean early childhood teachers' professional experiences during the COVID-19 school disruption. *Early Childhood Education Journal, 51,* 431–441. https://doi.org/10.1007/s10643-022-01320-7

Abduraxmanova, Sh A, & Jo'rayev, X (2022). Modern web technologies. *Conference Zone,* 178–179. Retrieved from http://www.conferencezone.org/index.php/cz/article/view/248

Avidov-Ungar, O, Merav, H, & Cohen, S (2023). Role perceptions of early childhood teachers leading professional learning communities following a new professional development policy. *Leadership and Policy in Schools*, *22*(1), 225–237. https://doi.org/10.1080/15700763.2021.1921224

Byun, S, & Jeon, L (2023). Early childhood teachers' work environment, perceived personal stress, and professional commitment in South Korea. *Child Youth Care Forum*, *52*, 1019–1039. https://doi.org/10.1007/s10566-022-09722-9

Carpenter, JP (2016). Unconference professional development: Edcamp participant perception and motivation attendance. *Professional Development in Education*, *42*(1), 78–99. https://doi.org/10.1080/19415257.2015.1036303

Dahri, NA, Vighio, MS, Al-Rahmi, WM, & Alismaiel, OA (2022). Usability evaluation of mobile app for the sustainable professional development of teachers. *International Journal of Interactive Mobile Technologies*, *16*(16). https://doi.org/10.3991/ijim.v16i16.32015

Duran, M (2021). The effects of COVID-19 pandemic on preschool education. *International Journal of Educational Methodology*, *7*(2), 249–260. https://doi.org/10.12973/ijem.7.2.249

Eddy, PL, Macdonald, RH, & Baer, EM (2021). Professional development during a crisis and beyond: Lessons learned during COVID. *New Directions for Community Colleges*, *2021*(195), 199–212. https://doi.org/10.1002/cc.20477

Eurydice (2023). *Continuing professional development for teachers working in early childhood and school education*. Retrieved from: https://eurydice.eacea.ec.europa.eu/national-education-systems/croatia/continuing-professional-development-teachers-working-early

Evans, L (2002). What is teacher development? *Oxford Review of Education*, *28*(1), 123–137. https://doi.org/10.1080/03054980120113670

Gawlik, K (2018). Focus groups interviews. In M. Ciesielska & D. Jemielniak (Eds.) *Qualitative Methodologies in Organization Studies Volume II: Methods and Possibilities*. (pp. 97–126) Palgrave MacMillan. https://doi.org/10.1007/978-3-319-65442-3

Gomes, J, Almeida, SC, Kaveri, G, Mannan, F, Gupta, P, Hu, A, & Sarkar, M (2021). Early childhood educators as COVID warriors: Adaptations and responsiveness to the pandemic across five countries. *International Journal of Early Childhood*, *53*, 345–366. https://doi.org/10.1007/s13158-021-00305-8

Hindin, A, & Mueller, M (2016). Assessing and understanding teacher candidates' dispositions toward and knowledge of parent involvement. *The Teacher Educator*, *51*, 9–32. https://doi.org/10.1080/08878730.2015.1107673

Hooper, A, Potts, C, & Walton, M (2023). Novice early childhood teachers' perceptions of their professional development experiences: An interpretive phenomenological approach. *Journal of Early Childhood Teacher Education*, *44*(3), 310–329. https://doi.org/10.1080/10901027.2022.2043495

Hu, D, Yuan, B, Luo, J, & Wang, M (2021). A review of empirical research on ICT applications in teacher professional development and teaching practice. *Knowledge Management & E-Learning*, *13*(1), 1–20. https://doi.org/10.34105/j.kmel.2021.13.001

Hyman, MR, & Sierra, JJ (2016). Focus groups interviews. *Business Outlook 14*(7).

Jen, E, Mathijssen, S, & Hoogeveen, L (2022). Supporting professional development for educators during the pandemic: Lessons from an international blended learning diploma program. *Prospects*, *51*(4), 583–587. https://doi.org/10.1007/s11125-021-09591-5

Jin, M (2023). Preservice teachers' online teaching experiences during COVID-19. *Early Childhood Education Journal*, *51*(2), 371–381. https://doi.org/10.1007/s10643-022-01316-3

Kamberelis, G, Dimitriadis, G, & Welker, A (2017). Focus group research and/in figured worlds. In: N.K. Denzin & Y.S. Lincoln (Eds.) *The SAGE Handbook of Qualitative Research* (pp. 1202–1239). Sage.

Lestari, NGAMY, Sumantri, MS, & Dhieni, N (2022). Development of early childhood education teacher competency: Reviewed from perception and teacher's motivation. *Jurnal Kependidikan: Jurnal Hasil Penelitian dan Kajian Kepustakaan di Bidang Pendidikan, Pengajaran dan Pembelajaran*, *8*(2), 491–499. https://doi.org/10.33394/jk.v8i2.5145

Li, J, & Luo, Q (2022). Early childhood teachers' professional development paths from a cultural ecology perspective. *Journal of Global Humanities and Social Sciences*, *3*(4), 114–117. https://doi.org/10.47852/bonviewGHSS2022030408

Ministry of Science, Education and Sport [MSES] (2014). *Regulation on the content and duration of the short preschool programmes.* Retrieved from: https://narodnenovine.nn.hr/eli/sluzbeni/2014/107/2081

Ministry of Science, Education and Sports [MSES] (2015). National curriculum for early childhood education and care. *Official Gazette.* NN05/15.

Mystakidis, S, Fragkaki, M, & Filippousis, G (2021). Ready teacher one: Virtual and augmented reality online professional development for K-12 school teachers. *Computers*, *10*(10), 134. https://doi.org/10.3390/computers10100134

Nadeem, E, Shernoff, ES, Coccaro, C, & Stokes-Tyler, D (2022). Supporting teachers during the COVID-19 pandemic: A community-partnered rapid needs assessment. *School Psychology*, *37*(4), 309–318. https://doi.org/10.1037/spq0000503

Nagasawa, M, & Tarrant, K (2020). *Who Will Care for the Early Care and Education Workforce? COVID-19 and the Need to Support Early Childhood Educators' Emotional Well-being.* New York Early Childhood Professional Development Institute, CUNY. https://educate.bankstreet.edu/sc/1

Negrín-Medina, MÁ, Bernárdez-Gómez, A, Portela-Pruaño, A, & Marrero-Galván, JJ (2022). Teachers' perceptions of changes in their professional development as a result of ICT. *Journal of Intelligence*, *10*(4), 90. https://doi.org/10.3390/jintelligence10040090

Perry, E (2022). Teacher professional development in changing circumstances: The impact of COVID-19 on schools' approaches to professional development. *Education Sciences*, *13*(1), 48. https://doi.org/10.3390/educsci13010048

Peeters, J, & Vandenbroeck, M (2011). Childcare practitioners and the process of professionalization. In: L. Miller and C. Cable (Eds.) *Professionalization, Leadership and Management in the Early Years* (pp. 62–76). Sage. https://doi.org/10.4135/9781446288795

Pölzl-Stefanec, E, & Geißler, C (2022). "Micro-steps" on the route to successful online professional development for Austrian Early Childhood Educators. *International Journal of Educational Research*, *115*, 102042. https://doi.org/10.1016/j.ijer.2022.102042

Powell, CG, & Bodur, Y (2019). Teachers' perceptions of an online professional development experience: Implications for a design and implementation framework. *Teach. Teach. Educ. 77*, 19–30. https://doi.org/10.1016/j.tate.2018.09.004

Redecker, C, & Punie, Y (2017). *European Framework for the Digital Competence of Educators: DigCompEdu*. EUR 28775 EN. Luxembourg: Publications Office of the European Union.

Roberts, AM, LoCasale-Crouch, J, Hamre, BK, & Jamil, FM (2020). Preschool teachers' self-efficacy, burnout, and stress in online professional development: A mixed methods approach to understand change. *Journal of Early Childhood Teacher Education, 41*(3), 262–283. https://doi.org/10.1080/10901027.2019.1638851

Saxena, A, & Chiu, MM (2022). Developing preschool teachers' computational thinking knowledge, attitudes, beliefs, and teaching self-efficacies: A curriculum-based professional development program. *Frontiers in Education, 7*, 889116. https://doi.org/10.3389/feduc.2022.889116

Tokić, S, & Vukašinović, A (2020). Continuity of educational process through virtual kindergarten during COVID-19 outbreak – case study from Croatia. In: U.L. Gómez Chova, A. López Martínez, & I. Candel Torres (ur.) *EDULEARN20 Proceedings*. doi:10.21125/edulearn.2020.1981

Stewart, C (2014). Transforming professional development to professional learning. *Journal of Adult Education, 43*(1), 28–33.

Svanbjörnsdóttir, B, Macdonald, A, & Frímannsson, G (2016). Views of learning and a sense of community among students, paraprofessionals and parents in developing a school culture towards a professional learning community. *Professional Development in Education, 42*(4), 589–609. https://doi.org/10.1080/19415257.2015.1047037

Visković, I, & Višnjić Jevtić, A (2017). Development of professional teacher competences for cooperation with parents. *Early Child Development and Care, 187*(10), 1569–1582. https://doi.org/10.1080/03004430.2017.1299145

Visković, I, & Višnjić Jevtić, A (2018). Professional development of kindergarten teachers in Croatia – A personal choice or an obligation. *Early Years, 38*(3), 286–297. https://doi.org/10.1080/09575146.2017.1278747

Višnjić Jevtić, A, & Halavuk, A (2021). Early childhood teachers and burn-out syndrome–perception of Croatian teachers. *Early Years, 41*(1), 36–47. https://doi.org/10.1080/09575146.2018.1482260

Zhou, W, Nakatsubo, F, Wu, J, & Liu, K (2022). Digital ethnography of an online professional learning community based on WeChat for Chinese early childhood teachers. *Computers & Education, 191*, 104617. https://doi.org/10.1016/j.compedu.2022.104617

8

IMPACT OF NEOLIBERAL-INSPIRED POLICIES ON EDUCATORS' PROFESSIONAL IDENTITY IN FIVE COUNTRIES

Visions for a better future

Marg Rogers, Fabio Dovigo, Laura K. Doan, Khatuna Dolidze, and Astrid Mus Rasmussen

Introduction

Neoliberalism is the dominant paradigm in many high-income countries (Apple, 2006). The impact on the early childhood education and care (ECEC) sector is profound (Moloney et al. 2019), as the managerialism happening in the wake of the neoliberal policies has led to highly regulated work environments (Rogers, 2021; Sims, 2020). Previous research has shown that increasingly used quality assurance procedures in ECEC services can hinder the time educators spend on educational and counselling activities with children and families (Osgood 2006; Roberts-Holmes and Bradbury, 2016; Moss 2012). Moreover, the balance between fulfilling the demands of the system and promoting play and other quality learning activities can strongly influence how educators perceive their role as educators and their professional identity (Rogers, Dovigo & Doan, 2020).

This chapter presents findings from an international study of educators' perception of their highly regulated work environment. The topic was investigated through a mixed-methods approach. A questionnaire was administered to educators working in the ECEC sector in Australia, Canada, Georgia, Italy, and Denmark. The findings confirm that educators are facing multiple challenges affecting well-being and identity connected to the growing number of administrative tasks and the neglect of the sector. The chapter begins with a discussion of neoliberal policies and the impact specifically on the ECEC area. Subsequently, the methods applied are described, and then quantitative and qualitative results from the five countries are presented, compared, and

DOI: 10.4324/9781003471172-10

discussed. The chapter ends with a conclusion that summarises and points to the need for future research and what implications the findings could have for practice.

Critical Neoliberal Framework

Neoliberalism is a 'conceptual sprawl' (Dunn, 2017), a fuzzy concept that has been constantly modified over the last 50 years to adapt to changing economic and political circumstances, challenging the principle of non-contradiction. For example, it has strongly advocated for the deregulation of the public sector and at the same time has multiplied suffocating performance-based regulation procedures. However, throughout this evolution, some essential elements of the neoliberal doctrine have been preserved: capitalism, free market consumerism, privatisation, individual responsibility and accountability (Brown, 2019). It is now the dominant paradigm in high-income countries, subsuming parts of society (e.g. health care and education) traditionally underpinned by very different philosophies (Apple, 2006). As Monbiot (2017) argues, this paradigm results in competition, division, and neglect, rather than promoting community cooperation.

Under neoliberal policies, managerialism replaces management (Sims, 2020), positioning workers as untrustworthy and placing further demands on staff for compliance and subordination (Morrish, 2016). This distrust results in even higher levels of managerialism, usually in the form of accountability and micromanagement (Giroux, 2015; Rogers et al., 2020). The framework's requirements for registration and accreditation of programs that rely on public funding need large quantities of evidence, triggering a wicked self-feeding cycle (Graeber, 2019; Morrish, 2016). Accordingly, a regime of intense inspections produces a hyper-accountability culture in workplaces, while workers are intimidated through daily data collection and exhausting paperwork that generate a fear of performativity (Ball, 2006; Keddie, 2013). This results in increased stress, as time is diverted away from the type of work staff both value and believe they are skilled at performing. As a result, workers feel undervalued, become averse to innovate or follow regulations to the letter (Moore & Robinson, 2016). Ironically, these regulations and systems are meant to increase quality, whereas they engender poorer productivity, work quality, and education (Grant, Danby, Thorpe & Theobald, 2016; Sims, 2020).

Within educational services and institutions that were created to educate, question the way things work, and emancipate, the application of this business model corrupts moral reasoning (Beattie, 2019). It can also lead to neglect of education as a priority and to divert resources to more immediate profitable areas of investment (Allais, 2014).

72 Marg Rogers et al.

Neoliberalism in ECEC

The impact of neoliberalism on the ECEC sector 'is profound and enacted differently across different nation states' (Moloney et al. 2019, p. 2). Although not explicit in government documents, the accepted concept is that the marketisation of ECEC is the best way to improve the quality of ECEC services (Roberts-Holmes & Moss, 2021). As Lloyd and Penn (2012) state, understanding ECEC as a marketable commodity undermines quality and equity. However, it ensures compliance with government's agendas (Sims et al., 2022). Thus, the value of caring becomes a performativity directive that enforces detached steering mechanisms (Brown, 2015). These include educational interventions via rankings, targets, and accountability (Ball, 2006) that all require big data which educators are forced to collect (Roberts-Holmes and Bradbury, 2016).

Indeed, there is an enormous 'disjuncture between teachers' experiences and policy intent' in ECEC services in a neoliberal context (Grant et al., 2016, p. 44). Such disunion is created by intensifying control over educators' activity via management strategies. Thus, educators spend enormous amounts of time record keeping and data collecting. The emphasis on performativity and control not only harms the development of the holistic child but weakens the professional identity of educators (Vandenbroeck et al., 2022).

Educator identity

Educators' identity develops over time, given they have the right support (Katz, 1972). In Katz's theoretical model, four stages of educators' development are explained: survival, consolidation, renewal, and maturity. It is unclear whether all stages are passed through but the OECD suggests teacher development is a continuum (McKenzie & Santiago, 2005). Neoliberal-inspired practices impact educators' work identity (Rogers et al., 2020), including how educators view, value, and prioritize their work, as well as their role within the workplace. Additionally, neoliberal approaches involve a 'top down' approach (Sims, 2017), with educators at the bottom, which positions them as 'not knowing,' when in fact, educators have the expertise and the ability to lead (Doan, 2022). This is especially detrimental to newly hired ECEC educators. During a period when they should be able to receive additional support in their new professional role and identity (Doan, 2014), educators are instead spending increasing time on tasks determined through managerial practices, thus taking the focus off educators' ability to support each other through a workplace culture inspired by a community of practice approach (Lave & Wenger, 1991). More generally, researchers have found that managerialism, a product of a neoliberal approach, can lead to decreased professional identity, self-confidence, and commitment (Skinner, Leavey & Rothi, 2021).

In the present study, our research examples illuminate the way neoliberal policies erode the professional identity of ECEC educators. The next sections outline the methodology and present data that illustrate different aspects of the challenges to identity that neoliberalism generates.

Methods

The project uses a mixed-method approach (Bryman, Bell, Reck & Fields, 2022). The questionnaire contained both closed and open-ended questions and was administered to educators working in the ECEC sector in Australia, Canada, Georgia, Italy, and Denmark. Descriptive statistics and inductive thematic analysis have been used to examine, respectively, quantitative and qualitative data (Braun & Clarke, 2006). Ethics approval was gained by the Human Research Ethics Committee at the University of New England, Australia, then each researcher applied for ethical approval in their own university.

Three of us initially met through a Special Interest Group within the European Early Childhood Education Research Association. These authors organised a symposium on the topic of the impact of neoliberal approaches on early learning and care programs within three countries: Italy, Australia, and Canada. This led to ongoing discussions and a co-authored publication (see Rogers et al., 2020) discussing the similarities and differences of ECEC educators' experiences in different settings. To explore this further, we created an international study, using a survey approach which enabled us to reach a wide number of participants. The survey was initially launched in 2021 in the previously mentioned three countries and then extended for further comparison to Georgia and Denmark in 2022, through previous collegial collaborations.

ECEC educators were recruited through various methods (email, online learning platforms, or social media) and software (Qualtrics, SurveyXact), depending on the context. The participants were all ECEC educators with different qualifications and roles, working in various service types.

Results

Quantitative Results

A total of 1274 (n = 1274) educators participated from Australia (n = 82), Canada (n = 145), Georgia (n = 568), Italy (n = 251), and Denmark (n = 228).

Participant's demographics

The vast majority of the educators identified as female, with Denmark having the lowest figure at 89%. Most educators are in the 40–49 age range. Australia has a predominantly younger workforce (62%), whereas Italian and Danish

74 Marg Rogers et al.

educators are ageing, with more than 30% in the 50–69 range. Regarding the working experience, most educators have been working for 11–20 years in the ECEC sector. However, a significant share of Italian (34%) and Danish (36%) educators have been employed for a longer time (21–40 and more years) compared to their peers in Australia, Canada, and Georgia. It should be noted that Danish participants tended to skip this and other questions, so some data is not available, or, the results might seem unusual.

In this study, one-third of Australian participants are located in regional towns, while in Canada most of them work in state, provincial, or regional cities. In contrast, 55% of Georgian educators are employed in rural towns, while in Italy educators are more homogenously distributed among different areas.

Concerning the qualification level of participants, most educators have a diploma, which is especially common in Australia (79%). However, it is worth noting that 33% of Georgian educators have a bachelor's degree, whereas 26% of Italian educators also have a master's level degree. This can explain why almost 80% of Australian educators want to upskill, while a large portion of those working in Italy are not interested in pursuing further qualifications.

Educator identity

Educator identity is both critical and multi-layered and is made more complex with educators being asked to take on more tasks and responsibilities with less time and funding. Through an inductive analysis of qualitative data, themes emerged, reflecting key parts of educator identity. These themes point to the wisdom, resilience, and dedication of educators, illustrated by the data in Table 8.1. Themes included educators identifying themselves as *knowledge creators*, recognising they had knowledge and skills to pass on to the children or other educators. Others identified themselves as *balancers*, identifying the need of balancing the sacrifices made to make a difference in children's lives with an acknowledgement of this through appropriate compensation, which is due to a lack of acknowledgement from their governments and society. Educators also identified themselves as *drivers*, with the potential to further develop their activity in the ECEC field. Some educators identified their role as *leaders*, or future leaders within the profession. Others had ideas about how leadership could be different. Educators identified their role as *advocates*, wishing to be acknowledged for the work they do to support children, families, and communities, including the fact that they have specialised training. As *change makers*, educators also identified the need for reform in the sector and their role in this change. Additionally, educators have specific ideas on how and what change can occur. Lastly, as *optimists*, a few educators recognised their natural fit and commitment within the sector, despite the challenges.

Impact of neoliberal-inspired policies on educators' **75**

TABLE 8.1 Educators' expressions of identity

Theme	Participant Quote	Nationality
Knowledge creator	*I'm too old to change profession now. I feel I have a lot to offer to the children.*	Australian
	The program I have created was recognized by the highest honour in Canada; both myself and my centre received the Prime Minister's Awards for excellence... I have been and continue to be invited to sit on expert panels both provincially and pan-Canadian.	Canadian
Balancers	*I know I can make a difference ... even it does take a huge toll on myself and my family.*	Australian
	I love what I do, however, I am reaching burnout.	Canadian
	We are asked for high professionalism, but the compensation is not adequate. Working hours continue to increase, but salary is the same.	Italian
	The state should take care of the constant improvement of educators' qualifications, the periodic increase of salaries, the regulation of the number of children in each group, and the development of the medical insurance package for caregivers.	Georgian
Drivers	*I wish to open my own community children service centre.*	Australian
	I want to influence the next generation of educators.	Canadian
	I think I will develop professionally and move to a higher level.	Georgian
Leaders	*When I finish my degree, I would like to be in a position to advocate for better conditions. I would also like to teach early childhood educators.*	Australian
	It would be great if the government could develop a career path for early childhood educators both professionally and financially so that those who stay longer could be rewarded and ... motivated.	Canadian
	Too much bureaucracy, too much time spent filling out, reading, understanding, and seeking information where there is no clarity...the time spent on bureaucratic tasks expands significantly. At times, one feels overwhelmed by bureaucracy, we became secretaries.	Italian

(*Continued*)

76 Marg Rogers et al.

TABLE 8.1 (Continued)

Theme	Participant Quote	Nationality
	I try to change the current situation. I want to develop more and be able to create a developing environment regardless of challenges.	Georgian
Advocates	*I hope in the next five years to be the advocate of change towards an affordable national childcare plan.*	Canadian
	Preschool education is underestimated, and educators are considered second-class teachers. I wish that the work of the teacher would be more appreciated, also considering the demands of families, which are very high.	Italian
	Recognize that our profession is paramount in our society, for future generations.	Danish
	Our work is undervalued, with very low wages.	Georgian
Change makers	*I want to continue being part of the change.*	Australian
	The Early Learning Framework gives educators a place to orient from and think deeply about practice. This work calls us to think about colonization, confronting bias, inclusion, common wording, etc.	Canadian
	The number of students per class must be reduced by increasing staff, and teacher salaries raised. The value of preschool education must be recognised, along with the way we take care of spaces. The profession should be valued, and innovation supported.	Italian
	We need formal and economic recognition of the time and resources we invest working extra-hours. Preschools need to be provided with good learning and play materials, considering them an essential educational service rather than a space for "dropping children while parents ... work".	Italian
	The whole system ... needs to be changed.	Georgian
Optimists	*I have been in the industry for 25 years...(I) have left a couple (of) times but always come back. It is where my heart is.*	Australian
	The importance of ECEs and Early Learning has only just come to the forefront in Canada. After 20 years in the field, it is wonderful to finally see the government recognizing what I have always known.	Canadian

(*Continued*)

Impact of neoliberal-inspired policies on educators' **77**

TABLE 8.1 (Continued)

Theme	Participant Quote	Nationality
	Despite everything, I love my job. I still have a lot to give and learn.	Italian
	I'm driven by the desire that children deserve a better everyday life in day care.	Danish
	(After) 21 years; I cannot imagine myself anywhere else.	Georgian

In the next sections, we discuss the findings and their limitations, identify areas for further research, and then draw conclusions.

Discussion

The outcomes emerging from the investigation conducted across the five examined nations reveal a shared trend concerning the escalating work–life imbalance, levels of stress, and consequent professional burnout. This negative trend can be partly attributed to longstanding structural issues that traditionally afflict the sector, such as inadequate educational spaces and materials, an imbalanced educator-to-child ratio, low salaries, and a general lack of recognition for the importance and quality of work undertaken by educators. However, the neoliberal shift in service management has added new elements to these longstanding problems, significantly worsening the professional activities of educators. As attested by the interviewees, a substantial portion of their work is now directed towards managing increasingly pressing administrative and bureaucratic demands purportedly made in the name of transparency and accountability. However, these demands, far from enhancing service transparency and accountability, generate a nonsense documentation that effectively diverts time and attention away from the daily requirements of working with children and families.

Accordingly, the professional identity of educators is substantially weakened by the requirement to adhere to impossible standards. Nonetheless, the questionnaires also highlight educators' capacity to critically reflect upon these forces that deteriorate their working conditions. This enables them to identify significant forms of resistance on both an individual level (for instance, by emphasising the value of their work with children and their families) and on a group level, by exploring new ways with colleagues of reorganising the daily workflow to reduce the increasing work-related pressure. This way, educators foster a sense of personal control and collective empowerment that helps recognise their own abilities and potential as knowledge creators, balancers, drivers, leaders, advocates, change-makers, and optimists.

Opportunities to support educators' professional identity

To support professional identity and increase educator efficacy, a funded peer mentoring program was started in British Columbia, Canada (Doan, 2019). This co-created program, which began as a pilot in 2016, has grown to an established province-wide program, involving hundreds of educators. This program, which has undergone several iterations, intentionally positions educators as the expert, knowing what is best for their development. This is in contrast to a top-down approach where educators are viewed as technicians and their work is reduced to simple care. The Peer Mentoring Program for Early Childhood Educators in BC (PSPECEBC) involves twelve educators coming together in a peer mentoring community of practice (CoP), meeting once a month. Each CoP has one or two facilitators who work with the educators, creating an environment where each person feels valued, respected, and a sense of belonging. Within each CoP, educators take part in peer mentoring, meeting weekly in pairs. The program intentionally uses a non-hierarchical peer mentoring approach as new educators acknowledged that while they had needs, they had much to offer as well (Doan, 2014).

Professional development takes place within each CoP and is determined by the early childhood educators themselves, which is based on the belief that educators know what they need and can determine their best next step. Additionally, the time that educators spend together as pairs, and in the CoP is viewed as professional development. In other words, professional development is not reduced to workshop or presentation by an expert, but is understood as a practice that educators themselves are active agents in.

Research has found it is effective in increasing educator leadership, learning and development, as well as retention. In a survey of 179 program participants, educators reported a 96% increase in learning; a 78% increase in their leadership; a 90% increase in their development. Additionally, 68% reported that their participation in the program made a difference in their ability to stay in the field; and 97% saw themselves staying in the field (Doan & Mughal, 2023). Educators have shared the ways this program has impacted their professional identity, including how they perceive themselves and the work itself:

> Interacting with experienced early childhood educators has ... develop(ed) my leadership skills. They have shared valuable insights on how to handle daily tasks ... which has been truly enlightening... my leadership capacity has grown substantially.
> [Being] able to learn the different pedagogies and practice ... through sharing by different educators and my peer mentor enhanced my professional development. It improved my perception of the profession and practice.

> I believe this program is invaluable and needs to be accessible to all ... (it) creates relationship, which is at the heart of what we do and has a many layered positive trickle-down effects into our lives ... professionally and personally... the reconnection ... I am experiencing ... has made my professional career more meaningful because it feels good to make a positive difference in someone else's professional life. I feel purposeful and valued.

For sustainability, the program, which currently involves 35 peer mentoring communities of practice, is moving from a university-based program into the Early Childhood Educators of BC, the professional association representing educators in the province. The program is also being piloted in Australia in 2023.

Limitations

The current study faced challenges due to low response rates within the Danish survey, impacting cross-country comparisons. This may have been due to the setup of the survey on different software programs, allowing some participants greater autonomy over which questions they had to answer. Conducted during the disruptive 2021–2022 COVID-19 pandemic, variations in timing and stress levels were observed both between and within countries.

Need for further research

Previous research indicates that educators have a relatively weak identification with their professionalism, due to the absence of a clear core sense of belonging to the profession. Although it was beyond the scope of this study, it would be interesting to deepen the knowledge gained regarding ECEC educators' identity and compare it to previous research.

Conclusions

In conclusion, the research underscores the passion and commitment of early childhood educators, driven by their dedication to children's well-being and development. However, the application of neoliberal policies has led to a worsening of their professional identity. The demands of bureaucratic paperwork and regulatory pressures have created a culture of stress, burnout, and detachment from the meaningful aspects of their work. Some of these have worsened further due to the COVID-19 pandemic (Sims et al., 2022; Sims, Rogers & Boyd, 2023).

Many governments have much to deal with as they face increasing rates of educator burnout (Ng, Rogers & McNamara, 2023) and attrition post pandemic, when ECEC educators were at the same time essential, yet remained invisible (Rogers, Boyd & Sims, 2023). To address workforce attraction and retention challenges, policymakers, like educators, need to find new ways of working (Boyd et al., 2023). For governments, this will need to include tapping into the three key elements of human motivation: autonomy, competence, and relatedness (Ryan, 2019). Managerial systems remove autonomy from educators' workplaces, and assume incompetence, replacing it with compliance. Additionally, the relatedness aspect of the job is severely affected, as educators have less time to spend with the children. Therefore, urgent changes are needed in this vital sector, and much can be gained from peer support programs to nurture educators' well-being and professional identity.

To take these insights forward into practice, it is crucial for policymakers, education administrators, and stakeholders to hear the voices of educators and recognise the importance of adequate resources, improved working conditions, and fair compensation. Creating a supportive environment for educators will not only enhance their professional satisfaction but also have a direct positive impact on the quality of education and care provided to children and families.

Educators themselves can use these findings to advocate for necessary changes within their respective countries. By identifying as knowledge creators, balancers, drivers, leaders, advocates, change-makers, and optimists, they can collaborate and engage in meaningful dialogue with policymakers and community leaders to address the structural and administrative challenges that hinder their practice.

References

Allais, S (2014). *Selling Out Education: National Qualifications Frameworks and the Neglect of Knowledge.* https://doi.org/10.1007/978-94-6209-578-6

Apple, MW (2006). Understanding and interrupting neoliberalism and neoconservatism in education. *Pedagogies, 1*(1), 21–26.

Ball, S (2006). *Education Policy and Social Class: The Selected Works of Stephen J Ball.* Routledge.

Boyd, W, Rogers, M, & Sims, M (2023). New ways of working and new opportunities: Early childhood leaders' professional practice post-COVID. In K. Marsh-Davies & C. Burnett (Eds.), *Teachers and Teaching Post-COVID* (pp. 18). Taylor & Francis. https://www.taylorfrancis.com/chapters/edit/10.4324/9781003352129-12/new-ways-working-new-opportunities-wendy-boyd-marg-rogers-margaret-sims

Beattie, P (2019). The road to psychopathology: Neoliberalism and the human mind. *Journal of Social Issues, 75*(1), 89–112. https://spssi.onlinelibrary.wiley.com/doi/10.1111/josi.12304

Braun, V, & Clarke, V (2006). Using thematic analysis in psychology. *Qualitative Research in Psychology, 3*, 77–101. https://www.tandfonline.com/doi/abs/10.1191/1478088706qp063oa

Brown, W (2015). *Undoing the Demos: Neoliberalism's Stealth Revolution.* London: MIT Press.

Brown, W (2019). *In the Ruins of Neoliberalism: The Rise of Antidemocratic Politics in the West*. New York: Columbia University Press.

Bryman, A, Bell, E, Reck, J, & Fields, J (2022). *Social Research Methods*. Oxford University Press.

Doan, LK, & Mughal, A (2023). Peer Mentoring Program for Early Childhood Educators in BC Year End Report 2022–2023.

Doan, LK (2022). Peer-mentoring communities of practice: A place to belong, ask questions, and grow. *The Early Childhood Educator, 37*(2), 16–21.

Doan, LK (2019). Finding community: An exploration into an induction support pilot project. *Journal of Childhood Studies, 44*(1), 68–79.

Doan, LK (2014). *The Early Years: An Exploration of the Experiences and Needs of Novice Early Childhood Educators in British Columbia*. Unpublished dissertation, University of Calgary.

Dunn, B (2017). Against neoliberalism as a concept. *Capital & Class, 41*(3), 435–454. ISSN (print) 0309-8168

Giroux, H (2015). *Dangerous Thinking in the Age of the New Authoritarianism*. Paradigm Publishers.

Graeber, D (2019). *Bullshit Jobs The Rise of Pointless Work and What We Can Do About It*. Penguin Random House.

Grant, S, Danby, S, Thorpe, K, & Theobald, M (2016). Early childhood teachers' work in a time of change. *Australasian Journal of Early Childhood, 41*(3), 38–45.

Katz, LG (1972). Developmental stages of preschool teachers. *The Elementary School Journal, 73*(1), 50–54.

Keddie, A (2013). Thriving amid the performance demands of the contemporary audit culture: A matter of school context. *Journal of Education Policy, 28*(6).

Lave, J, & Wenger, E (1991). *Situated Learning: Legitimate Peripheral Participation*. Cambridge University Press.

Lloyd, E, & Penn, H (2012). *Childcare Markets: Can They Deliver an Equitable Service?* Policy Press.

Ng, J, Rogers, M, & McNamara, C (2023). A systematic review of burnout and quality of life of early childhood educators. *Issues in Educational Research, 33*(1), 173–206. http://www.iier.org.au/iier33/ng.pdf

McKenzie, P & Santiago, P (Éds.) (2005). *Teachers Matter: Attracting, Developing and Retaining Effective Teachers*. Paris: Organisation for Economic Co-operation and Development.

Moloney, M, Sims, M, Rothe, A, Buettner, C, Sonter, L, Waniganayake, M, Opazo, M-J, Calder, P. & Girlich, S (2019). Resisting neoliberalism: Professionalisation of early childhood education and care. *International Journal of Elementary Education, 8*(4), 1–10. https://www.sciencepublishinggroup.com/journal/paperinfo?journal id=192&doi=10.11648/j.ijeedu.20190801.11

Monbiot, G (2017). *Out of the Wreckage A New Politics for an Age of Crisis*. Verso.

Moore, P & Robinson, A (2016). The quantified self: What counts in the neoliberal workplace. *New Media & Society, 18*(11), 2774–2792.

Morrish, L (2016). Metaphors we work by. *Academic Irregularities*. Retrieved from: https://academicirregularities.wordpress.com/2016/11/11/metaphors-we-work-by/

Moss, P (2012). Need markets be the only show in town? In: E. Lloyd & H. Penn (Eds.), *Childcare Markets: Can They Deliver an Equitable Dervice?* (pp. 191–208). The Policy Press.

Osgood, J (2006). Deconstructing professionalism in early childhood education: Resisting the regulatory gaze. *Contemporary Issues in Early Childhood*, *7*(1), 5–14.

Roberts-Holmes, G & Bradbury, A (2016). The datafication of early years education and its impact upon pedagogy. *Improving Schools*, *19*(2), 119–128. https://doi.org/10.1177/1365480216651519

Roberts-Holmes, G, & Moss, P (2021). *Neoliberalism and Early Childhood Education: Markets, Imaginaries and Governance*. Abingdon: Routledge.

Rogers, M (2021). Contextualised, not neoliberalised professionalism in early childhood education and care: Effects of prescribed notions of quality on educator confidence in Australia. *International Electronic Journal of Elementary Education*, *13*(4), 549–564. https://www.iejee.com/index.php/IEJEE/article/view/1447/532

Rogers, M, Boyd, W, & Sims, M (2023). "Burnout central": Australian early childhood educational leaders' experiences during the Covid-19 pandemic. *Issues in Educational Research*, *33*(1), 284–306. http://www.iier.org.au/iier33/rogers.pdf

Rogers, M, Dovigo, F, & Doan, L (2020). Educator identity in a neoliberal context: Recognising and supporting early childhood education and care educators. *European Early Childhood Education Research Journal*, *28*(6), 806–822. https://doi.org/10.1080/1350293X.2020.1836583

Ryan, R (2019). *The Oxford Handbook of Human Motivation*. Oxford University Press, Incorporated. https://books.google.ca/books?id=jCeeDwAAQBAJ

Sims, M (2017). Neoliberalism and early childhood. *Cogent Education*, *4*(1), 136–141. https://doi.org/10.1080/2331186X.2017.1365411

Sims, M (2020). *Bullshit Towers: Neoliberalism and Managerialism in Universities in Australia*. Peter Lang.

Sims, M, Rogers, M, & Boyd, W (2023). The more things change the more they stay the same: Early childhood professionalism in COVID-19 times. *Issues in Educational Research*, *33*(4). http://www.iier.org.au/iier33/sims.pdf

Sims, M, Calder, P, Moloney, M, Rothe, A, Rogers, M, Doan, L, Kakana, D, & Georgiadou, S (2022). Neoliberalism and government responses to Covid-19: Ramifications for early childhood education and care. *Issues in Educational Research*, *32*(3), 1174–1195. http://www.iier.org.au/iier32/sims.pdf

Skinner, B, Leavey, G, & Rothi, D (2021). Managerialism and teacher professional identity: Impact on well-being among teachers in the UK. *Educational Review*, *73*(1), 1–16. DOI:10.1080/00131911.2018.1556205

Vandenbroeck, M, Lehrer, J, Mitchell, L, Alasuutari, M, Cadart, ML, Karila, K, Musatti, T, Rupin, P, & Yuen, G (2022). Resisting the consumentality of parents. In M. Vandenbroeck, J. Lehrer, & L. Mitchell (Eds.), *The Decommodification of Early Childhood Education and Care: Resisting Neoliberalism* (pp. 81–146). Routledge. https://doi.org/10.4324/9781003218104-4

9

FOSTERING PRACTICE-BASED PHILOSOPHY IN EARLY CHILDHOOD EDUCATORS

Reflections on developing a pedagogic creed

Lewis Stockwell and Michael Young

Module Design: Socratic Dialogue

Imagine the scene: Lecturers Lewis and Michael are in a tricky development meeting for the BA (Hons) Early Childhood Education programme. They are being challenged about a proposed final-year undergraduate module that focuses on philosophy of education in early childhood professional practice. Very few of them exist in the UK, let alone as a way of bringing the threads of a degree together. The Head of Academic Quality (AQ) is asking probing questions, the kind of questions we are likely to get from an external examiner at the validation event. These are good questions that make Michael and Lewis assert the underpinning values of the module in much the same way, it turns out, that students will eventually be required to do in their final summative assignment:

Michael:	I believe that early childhood education is for the empowerment of young children to develop an individual and community identity that enables them, and their communities, to resolve the problems they face.
Head of AQ:	How are you going to relate such a position to early childhood practice?
Lewis:	Interesting question, well, clearly in order for young children to shape and develop their individual identities they require knowledgeable and supportive others to lay the foundations for them...
Michael:	Absolutely - and ensuring that early childhood educators are suitably equipped in recognising and understanding how

DOI: 10.4324/9781003471172-11

	young children make sense of themselves and the world around them is absolutely crucial.
AQ Head:	And this is the purpose of the module then?
Michael:	Yes, and as part of this process these professionals first need to establish, be aware of and feel comfortable with their own values and beliefs about early childhood education before they leave a mark on the lives of children.
Lewis:	To be really honest, I'm not entirely sure they are, on the whole. Reflecting on placement visits, I cannot be sure that most practitioners are as clear as this module, this degree even, requires them to be. I think many of them would feel a great deal of empowerment should they have the opportunity to develop their own sort of manifesto or 'creed'. Being able to identify what is most important to them in relation to their early childhood practice could be beneficial for them and for achieving the goal Michael's just stated.
Michael:	Yes, and two further things: first, it shows that practitioners can take hold of their practice and work to improve it from the inside. Second, it requires the students to be critically aware of the powerplays and policy structures that can disempower practitioners, leaving them as technicians of policy rather than critically-conscious pedagogues. Is that not also indicative of what's expected in the final year of an undergraduate degree?
AQ Head:	Well, I can't argue with you. But there are a few things that you're going to need to consider. How are you going to scaffold their learning? They've not done this kind of explicit philosophical work before.
Lewis:	Well… most educators draw upon previous experiences, whether these are on a personal or professional level, that either consciously or unconsciously influence their own pedagogies in some way. In the case of these students, some of them are practitioners already, all of them have placement experience, and they'll have the previous five semesters' worth of study to draw upon. So, I think we'll have enough sources of inspiration for purposeful reflection. These can act as a kind of 'starting point' for our developing early childhood educators to begin setting out their own values or beliefs…?
AQ Head:	That seems logical to me, but logic aside for a moment… what about their emotional selves, the satisfaction levels… this module seems awfully hard and challenging to me. You're asking them to put themselves on the line, to display their values – personal and professional.
Michael:	I take that point. I think we will have some students who won't want to go there… but isn't it our job to provide students with

what they *need*, not necessarily what they *want*. What is it that Freire says, 'the oppressed become the oppressors'? If we continue to perpetuate what's going on out there, in practice, we'll continue to have significant issues of low status, low expectations and a lack of drive to make change. It is no coincidence that those striving for change are critically aware of how the government operates in early childhood education and care. Isn't it our job to create a place where learners' consciousness is challenged to expand, where they critically analyse their beliefs and how they translate into action?

Lewis: That's virtue ethics, right there. We are trying to create a sustainable change to practice with our students. We meet the requirements for a final year module, we'll make sure that discomfort is reasonable and for educational purposes. We'll enable them to succeed.

AQ Head: Right, well then… I'm satisfied. Let's review after the module has run a couple of times. Good luck.

Introduction

The Socratic-style dialogue above is the starting point of this chapter, which draws inspiration from a final-year undergraduate module, *Developing my Pedagogical Creed*, which is part of the BA (Hons) Early Childhood Education programme delivered at the University of Hertfordshire, England. We – the authors who are also the lecturers – have shared the initial discussions about the key considerations that were identified in designing the module and managing the student experience. In what follows, we share some of the philosophical concepts, arguments and educational readings to support nascent early childhood educators in developing authentic professional values. We discuss the aims of the module that enable students to develop their own set of values and beliefs as graduate practitioners in early childhood (EC) care and provision. We then turn to explain, and seek to justify, the essential components that underpin an authentic 'pedagogic creed' for EC educators and aim to support the idea that, in practice, it is possible to 'live out one's creed' with authenticity. Throughout we reflect on the pedagogic and ethical underpinnings of the module and reflect on insightful learning and teaching moments. We conclude by offering some thoughts as to how similar learning could take place within wider early childhood education (ECE) practice.

Module Design

As the dialogue above shows, the main 'aims' of the module were for students to gain an understanding of the philosophy of education specifically in an ECE context and be able to express their own values and beliefs or 'pedagogic creed' based on the philosophical discussions that resonated with them. We wanted them to have a graduate-level understanding and confidence about themselves as EC practitioners who could seek to make positive and informed change.

As a module team we felt that in order to underpin this 'creed' there should be a systematic understanding of the nature of philosophical educational enquiry in ECE: As a result, students were directed to compare and contrast competing philosophical positions through weekly class discussions and reflect upon how these readings/perspectives align with or, more importantly, challenge their own professional practice experience and values. Underpinning this was an acknowledgement of Dewey's second statement in his *Pedagogic creed* which outlines that education occurs through the stimulation of a learner in a social situation. In such a position, the learner needs to gain an understanding of their role by acting as a member of a unified group and to 'emerge from [their] original narrowness of action and feeling and to conceive of [themselves] from the standpoint of the welfare of the group to which they belong' (Dewey, 1964, p. 427).

To make this come alive for the students, we modelled how communities of philosophical enquiry could be developed with young children, using methods and tools from Philosophy for Children (P4C) (for example, Gaut and Gaut, 2011). As part of this approach, we aimed to enable students to move away from a typically individualistic 'student-self', representative of the modern neoliberal education agenda (Ball, 2012). This would help them to develop their practice-based identity which, in order to be called 'practice', requires not only an acknowledgement of but a conscious striving toward the enhancement of the practice (MacIntyre, 2007). P4C not only enables learners to engage in deliberation, contestation and critical reflection, but it also models a democratic identity 'as a way of living that connects individuals to each other and their society, and to an awareness of the need for social reconstruction' (Echerverria and Hannam, 2017, p. 9).

Weekly lectures were shared with the students on aspects of philosophy of education, which aimed to show how philosophical issues were present in practice-based contexts. The teaching attempted to model and explain the ethical underpinnings of pedagogical decision-making and to highlight, in ways perhaps many of them had not experienced before, the il/logical steps educators can take when engaging in the education of others. Prior to and after lectures, practical activities added a concrete and authentic dimension to their learning. The activities encouraged students to 'problem-solve' philosophical dilemmas and thought experiments, by clarifying questions and critiquing alternative arguments. They might be put in the role of party-policy manifesto makers trying to please an indecisive electorate or in the position of parents seeking justifications for *this* or *that* action in an EC space. As a result, they learned to ask challenging questions of each other, while constructing cogent arguments in reply. Some examples were fictitious – generated by the teaching team – and other examples were representative of actual educational dilemmas across age phases.

Philosophy and theory of education texts were selected carefully: some for their introductory and invitational qualities, and some for their potential to elicit emotion responses, which would lead to appraisals of arguments. Our aim was to create a place and pedagogical approach whereby students, who held pluralistic identities, were not forced into a particular way of being and becoming, rather we aimed to work in a form of authentic partnership with students (Dickerson, Jarvis and Stockwell, 2016; Stockwell, Smith and Woods, 2020). For instance, we supported students to engage with aspects of Aristotle's *Nicomachean Ethics* (2001), Freire's (1970) *Pedagogy of the Oppressed*, along with feminist philosophy of education by Noddings (2012), the aims of education (Peters, 1966; Mezirow, 1990; Dewey, 1997; Kolb, 2014), political philosophy of parenting by Suissa (2013), literature and thought experiments on justice (See: Sandel, 2010; Ruitenberg and Vokey, 2014), rule following in and for the life of the child (O'Neill, 1992, 2010), moral education and discipline in educational contexts (see: MacAllister, 2011, 2014; Hand, 2018), and racial awareness in education practice (Bhopal, 2018). In seminars and workshops we created learning opportunities for students to bring their analyses of philosophy of education, and to reflect on practice experiences and prominent policy, that held significant sway in the field such as (but not limited to) the Early Years Foundation Stage (UK Department for Education, 2017) and its accompanying curriculum guidance Development Matters (The British Association for Early Childhood Education, 2012), the National Curriculum for English primary schools (UK Department for Education, 2013), human and child rights legislation and other pertinent publications concerning the EC workforce. Depending upon the unique nature of the values and beliefs of each individual, there was also an emphasis on students exploring a number of EC issues in relation to political philosophy of education more broadly, including specific cases focussing on wellbeing, diversity, equity and inclusion affecting the work with young children, their families and communities (including issues of race and gender in educational settings).

Philosophical Underpinnings

In *My Pedagogic Creed* Dewey (1964) takes his stand as a philosopher and practitioner of education. Each proposition is preceded with the phrase 'I believe that…' and is followed by succinct arguments about what education is, what the school is; he then goes on to argue what the focus of subject matter ought to be, how teaching and learning ought to take place and argues that the role of schooling (and education more broadly) is, 'the fundamental method of social progress and reform' (Dewey, 1964, p. 437). It was from these overarching, yet pointed arguments, that we were able to provide the framework for the philosophically-informed teaching and learning that we wanted to engage our students in. Although students had engaged with pedagogic theory, explored key arguments and justifications for different approaches in historical and contemporary EC discourse and practice, it was in this final module that they were confronted explicitly with taking a position on what ECE should be for, and how they believed such purposes should be achieved. While teaching and learning was designed using Deweyan insight, his voice was one of many in the module. Knowing that the students had not been challenged in this way, we first needed to provide a rationale for this 'new' way of thinking and educating. Firstly, we introduced the students to adult transformative education: this would be a recurring theme throughout their studies and centred on their own learning development prior to thinking about EC practice and culture.

We start with Mezirow for similar reasons that Calleja (2014, p. 117) states about his work:

> Tracking Jack Mezirow's extensive contribution to the understanding of adult transformative learning experience helps one understand the deep, structured shift experienced by individuals who allow themselves to learn from their own experience within a community of practice.

We knew that the students came to the module with rich practice-based experiences, along with significant prior degree-related learning. It was with these experiences and other earlier training and education that we, as educators, were dealing – we started by making them aware of their own *frames of reference* in order for them to be better placed to transform them:

> Transformative learning requires a form of education very different from that commonly associated with children. New information is only a resource in the adult learning process. To become meaningful, learning requires that new information be incorporated by the learner into an already well-developed symbolic frame of reference, an active process involving thought, feelings, and disposition. The learner may also have to be helped to transform his or her frame of reference to fully understand the experience.
>
> *(Mezirow, 1997, p. 10)*

By acknowledging and drawing on their previous learning and reminding them of their unique human capacities for reflection, meaning-making and reflection-in-action, we provided students with conceptual literature that would enable them to consolidate their learning or a purpose greater than their own personal growth. For instance, we created space in the learning environment for students to track the socio-cultural, political and economic influences (amongst others) that had led them to their current ethnocentric lens. This kind of activity was developed, as Mezirow (1997, p. 11) concludes, 'to help the individual become a more autonomous thinker by learning to negotiate his or her own values, meanings, and purposes rather than to uncritically act on those of others'. Through introducing these learners to Mezirow's thinking in the first instance, they were able to realise that in order for them to become 'graduate-level' EC educators, they would need to have grounded arguments for their pedagogical beliefs and decisions. They would need to be prepared to be challenged by a range of stakeholders – parents, managers, colleagues, policymakers, among others – in their attempts to improve and bring about ethical 'goods' in their practice. In order to do this, we made space to revisit a range of practices, policy and theory along with introducing concepts that would help them give voice to phenomena. In a very real sense, we constructed the learning environment on the collective striving for *practical wisdom* (Aristotle, 2001; Birmingham, 2004; MacIntyre, 2007).

While we were not attempting to educate for a particular image or narrative of *the* archetypal EC graduate, we were unapologetically attempting to educate them in ways that would challenge their practice. In equal measure, we further wanted to build their confidence in articulating how the theories they were engaging with could be challenged by their practice-based lived experience. The means by which we did this was through exploring selected features of Aristotelean virtue ethics. Building on their learning from Mezirow, students were introduced to the concept of *phronesis – practical wisdom* – in educational contexts. Phronesis, unlike knowledge or skill, is a different kind of thought and action that aims toward reasoning what actions will bring about the good for the human being (Aristotle, 2001). For the educator, it is a form of moral imagination that centres on a deep and situated knowing and reflection but moves beyond thought alone. Phronesis has a component of realisation that is produced in moral action. Thus, the combination of reflective thought and action toward carefully reasoned moral goods is central to Aristotle's arguments and to subsequent educational discussions (Birmingham, 2004). It centres on carefully *thinking* about doing the right thing in an education context and then *actually doing it*. The educator then carefully attends to the outcomes of the action, takes that learning and applies these insights in other situations that demand it. Such *doings* are displays and expressions of the educator's moral dispositions. When enabling students to consider what the morally desirable features of ECE, practice and their own professional lives are, they are able to reason what moral goods should come about and, importantly, *how* they should be brought about. Hence, drawing on Dewey's *Pedagogic Creed*, students were able to begin thinking about how theories were influencing their moral decision-making at different levels, whether that was their orientation with ECE policy, their thinking about their own pedagogical beliefs and values, and how they fitted (or not) with their current employment, or indeed the practice as a whole. Metaphorically these inquiries provided a theory-practice 'call and response' centred on the learners' own moral values, frames of reference and capacities for phronesis in order to enable them to begin to consider how they would meet likely criticism or challenges within practice itself. In other words, once they could gather a good understanding of themselves as educational professionals, they would be able to unpick and mount responses to what they believed were ethically questionable situations within EC practice.

While we cannot go into all of the philosophy we discussed with the students here, we built upon those ideas explored above and moved into a range of discourses. Managerialism and performativity were discussed, authenticity and human flourishing were repeatedly explored, and then topic areas were selected to nurture students' critical capacities about, what we suspected were, strongly-held beliefs: for example, parent partnerships, multi-agency working and particular pedagogies (such as Montessori, Froebelian education, Forest School, etc.). One illustrative interaction of subject-based teaching we will share here.

It is challenging to find credible sources that philosophically critique the educational value of play-based education. In Dearden (1970) we found an argument that we knew would trouble the students' frames of reference and their moral and pedagogical values. In a short and sharp summary, Dearden's argument runs as follows: (1) It is often asserted that play is a valuable educational tool, but when we dig deeper it is near impossible to find a satisfactory definition of play for the educational context. We can find a range of concepts which have shared features but no clear definition. Schooling is often framed not around the notion of play, but work. Even then, there are many activities in the life of the child that are both not-play and not-work. (In more recent years, of course, ECE is not framed toward the moral good of play, but rather toward school readiness and all that comes with that). (2) Play is often valued for its self-contained non-seriousness and self-satisfaction; it does not have to have any greater purpose than the play itself entered into for fun – a self-contained activity without purpose may only haphazardly be educational and, furthermore, does not require an educator. (3) While it is acknowledged that nursery education may help achieve a range of other goods in learners such as social cohesion, emotional development, learning to talk and so on, play fails to meet the conditions of an education, where an education is centred on the purposeful development of worthwhile knowledge and understanding. There is no guarantee that, according to Dearden, play can lead to such developments or engagement with such outcomes; he continues: 'it is doubtful whether much of *substantial* educational value could be learned by a process of unconscious 'picking-up' during play activities' (Dearden, 1970, p. 90).

Whether one seriously agrees with Dearden's arguments or not, the purpose of sharing this text with the students was to get them to see that not everyone thought the way they did – it is fairly universal that many EC educators in England place a high value of play-based learning. In one interaction, one student entered into such frustrated rage they clenched their fists, banged the table and shared their uncensored response to our Dearden-supported philosophical challenges... This was not an isolated incident. In such moments we returned to concepts in Mezirow and Aristotle to enable the students to formulate clearly articulated arguments rather than surface-level retorts on the knife-edge of verbal and physical violence. The goal was to enable them to draw on their previous learning and to articulate considered and ethically wise responses to such attacks from outside EC practice. Indeed, in a 'Harry Potter' context, it was an attempt to provide a defence against the 'dark arts' of ill-informed education policy and, to some extent, partially informed or misguided parental expectation. We used such experiences to build in further analyses to support the students' development of autonomous and critical thinking. This enabled students to resist a fairly typical reverential treatment of theorists and policy similar to that displayed within play-based education theory, helping them gather intellectual and ethical knowledge and reasoning skills to articulate the moral purposes of ECE and educators' practice.

The assessment: 'I believe that early childhood education should...'

Both in keeping with and to embrace the 'philosophical' nature of the module, we as a production team decided that the most effective means for students to convey a purposeful overview of their 'pedagogical creeds' would be to ask them to deliver an oral presentation of their set of underpinning values and beliefs around ECE. In so doing, we felt that students would be offered the best opportunity to express their overarching 'creed' and convey a sufficient level of passion in relation to their own values and beliefs that had accumulated throughout their degree studies and previous experiences. Whilst we deliberately wanted students to eschew a written explanation of their 'creed', it was decided that a series of PowerPoint slides to merely support and provide a visual 'backdrop' to the students' own presentations would help them to demonstrate additional literature and theoretical understanding to complement their verbal expositions.

Initially, students were prompted to state each of the values and beliefs that comprised their pedagogical creed, critically explaining their origins with supporting citations and why they were important, almost 'indispensable', to their EC practice. They were encouraged to draw upon various influences on these values and beliefs such as a 'timeline' of their life experiences, work placement examples and previous module content.

Students then focused on one main value or belief and discussed this in greater depth: they were encouraged to support their discussions with appropriate readings from the module, key philosophical concepts and relevant EC policy (for example, the EYFS and children's rights legislation). A number of question prompts were provided: 'Are there authors that confirm or contrast with your own view? Are there particular session activities that you have completed that have made you think more deeply about your main value or belief?' Crucially, students were urged to make links between this main value or belief and some of the others that were stated at the beginning of their presentation as a way of illustrating how these ultimately interconnected and comprised a single 'pedagogical creed'.

Toward the end of their presentations, students were asked to not only identify some of the 'challenges' of 'living out' their creed in practice but also to suggest possible solutions or alternative actions (which occasionally might involve them in applying their 'creed' beyond the EC context). Examples of 'barriers' to fully implementing one's creed included the values and beliefs held by other practitioners and parents, and restrictive setting policies/procedures. As a brief 'conclusion' to their presentations students would reflect upon and convey the overriding purpose to their set of values and beliefs: 'What will you now do with your 'creed'? How might it support you in your future career?'

Concluding thoughts

By way of conclusion, we would like to share practical ways of developing such an approach for yourself as a developing or established EC practitioner. While the *pedagogic creed* module runs as part of a degree, it is well within the grasp of all EC educators to extend their critical capacities. The first task, or challenge, is to be able to articulate our values authentically, to exemplify autonomous thinking and demonstrate self-respect. By asking ourselves questions like 'Why do I think that?' or 'What is motivating this/their decision-making?' we can soon start to become aware of the hidden concepts and norms at work in our everyday lives. Once we garner some suggested answers to these questions, we can start to search out insights from literature, videos and podcasts to get us thinking in different ways that can lead to action: what Freire (1970) calls *critical consciousness for new social realities*. If you have a set of mandated values in your organisation like all EC and school settings, then you could generate and analyse your own professional creed that works with, challenges, and extends those mandated values from your perspective. This can enable you to hold elements of policy and practice to account while striving for positive and informed change. As a result, we see this approach as elevating the status of philosophy, theory and practice in the EC collective consciousness, providing much-needed recognition for the underpinnings of practice in policy, public discourse and parental engagement at all levels. We believe that this can give all, not only graduate-level, practitioners a fighting chance against and the capacity to move beyond the tokenism endemic in early childhood practice.

Acknowledgement

We would like to thank Christine Collins for her important role in our team. Her creative and inspiring contributions to the teaching on the pedagogical creed module are very much a part of how we have attempted to capture the dialogues and reflective writing within this chapter.

References

Aristotle (2001) 'Ethica Nicomachea', in Mckeon, R. (ed.) *The Basic Works of Aristotle*. London: Random House, pp. 927–1112.

Ball, SJ (2012) 'Performativity, commodification and commitment: An I-Spy guide to the neoliberal university', *British Journal of Educational Studies*, 60(1), pp. 17–28. doi:10.1080/00071005.2011.650940

Bhopal, K (2018) *White Privilege: The Myth of a Post-Racial Society*. Bristol: Policy Press.

Birmingham, C (2004) 'Phronesis: A model for pedagogical reflection', *Journal of Teacher Education*, 55(4), pp. 313–324. doi:10.1177/0022487104266725

Calleja, C (2014) 'Jack Mezirow's conceptualisation of adult transformative learning: A review', *Journal of Adult and Continuing Education*, 20(1). doi:10.7227/JACE.20.1.8

Dearden, RF (1970) 'The Concept of Play', in Peters, R. S. (ed.) *The Concept of Education*. London: Routledge & Kegan Paul, pp. 73–91.

Dewey, J (1964) 'My Pedagogic Creed', in Archambault, R. D. (ed.) *John Dewey on Education: Selected Writings*. Chicago: University of Chicago Press, pp. 427–439.

Dewey, J (1997) *Experience and Education*. Kappa Delt. New York: Touchstone.

Dickerson, C, Jarvis, J, & Stockwell, L (2016) 'Staff–student collaboration: student learning from working together to enhance educational practice in higher education', *Teaching in Higher Education*, 21(3). doi:10.1080/13562517.2015.1136279

Echerverria, E and Hannam, P (2017) 'The Community of Philosophical Inquiry (P4C): A pedagogical proposal for advancing democracy', in Rollins Gregory, M., Haynes, J., and Murris, K. (eds) *The Routledge International Handbook of Philosophy for Children*. Abingdon: Routledge Ltd, pp. 3–9.

Freire, P (1970) *The Pedagogy of the Oppressed*. London: Penguin

Gaut, B and Gaut, M (2011) *Philosophy for Young Children: A Practical Guide*. London: Taylor & Francis Group.

Hand, M (2018) *A Theory of Moral Education*. London: Routledge.

Kolb, DA (2014) *Experiential Learning: Experience as the Source of Learning and Development*. Second. Upper Saddle River, New Jersey: Pearson Education Inc

MacAllister, J (2011) *Wisdom and the Life of Virtue: What Should Discipline be for in Schools?*. The University of Edinburgh. Retrieved from: http://www.era.lib.ed.ac.uk/handle/1842/5841

MacAllister, J (2014) 'Why discipline needs to be reclaimed as an educational concept', *Educational Studies*, Routledge, *40*(4), pp. 438–451. doi:10.1080/03055698.2014.930341

MacIntyre, A (2007) *After Virtue*. Third. London: Bloomsbury.

Mezirow, J (1990) *Fostering Critical Reflection in Adulthood: A Guide to Transformative and Emancipatory Learning*. San Francisco: Jossey-Bass.

Mezirow, J (1997) 'Transformative learning: Theory to practice', *New Directions for Adult and Continuing Education*, *1997*(74), pp. 5–12. doi:10.1002/ace.7401

Noddings, N (2012) *Philosophy of Education*. Boulder: Westview Press.

O'Neill, O (1992) 'Children's rights and children's lives', *International Journal of Law and the Family*, 6, pp. 24–42.

O'Neill, O (2010) 'Rights, obligations, priorities', *Studies in Christian Ethics*, *23*(2), pp. 163–171. doi:10.1177/0953946809359468

Peters, RS (1966) *Ethics & Education*. London: Urwin University Books.

Ruitenberg, C & Vokey, D (2014) 'Equality and Justice', in Bailey, R. et al. (eds) *The Sage Handbook of Philosophy of Education*. London, pp. 401–414.

Sandel, MJ (2010) *Justice: What's the Right Thing to Do?* London: Penguin Books.

Stockwell, L, Smith, K & Woods, PA (2020) 'That which is worthy of love: A philosophical framework for reflection on student-student partnership for the future university', *Philosophy and Theory in Higher Education*, *2*(3), pp. 71–98. Retrieved from: https://www.peterlang.com/fileasset/Journals/PTIHE/PTIHE032020_book.pdf

Suissa, J (2013) 'Tiger mothers and praise junkies: Children, praise and the reactive attitudes', *Journal of Philosophy of Education*, *47*(1), pp. 1–19. doi:10.1111/1467-9752.12016

The British Association for Early Childhood Education (2012) *Development Matters in the Early Years Foundation Stage (EYFS)*. London. Retrieved from: www.early-education.org.uk

UK Department for Education (2013) 'The national curriculum in England Key stages 1 and 2 framework document September 2013 2 Contents'. London, United Kingdom: HMGov, p. 201.

UK Department for Education (2017) *Statutory Framework for the Early Years Foundation Stage*, DfE publications. doi:10.1163/15685314-04306007

10

THE LEYF MODEL

A sustainable ECEC model that addresses the disadvantage gap

June O'Sullivan

Introduction

Our first five years profoundly shape our future life outcomes. Early Childhood Education and Care (ECEC) has the potential to transform children's lives, especially those from disadvantaged backgrounds. The early years are acknowledged as crucial for children's outcomes, the poorest of whom will start school already 11 months behind their more affluent peers. Attendance at high-quality early years provision offers a vital opportunity to narrow a gap that will only widen throughout the school years. Yet, in the United Kingdom (UK) we operate ECEC within a mixed market model which does not meet the needs of these children. This chapter examines how the social enterprise model can be used to set nurseries apart from mainstream provision and the prevailing neoliberal paradigm that characterizes ECEC in many countries, including the UK (Moloney et al., 2019). I will use the London Early Years Foundation (LEYF), where I am the CEO, as a case study.

Setting the ECEC Context

In the UK, ECEC is shaped by the mixed market model, which has resulted in a fragmented sector. Nearly two-thirds of settings describe themselves as "private-for-profit", and the rest are charitable, social enterprise, community and state provision. Private providers have many business structures ranging from family-run single-site nurseries, childminders providing ECEC in their own homes right up to large nursery chains funded by private equity. While some of these businesses generate large profits, contentiously channelled to

DOI: 10.4324/9781003471172-12

shareholders, many are financially precarious and struggle to make ends meet year on year (O'Sullivan and Sakr, 2020).

The mixed market leads to many difficulties from financial instability to a weak un-coordinated voice. A recent Early Years Alliance survey (Gibson, 2023) found that 25% of private nurseries in the UK live "hand to mouth", and the National Day Nurseries Association (NDNA) (2021) identified a continual decline in the numbers of settings especially in areas of disadvantage which they said was supported by Ofsted's own data. Providers in areas of disadvantage therefore appear more vulnerable to market forces. Places for children are less available and of lower quality. This is despite the benefit those children would gain from high-quality ECEC.

The mixed economy is also unhelpful when trying to agree a shared voice, a clarity of social purpose and a collaborative approach. For example, the lack of insight into ECEC among the public is a challenge because it leads to a failure to understand the significant importance ECEC has for children's development, especially those children from disadvantaged backgrounds. Instead, providing childcare is considered an economic benefit for working parents. It is only through recent campaigns driven by the very high fees crisis that the public has become more aware of the complexity of the ECEC issue. The Royal Foundation Centre for Childhood found only 17% of the public recognise the importance of children's development from pregnancy to age 5. This has led to their long-term ambition to transform public awareness to a point that everyone in society understands their part in changing the situation for children and families (Ipsos Mori, 2020).

I was always struck by the unfairness that the childcare market model operating within a neoliberal context reshaped childcare into a commodity accessible mainly to those who could afford it. I designed London Early Years Foundation (LEYF) to operate in stark contrast and as a challenge to the exclusivity and profit-driven motives associated with mainstream ECEC systems. LEYF provides an example of how to deliver an accessible service to all children but especially to those from disadvantaged backgrounds. The LEYF social enterprise is a business model with social purpose, shaped around the three pillars of sustainability (economic, social and environmental), underpinned by a pedagogy for social justice and a social leadership model. LEYF, established in 2008, is a clear example that ECEC is a political space, and leading a social enterprise is a political act.

The LEYF Model: A Social Enterprise in Action

A social enterprise is a purposeful business with long-term objectives designed to address complex social, economic and ecological issues. The concept of social enterprise first appeared in the 1970s in the United States of America and picked up steam in the 1990s, particularly in the UK as the social solidarity movement started to build the vision of businesses that embed the economic viability of the enterprise with societal needs and aspirations. It is no surprise that this movement continues to grow and deepen its roots in communities across the globe (Royal Society Arts, 2022). Mainstream thinkers like Handy (2011) and Porter (2011) predicted that business transformation would be underpinned by producing shared economic value which in turn created value for society. Pioneering social enterprises have stepped into this space and demonstrated a willingness to reimagine a different future by operating in chaos created by uncertainty and adversity and to build new mechanisms that can effectively tackle and influence whole systems towards better futures for people, places and the planet.

As a social enterprise, LEYF differs from the mainstream private ECEC sector. Although it uses a business model, the social purpose is embedded through an asset lock, in our case the charitable articles of association which state that we support children from disadvantaged backgrounds. We do this by subsidising a significant proportion of places (35% is our minimum target in a context where there is no requirement for settings using the funded entitlement to offer any places) and by operating nurseries in areas of deprivation. Right now, 77% of our nurseries are in areas in the lower quartile of the Indices of Deprivation Affecting Children scale which measures the proportion of all children aged 0–15 living in income-deprived families but they attract parents from all backgrounds who like the model. Therefore, the business strategy and operational plan are designed to ensure we achieve this annually.

LEYF does not have shareholders; our governance structure is that of a charity, led by a board of trustees. We do not need to generate sufficient profits to pay dividends but like every business we need to make a surplus to secure the business and to deliver improvements through research and development while operating within a level of financial sustainability. Unlike traditional charities we are not dependent on fundraising for survival but need to demonstrate a minimum of 55% of our income is earned by trading. There are probably small family-built community businesses as well as those settings delivering public services that operate within the social enterprise ethos but may not call themselves this. It begs the need for a social enterprise network.

All businesses need to be agile to address the unknown or unexpected. The UK ECEC sector is facing big changes from September 2024 as a result of the Government's childcare expansion plan, offering a funded entitlement of 15 hours of childcare to working parents of children aged 9 months to 3-year-olds. Apart from managing the actual realities of building new provision, finding staff to deliver it, and working out how to support low-income families access enough funded hours to make working worthwhile, there is the additional challenge of the Government purchasing over 80% of the places. This potentially makes childcare another arm of the welfare state and may position ECEC as a public responsibility in the same way as primary education. Alternatively,

98 June O'Sullivan

it also has the potential to create even further divisions with private settings providing a full service for more affluent families and the voluntary and state-funded sectors using the government entitlements for poorer and more disadvantaged children. Social enterprise could be the hybrid that fills the gap as state-funded provision is always at risk to the vagaries of government funding decisions while frequently demonstrating weak business competence. A model where children from all backgrounds learn together is significant on many levels including reducing the prejudices that become ingrained early on and divide our society (ICFE, 2021).

The LEYF Pedagogy Approach: A Pedagogy for Social Justice

At LEYF, pedagogy means "leading to learn" and focuses on how staff teach and support children's learning and development. Teaching and caring are integrated, and LEYF staff are called Early Years teachers. The LEYF pedagogy operates within the Early Years Foundation Stage statutory framework (EYFS) (Department for Education (DfE), 2023). We recognise that the EYFS, or its equivalents in other countries, often serve as foundational guidance for educators. However, the LEYF response to the EYFS is not about blind compliance but harnessing its principles to enhance the learning experience for children while nurturing a culture of innovation. We see the EYFS as a starting point for our practice, not a constraint. It provides a shared language and framework that ensures consistency and quality across our nurseries through planning and assessment, partnership with parents, equality of opportunity and anti-discriminatory practice, ensuring that every child is included, supported and safeguarded.

The LEYF pedagogy takes account of the four principles of the EYFS. We agree that every child is unique, learns and develops at different rates and in diverse ways. We also agree that children are strong curious beings who thrive with the right support, in an encouraging learning environment underpinned by strong positive relationships. The beauty of these principles is how they are translated into different pedagogical approaches and how they look in practice. Unlike some mainstream models that prioritise standardised curricula and assessments, we place children at the centre of their learning journey. Pedagogy is never about reproducing an educational model, and both the DfE and Ofsted allow settings to make their own judgement about how to operate within the EYFS. This has led to a plethora of pedagogies and curricula bandied about the sector. Getting the two terms confused is not unusual in the Early Years sector, and they are often used interchangeably. The LEYF pedagogy incorporates the EYFS but in a way that is culturally contextual and situated within the whole LEYF approach. And our relationship with the EYFS is one of synergy rather than constraint.

The LEYF social purpose is to change the world one child at a time, by creating a model where children can access high-quality education and care. To do this we needed a pedagogy that puts the child at the centre and aligns purpose with practice. If ECEC is to be an effective vehicle for social change, we need to understand how to shape a social pedagogy to fulfil this purpose (Stephen, 2010). In addition, rethinking leadership to deliver a social purpose was critical as getting leadership in ECEC right is "crucial for enabling learning, pedagogy, participation, distributed power, voice, challenge, stimulation, social equity, democracy, community and achievement to flourish in a positive and purposeful climate" (Cheesman & Reed, 2019, p. 183).

Our approach was very influenced by social pedagogy which is concerned with well-being, learning and growth (ThemPra, 2018). Social pedagogy is fundamentally concerned with four aspects of the human condition through its practice:

1 A multi-dimensional and holistic understanding of *well-being*.
2 *Learning* from a standpoint of the "competent" or "rich" child, where education does not impose but facilitates children's capacity to think for themselves;
3 Authentic and trusting *relationships* between professionals and young people that acknowledge and work with both the authoritative and affectionate, as well as retaining a sense of the private.
4 *Empowerment* or promoting active engagement in one's own life and within society, and as such social pedagogy is fundamentally concerned with children's rights and developing the skills for living in a democracy.

(Eichsteller & Holthoff, 2012)

From the outset, we chose to develop the LEYF pedagogy within some of social pedagogy thinking because it is an educational solution to social and economic upheaval which challenged social integration by blending the theory of social and moral education with a method of practice. The result was a set of ideas based on the values of humanity, continually reviewed and refreshed by thinkers and practitioners who refine their pedagogical responses to changing political, social and economic issues with the ultimate intention to create a more just society through educational means. It is a departure from neoliberal approaches that tend to overly standardise ECEC. Our pedagogical model encourages reflective practice and values the unique contributions of each staff member.

The LEYF pedagogy also fitted very comfortably within the concept of social pedagogy because of our ambition to recognise everyone's intrinsic worth and ability to reach their full potential. Hämäläinen (2003) describes our commitment very neatly as "...promoting people's social functioning, inclusion, participation, social identity and social competence as members of society" (p. 76).

The guiding ethos of social pedagogy anchored the social purpose and the values of LEYF despite the many changes and shifts we implemented to develop a workable model. The LEYF pedagogy, in the spirit of social pedagogy, is dynamic, creative, and process-orientated rather than mechanical, procedural and automated. This pedagogical fluidity has shaped our approach as we discovered more about children's development and adjusted to the changing context of their lives. We believe that innovation and compliance are not mutually exclusive. We view the EYFS as a foundation upon which we can build innovative and responsive pedagogical practices. Our nurseries are hubs of experimentation, where staff are encouraged to try new approaches, integrate emerging research, design responsive pedagogical practices, and engage in professional development to keep our practice dynamic and fresh. The resulting LEYF pedagogy is made up of seven interwoven strands, each one made from thousands of threads, all of which combine to form a strong learning rope which supports children, families and staff (see Figure 10.1).

The pedagogy at LEYF is delivered by teachers concerned with the 'three Ps': the professional, the personal and the private. It is underpinned by the idea that 'every person has inherent potential, is valuable, resourceful and can

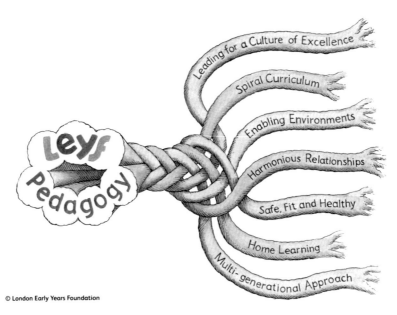

FIGURE 10.1   LEYF Social Pedagogy. Image by June O'Sullivan/London Early Years Foundation.

make a meaningful contribution to the wider community if we find ways of including them' (ThemPra, 2018). Stephens (2013) insists that these relationships have to be underpinned by the notion of *caritas*, a Latin word for the 'benevolent concern for others which signals a sense of solidarity' (Stephens, 2013, p. 23) and goes further than kindness. Freire (1970) refers to education as an act of love when educators intentionally choose to build valuing and loving the children into the pedagogical process. At LEYF this connected to the Harmonious Relationship element of the pedagogy with the focus on loving harmony with the children, each other, parents, colleagues, community and wider society.

According to Eichsteller and Holthoff (2012), social pedagogy is concerned with the theory and practice of creating a 'thriving garden for children', creating a fertile self-sustaining ecosystem connecting the child's well-being, learning and resources to their surroundings. Social pedagogy continues to evolve as a pedagogical response that identifies the educational pathways to promote critical consciousness in all children to enable them to respond to societal changes that affect the relationship between the individual and society especially when there are risks of fragmentation and social exclusion. It will therefore continue to be shaped by social pedagogues who courageously embrace a level of pedagogical fluidity that is driven by continual discussion and reflection as we observe and understand the changing world faced by our children. For example, the COVID-19 pandemic tested us in unprecedented ways, however, our unwavering commitment to the well-being of children, families and staff members remained constant. By prioritising support, resilience and adaptability, we navigated the challenges and emerged stronger, reaffirming our belief in our pedagogy. The impact of the pandemic continues not least in children's delayed development, higher levels of separation anxiety and more entrenched levels of poverty. We continue to evolve a range of responses, for example, extending places to more children in poverty, building home learning bridges and extending our SEND support. The pandemic also reinforced the need to strengthen our sustainability approach.

The LEYF Approach to Sustainability

Building a social enterprise automatically frames the business within the three pillars of sustainability based on the Brundtland Report (1987) which identified the importance of the 3 E's of sustainability: economic prosperity, equitable societies and environmental regeneration and stewardship. This description helps us see how the economy and our natural resources are firmly interlinked and underpinned by fairness, which in turn is important as we begin to think of ourselves as guardians of our children's future.

The Economic Pillar of Sustainability

The economic pillar of sustainability is shaped by the LEYF business model of a charitable social enterprise providing all children with access to a high-quality nursery irrespective of their backgrounds. Our business strategy looks at sustainability through governance, pedagogy and operations. It filters through all business decisions from setting the budget and paying staff to developing growth plans. The wellbeing of staff is central to economic sustainability, and as we are a not-for-dividend organisation, all our surplus is reinvested in places for children and family support plus fair salaries, good benefits, generous pensions as well as career and development opportunities from entry qualifications to a higher education degree for staff.

The Social Pillar of Sustainability

Our understanding of social sustainability has shaped our inclusive and equitable business and our pedagogical model which is centred around fairness and equity for children, their families and staff. We actively campaign and lead the way for change, for example, by demonstrating how we have increased the number of men in childcare. We also established the first Early Years Chef Academy to train chefs to be better able to provide nutritious meals, offer food education and promote healthy life choices as a response to child obesity and food poverty. Whether it is through the LEYF Apprenticeship Academy which actively recruits learners from complicated backgrounds such as looked after care leavers or our partnership to support young Dads in local prisons, our pedagogy promotes harmonious relationships and community engagement, while partnerships are key to how we support children, families and staff.

The Environmental Pillar of Sustainability

Environmental sustainability is understood throughout life as the way we look after our planet. ECEC is a natural starting point, and children are much more competent and thoughtful than we give them credit for. Indeed, if sustainable development is relevant to children's lives, then we need to prepare them for their role in dealing with the problems they are facing. We want to educate our children to become curious about the wider world and learn to take responsibility about how they can be kind and respectful to their environment, nature and wildlife and learn about the impact their decisions can have on the planet. This approach filters through our operations, procurement, resourcing, pedagogy and governance.

Social Leadership

To enable us to put our commitment to sustainability and social justice into practice, we use a model of social leadership. This involves developing innovation, agility and responsiveness in organisational culture by drawing on the talents and ideas of everyone in the organisation. Social leaders avoid traditional hierarchies and create a culture, as well as systems and processes, that support leaders to harness 'social energy' across the organisation. This is very relevant today, as we see so many staff leaving the sector because they are dissatisfied by lack of status and value for their work, by low pay and poor conditions and with no meaningful professional development opportunities. A review produced by the OECD (2018), more than ten years ago, highlighted the wealth of evidence to show that high-quality staff in itself is not enough for high-quality provision, since staff also need to be fairly treated and remunerated, and receive sufficient professional development. This triangle of support is more likely to drive high-quality ECEC provision as confirmed by the Education Policy Institute review (Bonetti, 2020). At LEYF our leadership model has seven elements which is central to developing a culture of excellence (see Figure 10.2).

Social Leadership and Social Pedagogy

Social leaders consider social pedagogy in ECEC as a combination of social, pedagogical and political practices, and the boundaries between these disciplines must be crossed to provide useful services to children and adults (Stephen, Ellis & Martlew, 2009). For social leaders this is essential to how they deliver a strong social pedagogy which is aligned to the values and ambitions of the organisation and supports a culture of wellbeing, empowerment and strong empathetic relationships. If social purpose is the heart of social

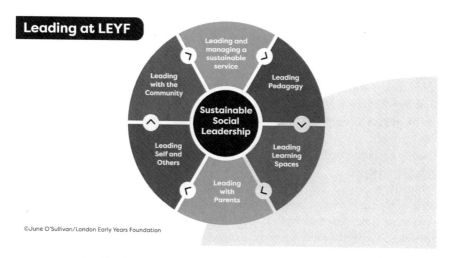

FIGURE 10.2 Leading at LEYF. Image by June O'Sullivan/London Early Years Foundation.

leadership, social pedagogy is the heartbeat – it is the process through which the social purpose does its work and brings life to the organisation.

There are three ways that social leaders use social pedagogy to strengthen their leadership. Firstly, it helps them create a culture of wellbeing and empowerment which reinforces the importance of the social purpose throughout the organisation. Secondly, social leaders use the social pedagogical approach to develop staff to be reflective and empathetic which is key to securing the social purpose. Thirdly, social leaders use the principles of social pedagogy to open a wider debate about the purpose of education and how we need to rethink modern ECEC policy in so many parts of the world.

Social leaders support staff to bring their hearts to their work recognising and encouraging their contribution as ethical and emotional beings. In social pedagogy this is also known as 'Haltung', which roughly translates as the mindset, values or personal moral codes that shape the way we think and drive our behaviour and attitudes to the world we live in at work and at home, the situations we face, our relationships and how we apply a profound respect for human dignity (Eichsteller & Holthoff 2012; Gardner & Charfe, 2019). This is best delivered in a culture of ambition and growth mindset led by social leaders who build optimism, hope and empowerment.

Dweck (2007) popularised the concept of the growth mindset which describes the belief that our intelligence and abilities can develop over time. In contrast, a fixed mindset regards intelligence or talents as unchangeable. She noted that low-income students were twice as likely to have fixed mindsets compared to their more affluent peers; yet having a growth mindset is a key predictor of achievement. The importance of thinking big and having ambition for children from more disadvantaged families must begin early. In their work about how to cultivate social justice via education, Gorski (2017) found that a deficit attitude to teaching children from disadvantaged and poor communities was commonplace among teachers. Teachers often saw poverty as the result of personal negative attitudes towards education and an unwillingness to work hard. They were surprised to discover that poor people had similar educational aspirations to those of more affluent families but believed the structural factors that led to poverty overwhelmed their abilities. If social leaders are to deliver their social purpose which is most often addressing a level of disadvantage and poverty, then staff need to be truly reflective of their contributions and the impact they can have on ensuring a fair, inclusive and democratic service.

Finally, to widen the debate, social leaders need to understand the importance of telling stories. They know that to influence an audience it is important to involve their heart as well as their mind; when they share some of their emotions, they tell a more inspirational story. Being surrounded by adults who use their heads, hearts and hands to drive their practice as well as being willing to bring their professional, private and personal selves to work provides a great source of stories and generates a wider discussion. Telling genuine stories and demonstrating values-driven practice is key because, as Freire (1970, p. 70) reminds us:

> Dialogue cannot exist in the absence of a profound love of the world and for people … Because love is an act of courage, not of fear, love is a commitment to others.

Managing Change by Building a Community of Practice

Social leaders in any context need to find ways to collaborate and build a shared voice. This is particularly true in our sector if we want to increase children's access to high-quality ECEC. Our sector needs people who can operate well in complexity, are comfortable with uncertainty and likely to keep their heads, hearts and hands while all around are losing theirs. We need to be ambidextrous working with the old system while building the new. I often describe this as building the bridge while we are also on it!

When we are thinking about new ways of doing things, we have to address change. For example, to be successful, the LEYF model needed to be scalable and replicable so that many more childcare social enterprises could be created. This was particularly challenging as in increasingly complex societies social exclusion becomes resistant to simple solutions like fiscal measures and standardised services. We developed the LEYF change model of 7A's (see Figure 10.3) because we needed a way of articulating the change process and identifying the points of challenge, such as anchoring new practice. Choukeir, Kenyon and Meghti (2022) identified three forms of support that can benefit individual social entrepreneurs and entrepreneurial movements, which are, capacity and skills building, funding and investment, and connecting and platforming. These are a useful set of steps to begin making change happen, especially if we are to reshape the market model so that all children have access to ECEC services.

We need to start the change by building a community of new pioneers willing to step into the social enterprise space. This could operate as a community of practice as envisaged by Lave and Wenger (1991) who described it as a group of teachers coming together to build knowledge and skills around an area of interest. It is not an action learning project but a place to deconstruct their knowledge and practice, share their passion and worries, through reflection and analysis in an inclusive and collaborative way so that it operates as a collective. Collaborative efforts amplify our message and influence positive change. It is time for a social enterprise ECEC community of practice so we can innovate together!

FIGURE 10.3   Making change happen. Image by June O'Sullivan/London Early Years Foundation.

Conclusion

LEYF was designed to address the lack of childcare models which focus on providing sustainable high-quality accessible settings for children from disadvantaged backgrounds particularly as the current model of a patchwork of government-funded support has actually widened the disadvantage gap. Quality early childhood education must be a priority for every society. We cannot afford to let it remain at the mercy of the market and hasty political decisions. We need a way of providing services that align with the three pillars of sustainability, economically secure, socially inclusive and environmentally alert. In a world where neoliberalism often dominates ECEC, LEYF stands as a beacon of hope and innovation. Transitioning from government-imposed systems to a social enterprise and social pedagogy model such as LEYF demands courage and imagination but provides an example for educators, governments and local authorities wishing to rethink their ECEC for children from disadvantaged backgrounds.

It is time we stop doing the same thing over and over again hoping for a different outcome and start doing things differently!

References

Bonetti, S (2020). *Early Years Workforce Development in England: Key Ingredients and Missed Opportunities*. London: Education Policy Institute.

Brundtland, GH (1987). Brundtland report. Our common future. *Comissão Mundial*, 4(1), pp. 17–25.

Cheesman, S & Reed, M (eds.). (2019). *Pedagogies for Leading Practice*. Routledge.

Choukeir, J, Kenyon, T, & Meghti, Z (2022). Entrepreneurs for change. *RSA Journal*, 4, pp. 11.

Department for Education (2023). *Statutory framework for the early years foundation stage.* Retrieved from: https://assets.publishing.service.gov.uk/government/uploads/system/uploads/attachment_data/file/1170108/EYFS_framework_from_September_2023.pdf

Dweck, C (2007). *Mindset: The New Psychology of Success.* Ballantine Books.

Eichsteller, G & Holthoff, S (2012). The art of being a social pedagogue: Developing cultural change in children's homes in Essex. *International Journal of Social Pedagogy, 1,* pp. 30–45.

Freire, P (1970) *Pedagogy of the Oppressed.* London: Penguin Classics

Gardner, A & Charfe, L (2019). Social pedagogy and social work. *Social Pedagogy and Social Work,* pp. 1–160.

Gorski, PC (2017). *Reaching and Teaching Students in Poverty: Strategies for Erasing the Opportunity Gap.* New York: Teachers College Press.

Gibson, J (2023). *Alliance research shows families will struggle to access funded places at early years settings.* Retrieved from: Alliance research shows families will struggle to access funded places at early years settings | early years alliance (eyalliance.org.uk)

Hämäläinen, J (2003). The concept of social pedagogy in the field of social work. *Journal of Social Work 3*(1), pp. 69–80.

Handy, C (2011). *The Empty Raincoat: Making Sense of the Future.* New York: Random House.

International Commission on the Futures of Education (ICFE) (2021). *Reimagining our Futures Together: A New Social Contract for Education.* Paris: UNESCO.

IPSOS Mori (2020). *State of the Nation: Understanding Public Attitudes to the Early Years.* Retrieved from: https://assets.ctfassets.net/qwnplnakca8g/43b4Wotc8AYK4WPCh2oOvs/fbe9ed4e11d0d7ad2a0906693a481512/Ipsos-MORI-SON_report.pdf

Lave, J & Wenger, E (1991). *Situated Learning: Legitimate Peripheral Participation.* Cambridge: Cambridge University Press.

Moloney, M, Sims, M, Rothe, A, Buettner, C, Sonter, L, Waniganayake, M, Opazo, MJ, Calder, P, & Girlich, S (2019). Resisting neoliberalism: Professionalisation of early childhood education and care. *International Journal of Elementary Education.*

National Day Nurseries Association (NDNA) (2021). *Stop Underfunding – Start Building Futures England.* Retrieved from: www.NDNA.org.uk

O'Sullivan, J & Sakr, M (2020). *Social Leadership: An Introduction.* London: Bloomsbury

OECD (2018). *Building a High-Quality Early Childhood Education and Care Workforce. Further Results from the Starting Strong Survey 2018.* Retrieved from: https://www.oecd-ilibrary.org/education/building-a-high-quality-early-childhood-education-and-care-workforce_b90bba3d-en

Porter, ME (2011). *Competitive Advantage of Nations: Creating and Sustaining Superior Performance.* Simon and Schuster.

Stephen, C (2010). Pedagogy: The silent partner in early years learning. *Early Years, 30*(1), pp. 15–28.

Stephen, C, Ellis, J, & Martlew, J (2009). Turned on to learning active learning in primary one. *Applied Educational Research Scheme.*

Stephens, P (2013). *Heart and Head.* Bremen: Europäischer Hochschulverlag.

ThemPra (2018). *The professional, personal, and private self of the social pedagogue.* Retrieved from http://www.thempra.org.uk/social-pedagogy/key-concepts-in-social-pedagogy/the-3-ps/

11

INVOLVING FAMILIES

Lessons from updating Australia's approved learning framework

Fay Hadley, Linda Harrison, Leanne Lavina, Lennie Barblett, Susan Irvine, Francis Bobongie-Harris, and Jennifer Cartmel

Project Background

In January 2021 a research team was commissioned to lead a consortium of education and care researchers and practitioners to update Australia's Approved Learning Framework (ALF), Belonging, Being and Becoming: The Early Years Learning Framework (EYLF). The consortium comprised 34 experts in early childhood education and care (ECEC) and a transdisciplinary advisory team of six wise counsels who gave feedback on all stages of the work. This chapter describes the journey of the consortium leaders and the wider research community of practice across this 15-month research project in gathering the voices of families. Listening to families allowed for their rich insights to inform the EYLF updates, improving the acceptability of the updated EYLF, and highlighting how important it is for policymakers to include families in reform agendas.

The aim of the research was to gather diverse perspectives to inform the update of the EYLF and reflect contemporary understandings of amplifying children's learning, development, and wellbeing. Developed prior to the 2012 implementation of Australia's National Quality Standard (NQS) which provides a national benchmark for quality in ECEC, the nationally approved Framework – *Belonging, Being and Becoming: The Early Years Framework for Australia* (EYLF) (Department of Education, Employment and Workplace Relations [DEEWR], 2009) had been in use for nearly a decade. Consistent with the aspirations of the NQS, it is important that educational programs and practices are informed by contemporary research and evidence-based practice to guide educators in supporting each child's learning and development as well as building continuity across educational systems (i.e., ECEC and school).

DOI: 10.4324/9781003471172-13

Gathering perspectives: Principles and stages of engagement

To inform the Update, the project was underpinned by a comprehensive engagement plan that sought to optimise diverse perspectives, including the voices of children and their families. Stakeholder engagement followed eight principles: Inclusion, respect, accessibility, ethical collection and use of data, a positive and strengths-based approach, timelines, transparency, and collegiality and collaboration (see Hadley et al., under review). Strategies were primarily focused on providing balanced and objective information to assist understanding the Framework's strengths, as well as identifying areas for updating and opportunities to clarify or strengthen practice and knowledge to align with current research evidence. To obtain input and feedback on analysis, alternatives, and decisions, engagement involved working directly with stakeholders to ensure their aspirations were understood and considered. This involved analysing responses provided by over 5000 educators, service providers, families, children, and other professionals from various ECEC settings across Australia. This was an iterative process, and the design facilitated engagement at critical points in the project, placing the final decision-making in the hands of stakeholders and providing the key to formulating recommendations for updating the EYLF.

The importance of families' perspectives on policy

Listening to families about what happens in the educational spaces their children attend is critical. Families are a key stakeholder and hearing their perspectives supports moving beyond an individualised approach to conceptualising education as a social responsibility. As Vandenbroeck (2023, p. xx) notes: 'It means there are possibilities for thinking about alliances between parents and professionals that are truly social and democratic'. Inclusive participatory methods in shaping early years policy and decision-making are regarded as a fundamental democratic entitlement essential for validating the policy formulation process at local and national levels. As argued by Gramberger (2001), there is a growing consensus on this matter. Degotardi et al. (2022) assert that involving diverse voices through engagement processes empowers stakeholders and opens new channels of communication that may not always be accessible to families.

Methods of implementation

An iterative, mixed method approach over three stages was used to gather and analyse data from approved providers, teachers, educators, families, children, other professionals, and policymakers. Stages 1 and 2 involved engaging, gathering and including stakeholder voices to gauge satisfaction and strengths of the EYLF in practice, and as well as opportunities to strengthen, expand and improve areas within the Framework. Families participated through online surveys that were translated into five additional languages, Arabic, Chinese, Hindi, Korean and Vietnamese. Ethical approvals were granted by the three University Ethics Committees where the researchers worked. Across all stages, explanations about consent and children's assent were explained and all responses de-identified.

Stage 1: Families' voices informing the discussion paper

An online survey for all stakeholders was a key research tool in understanding perceived strengths and potential areas for updating the Framework. Stage 1 also included conducting a review of the contemporary literature and other Frameworks 'to identify areas of strength and potential areas for updating the ALF' (Barblett et al., 2021, p. 3). The analysis of Stage 1 data contributed to a discussion paper with recommendations for updating the EYLF.

Stage 1: Sample size and representativeness

A total of 361 families from all states and territories of Australia responded to the Stage 1 surveys. The majority (93%; n = 334) used centre-based ECEC settings (preschool/kindergarten and long day care [LDC] centres) and 7% (n = 28) used home-based family day care (FDC) settings which are licensed for children from birth to age 12 years. Family demographic details are provided in Table 11.1. The majority of participants identified as female, English-speaking and working in a professional role. The proportion of family members and children identified as Aboriginal or Torres Strait Islander (2% and 3%) was slightly less than the national population. Families' experience of using ECEC settings ranged from less than 1 year to more than 6 years.

Families responded to a series of questions about their knowledge and views about the EYLF in relation to their children in their ECEC service. The survey asked families to rate the importance of the Vision, Principles, Practices and Learning Outcomes using a 6-point scale from 'not at all' important to 'extremely' important. A 'not sure' option was also available. Three-quarters (74.6%) of families confirmed that they had heard of or were aware of the EYLF that educators use when working with their child/children.

Table 11.2 summarises families' ratings of the importance of the noted EYLF elements, reported as the proportion who selected 'very much' or 'extremely' important. Higher ratings (80–90%) suggest strong endorsement of the EYLF vision, principles, practices and learning outcomes, while lower ratings suggest areas for improvement and opportunities to update the Framework.

TABLE 11.1 Stage 1 Family Demographics

	Families using ECEC Total = 361	
	n	%
Family member identified as female[a]	298	83%
Family member is of Aboriginal or Torres Strait Islander origin	8	2%
Family member speaks a language other than English	86	24%
Family member is working or studying or both	292	81%
Family member (working) identified as a professional worker[b]	188	64%
Has used ECEC settings for less than 1 year	97	27%
Has used ECEC settings for 1 to 3 years	148	41%
Has used ECEC settings for more than 3 years	90	25%
Age of child/children		
- Under 3 years	156	43%
- 3 to 5 years	181	50%
- over 5 years but less than 8 years	24	7%
Child/children is/are of Aboriginal or Torres Strait Islander origin	10	3%
Child/children speak/s a language other than English	66	18%
Child/children have a disability or developmental delay	27	8%

[a] Others identified as male, preferred not to say, or did not complete this question
[b] Other working family members identified as technician/trades worker, community/personal service worker, clerical/administrative worker, or sales worker

TABLE 11.2 Percent of families who rated the EYLF Vision, Principles, Practices and Learning Outcomes as very to extremely important

	ECEC - EYLF
Vision	
All children experience learning that is engaging and build success for life	84.5%
Principles	
Secure, respectful and reciprocal relationships	98.3%
Partnerships with families and support professionals	89.8%
High expectations and equity for all children's capacity to succeed	91.6%
Respect for diversity of cultures, values, practices and beliefs	92.8%
Practices	
Learning through play	95.5%
Assessment for learning	58.7%
Learning Outcomes (LO)	
LO 1 Children have a strong sense of identity	95.4%
LO 2 Children are connected with and contribute to their world	92.7%
LO 3 Children have a strong sense of wellbeing	95.0%
LO 4 Children are confident and involved learners	96.1%
LO 5 Children are effective communicators	91.4%

112 Fay Hadley et al.

Results indicated endorsement of the Vision by a significant proportion of families (84.5% rated this as very or extremely important). Families' comments on how the Vision could be improved were insightful and fed into the recommendations. For instance, common themes raised included:

Cultural appreciation particularly learning about the Traditional Owners of the land.

(ECEC-FDC)

Results for the Principles reflected families' very strong support for supportive, secure relationships between educators and their children (98% rated this as very/extremely important). They also valued cultural responsiveness, agreeing the update needed to better reflect inclusiveness and genuine embedding of diverse perspectives and authentic partnerships.

Having trust between the school, parents and the children is the most important factor in helping them shape their identity when they can feel safe and respected to be who they are.

(ECEC-Preschool)

Over 95% of families rated the Practice of Learning through play (EYLF) as very or extremely important; commenting, for example, that:

For our family we place 'learning through play' very highly. So much research shows that play-based learning is the best for the early years. It should continue into prep and years 1-2 at Primary school too. They should be allowed to get messy, experiment, run, jump, and climb as they learn.

(ECEC-LDC)

In contrast, the Practice Assessment for learning received the lowest ratings: only 58.7% of ECEC families rated this as very/extremely important for their child/children. Feedback regarding this Practice focused on broadening the focus beyond assessment to ensure a holistic approach with relational and social strengths, rather than formalised methods of assessment that increase educators' workloads. For example:

It looks very complicated, how much time does it take educators to document this practice, time taken away from the children or time outside of work (non-paid) to complete? How many families appreciate all this paperwork of the framework?

(ECEC-FDC)

The five EYLF Learning Outcomes were all strongly endorsed by ECEC families (ratings of 91–96%). For example:

I think the target areas for the Outcomes are appropriate, easy to understand and well-balanced.

(ECEC-FDC)

They (educators) provide a wide range of activities. Identify individual's interests/strengths/weaknesses. Utilise this knowledge to help each child start building the fundamentals of learning new skills and advancing those they have already obtained.

(ECEC-LDC)

Stage 2: Families' voices informing the EYLF Update

Drawing on the literature review and stakeholder feedback in Stage 1, the Discussion Paper identified 20 opportunities for clarification, expansion and updating the EYLF. Of these, 15 were identified as most relevant to families' use and experience in ECEC and presented in an abridged, family-friendly paper (see: Hadley, et al., 2021).

Families were invited to consider each recommendation and provide their responses via an online survey, which was again translated into five additional languages. Analysis of Stage 2 data informed the draft Update to the Framework and the development of protocols to pilot prior to finalising the EYLF version 2.

Stage 2: Sample size and representativeness

A total of 215 families from all states and territories of Australia responded to the Stage 2 survey. The families were using one or a mix of ECEC services: 72% were using LDC centres; about a third (34%) were using school-based or centre-based preschool/kindergarten programs; and 14% used home-based FDC or other child and family support services. The majority of participants identified as female (94%) and from an English-speaking background (76%). A small but representative proportion of family members and children identified as Aboriginal or Torres Strait Islander (3.5% and 5.4%). The children of participating families included under 3-year-olds (39%) and 3 to 5-year-olds (61%). Families' experience of using ECEC settings ranged from 1 to 4 years.

The 15 recommendations were explained briefly for families and clearly stated in a sentence. Families were asked to rate the extent to which they agreed/disagreed with the recommended update, using a 7-point rating scale to (1 = disagree very strongly; 2 = disagree strongly; 3 = disagree; 4 = neutral neither disagree nor agree; 5 = agree; 6 = agree strongly; 7 = agree very strongly). For example, the Recommendation to update the Vision by strengthening Aboriginal and Torres Strait Islander perspectives was explained as follows:

Strengthening Aboriginal and Torres Strait Islander knowledge and perspectives throughout both ALFs is a priority that aligns with the Australian Curriculum and reflects the Alice Springs (Mparntwe) Education Declaration, 2019. This recognises 60,000 years of continual connection by Aboriginal and Torres Strait Islander peoples as a key part of the nation's history, present and future. Evidence suggests this is a way to move towards Reconciliation.

The question was then asked: To what extent do you agree/disagree with updating the EYLF by: Expanding the EYLF vision to recognise the role of ECEC in advancing Reconciliation.

The number of family members who provided rated responses to these 15 recommendations ranged from 187 to 250. Ratings of 'agree', 'strongly agree' and 'very strongly agree' were combined to provide an estimate of the number and proportion of families who were in favour of the recommendation. Table 11.3 provides the number and percentage of participants who endorsed each recommendation.

As in Stage 1, a figure of 80% agreement was seen as a strong endorsement of the recommended update to the EYLF framework. Nine of the 15 recommendations - Vision (1), Principles (5, 6, 7, 8), and Learning Outcomes (12, 13, 14, 15) were strongly endorsed. Updates to the Vision were seen as important by ECEC families (82.3% agreement), but with some uncertainties regarding reconciliation (74.7% agreement); for example, noting:

I can't fault the discussion paper proposals – specifically the repositioning of 'success for life' and the Traditional owner's content. How it translates to on the ground learning and experience will be interesting and exciting to watch.

(ECEC-FDC)

Keep things like the various cultural groups and the environment for when they are older and can actually understand what they are being presented.

(ECEC-Preschool)

There were lower levels of agreement about embedding Aboriginal and Torres Strait Islander perspectives. The recommendations for Principles (3, 4) received agreement by three-quarters (77.8% and 75.8%) of families. Qualitative responses indicated concerns that this could lead to less focus on other types of diversity and cultures that live in Australia, for example:

Definitely a focus on Indigenous perspectives is a must, however, we need to ensure we hold the same respect for our multicultural society and not lose the importance of all cultures as equals.

(ECEC-LDC)

TABLE 11.3 Percentage of families who agreed with the 15 recommended updates to the EYLF

Vision	%
1. Reconsidering the words 'success for life' in the vision and instead emphasise the vision as all children and young people become confident and creative individuals, successful lifelong learners, and active and informed members of the community.	82.3%
2. Expanding the EYLF vision to recognise the role of ECEC in advancing Reconciliation	74.7%

Principles	
3. Adding a principle about embedding Aboriginal and Torres Strait Islander knowledges and perspectives in the EYLF	77.8%
4. Making Aboriginal and Torres Strait Islanders cultures and ways of knowing more explicit in all of the learning outcomes to reflect family/community connections, connection to country, kinship systems, telling of stories (oral history), spirituality, and connecting with the extended family	75.8%
5. Expanding the principle of high expectations and equity to reflect modern understandings of diversity and inclusion	83.8%
6. Adding a principle of sustainability to include environmental, social and economic sustainability	92.5%
7. Revising the principle of secure, respectful and reciprocal relationships to include children and young people's connections with educators and their peers to underpin learning and teaching practices	88.8%
8. Strengthening the principle of partnerships to include working with diverse families, culturally safe spaces, and strengthening connections with child and family professionals and school communities	90.9%

Practices	
9. Reframing the practice of cultural competence to cultural responsiveness, which includes a genuine commitment to embedding Aboriginal and Torres Strait Islander perspectives in all aspects of service provision	74.3%
10. Re-aligning EYLF practices to: Assessment and evaluation for learning, development and well-being to reflect contemporary understandings of authentic and meaningful assessment approaches including children's role in assessing their own learning	69.7%

Learning Outcomes	
11. Expanding the guidance relating to Learning Outcome 1 to reflect contemporary perspectives of personal (e.g., gender) and social (e.g., customs and rituals) identity and Aboriginal and Torres Strait Islanders identities	69.5%
12. Strengthening concepts of sustainability in Learning Outcome 2, based on the broader definition of sustainability spanning environmental, social and economic sustainability	84.9%

(*Continued*)

116 Fay Hadley et al.

TABLE 11.3 (Continued)

13. Expanding the guidance relating to Learning Outcome 3 to reflect information about wellbeing and drawing on recent research and guidelines relating to children's health and wellbeing, social competence, embodied learning, fundamental movement skills, including mental health promotion, protective behaviours and resilience	95.2%
14. Strengthening the focus in Learning Outcome 4 on children's thinking, development of conceptual thinking (e.g., science and mathematics) and reinforcing the use of the language of learning	88.6%
15. Strengthening the guidance relating to Learning Outcome 5 to include oral, aural and non-oral languages, communication through the arts, mathematical thinking and a focus on children and young people as creative, safe, and critical users of technology for learning, leisure and creative expression	87.8%

Recommendations for Practices 9 received agreement from just under three-quarters (74.3%) of families. Families' comments for supporting embedding of Aboriginal and Torres Strait Islander perspectives focused on the need to move to more authentic approaches. For example:

> Ensuring 'being' is always in there as there is such a rush to grow up, continuing on supporting reconciliation and the importance of play.
>
> *(ECEC-LDC)*

As in Stage 1, the Practice of Assessment for learning (10) received a lower level of agreement (69.7%) from families.

> My child is in daycare, he will be educated at school. Education is only an unnecessary bonus in his daily routine. So assessment isn't of any significance to us at this stage. We know what he's doing and where he's up to more than the educators that spend more time with him.
>
> *(ECEC-LDC)*

> I marked 'Assessment for learning' as lesser rating because I feel assessments aren't exactly core practice for early childhood age young people. They are developing their mindset and so tasking them in assessment style test will not achieve much but it's good practice to begin as they enter pre-school to Kindergarten age.
>
> *(ECEC-LDC)*

Learning Outcome (11) recommendation also received lower agreement (69.5%) from families who questioned whether explicit teaching of some topics such as gender was appropriate. For instance:

I feel strongly about everyone feeling accepted and included, however don't want to overcomplicate topics (such as gender) by forcing the conversation with such young children. I believe children are naturally accepting of others (e.g. racism is taught) and we should encourage inclusion in organic ways and not in structured lessons or forced language.

(ECEC-LDC)

The other four recommendations relating to updates to Learning Outcomes 2, 3, 4 and 5 were strongly endorsed by families.

Listening to families to transform policy

Findings from stage 1 and stage 2 of the Update project have shown that families' voices are important, and they have a strong role to play in the transformation of policy. The ideas, and concerns families raised ensured concepts were strengthened or better explained in the updated EYLF. For information about the overall findings of the updates see: Barblett et al. (2021, 2023) and Cartmel et al. (2023a, 2023b).

Adopting a staged consultative approach with families yielded diverse perspectives which added to current understandings of strengths and update opportunities across the five elements of the EYLF. This section highlights the key areas where families' perspectives were critical to informing the updates: *Partnerships, Inclusion and diversity,* and *Assessment and learning.*

Partnerships

Families' views revealed different meanings about partnerships when compared to educators. This information was key to updating language and concepts informing the EYLF, especially how educator–family partnerships might be enacted in practice. In Stage 1 Families overwhelmingly supported the current EYLF principles (over 90%): *Secure, respectful, and reciprocal relationships, Partnerships with families and support professionals, High expectations and equity for all children's capacity to succeed, Respect for diversity of culture, value, practices and beliefs.* Responses reiterated the importance of placing families at the centre of practice where partnerships are built on respect, reciprocal communication, and shared decisions. Relationships guided by strengths-based approaches recognise families as experts and first educators in their children's lives (Australian Government Department of Education [AGDE], 2022). Authentic reciprocal partnerships based on mutual exchange communicate value for parents' perspectives and contributions, and these foundations are essential to forming responsive educator–family relationships (Almendingen, Clayton & Matthews., 2022; Hadley & Rouse, 2018).

Strengthening the Principle of *Partnerships* to include working with diverse families, culturally safe spaces, and strengthening connections with child and family professionals, and school communities was seen as very important by the families. The literature notes how partnerships can be understood differently by educators and families (Hadley & Rouse, 2018). Ensuring the updated EYLF reflected the contemporary perspectives and application of partnerships was important to strengthen environments of care, education and safety for children, and provide greater opportunities to recognise and develop coordinated responses that meet the diversity of families accessing settings. High educational quality and responsive learning environments are established when systems work in partnership to build and maintain connections across contexts (Cartmel & Hayes, 2016).

Inclusion and diversity

The focus on cultural competence across the Principles, Practices and Outcomes was identified as requiring updating, with additional representation of Aboriginal and Torres Strait Islander perspectives, histories, and stories of placed identities on Country as recommended from Royal Commission findings (e.g. Victorian Government, 2008). Based on a rights-based approach to knowing and understanding past and present contexts of shared experience, Australian children need opportunities to learn about and appreciate the diverse lived perspectives of Aboriginal and Torres Strait Islander peoples in their community (Barblett et al., 2020). Integrating Indigenous cultures and perspectives within ECEC settings recognises the importance of cultural competence for improving outcomes for Aboriginal and Torres Strait Islander peoples (Department of Education and Training Queensland, 2011). However, the updates also emphasised the importance of other cultural diversity considerations. This also involves educators and other professionals actively deconstructing issues of power, racism, and discrimination to ensure programs reflect the voices and experiences of children, young people, and families, to build an environment of cultural safety, acceptance, and belonging for all (Gerlach, Brown & Greenwood, 2017; AGDE, 2022).

Learning and Assessment

Stakeholder advocacy for updating Learning Outcome 1, the importance of children's strong identities for connecting to and positively relating with others (see Marwick, 2017) was affirmed by families. Consistent with the work of Solomon (2016), responses reflected the importance of valuing oneself as learner and engaged citizen. Although introducing perspectives around cultural and gender identities was seen as requiring sensitivity and boundaries on what is important content in ECEC settings. Early childhood research has highlighted better understanding of what play-based learning is and what it can look like (Leggett & Ford, 2013; McLean, Lake, Wild & Licandro, 2023). Families supported strengthening play-based approaches to practice, including children's agency in designing and leading their learning.

There were different views on *Assessment for learning*, which provided impetus to expand definitions of collaborative methods of assessing children's learning. Parents expressed negative views of assessment and cautioned against a move to formalised assessments. They considered play-based approaches more important and did not want formal testing to be the focus of their child's learning and development. It is clear there is a need to think about assessment practices that are authentic, reliable, and valid, and that do not create a deficit approach or label children. Keary, Garvis, Zheng, & Walsh (2020) call for this deeper understanding of assessment practices. Support for an inclusive approach is found in the Early Years Framework of Finland where children's views of their learning form part of assessment (OECD, 2016). Families overwhelmingly positioned the concept of assessment within understandings of learning, development and wellbeing and were clear in their expectations of educator and child roles in assessment with relationships being prioritised.

Families' views on Learning Outcomes also emphasised inclusive approaches with social and wellbeing aspects to be prioritised over 'academics'. Strengthening connections between the Vision, Principles, Practices and Learning Outcomes was key to adopting more socially and culturally responsive approaches. Additionally, Krieg (2011) notes benefits associated with bridging educators' content knowledge and methods used to build children's understandings through shared inquiry. Reflecting the same general focus toward Learning Outcomes, ECEC families spoke of the social and learning benefits that play-based experiences offered their child.

Conclusion

It is critically important that families' voices are sought and heard, and their perspectives considered when updating key policy and curriculum documents that impact their children's lives. It was clear in our project that families were knowledgeable about ECEC, and able to offer rich insights to inform curriculum and practice. This project affirmed the importance of gathering multiple perspectives to better understand and respond to the current needs, experiences, and expectations of children and families in partnership with ECEC settings and other professionals.

References

Almendingen, A, Clayton, O, & Matthews, J (2022). Partnering with parents in early childhood services: Raising and responding to concerns. *Early Childhood Education Journal, 50*, 527–538. https://doi.org/10.1007/s10643-021-01173-6

Australian Government Department of Education (2022). *Belonging, being & becoming: The early years learning framework for Australia V2.0*. Retrieved from: https://www.acecqa.gov.au/sites/default/files/2023-01/EYLF-2022-V2.0.pdf

Barblett, L, Barratt-Pugh, C, Knaus, M, & Cooper, T (2020). Supporting aboriginal families' and children's developing sense of belonging at KindiLink. *Australasian Journal of Early Childhood*, 45(4), 309–321. https://doi.org/10.1177/1836939120966079

Barblett, L, Bobongie-Harris, F, Cartmel, J, Hadley, F, Irvine, S, & Harrison, LJ (2023). "We're not useless, we know stuff!": Using children's voices to change policy. *Australasian Journal of Early Childhood*, 48(2), 134–147. https://doi.org/10.1177/183693912211399

Barblett, L, Cartmel, J, Hadley, F, Harrison, LJ, Irvine, S, Bobongie-Harris, F, & Lavina, L (2021). *National Quality Framework Approved Learning Frameworks Update: Literature Review*. Australian Children's Educations and Care Quality Authority, p. 65. Retrieved from: https://www.mq.edu.au/__data/assets/pdf_file/0005/1189427/2021NQF-ALF-UpdateLiteratureReview.PDF.pdf

Cartmel, J, Irvine, S, Harrison, LJ, Barblett, L, Bobongie-Harris, F, Lavina, L, & Hadley, F (2023a). Conceptualising the education and care workforce from the perspective of children and young people. *Frontiers in Education. Educational Psychology*, 8, 1167486. https://doi.org/10.3389/feduc.2023.1167486 (Research Topic *Stakeholders' Perspectives on Assessment and Improvement of Quality in Early Childhood Education and Care: A World-Wide Kaleidoscope*).

Cartmel, J, Hurst, B, Bobongie-Harris, F, Hadley, F, Barblett, L, Harrison, L, & Irvine, S (2023b). Do children have a right to do nothing? Exploring the place of passive leisure in Australian School Age Care. *Childhood*. https://doi.org/10.1177/09075682231212387

Cartmel, J, & Hayes, A (2016). Before and after school: Literature review about Australian school age child care. *Children Australia*, 41(3), 201–207. https://doi.org/10.1017/cha.2016.17

Degotardi, S, Waniganayake, M, Bull, R, Wong, S, Dahm, M, Hadley, F, Harrison, LJ, Sadow, L, Amin, J, Donovan, M, Tran, D, & Zurynski, Y (2022). Using a multidisciplinary, multi-method and collaborative research design to investigate the health communication power of the early childhood sector. *Australasian Journal of Early Childhood Special Issue*, 47(4), 245–259. https://doi.org/10.1177/18369391221120958

Department of Education, Employment and Workplace Relations [DEEWR] (2009). *Belonging, Being and Becoming: The Early Years Learning Framework for Australia*. Retrieved from: https://www.acecqa.gov.au/sites/default/files/201802/belonging_being_and_becoming_the_early_years_learning_framework_for_australia.pdf

Department of Education and Training Queensland (2011). *Embedding Aboriginal and Torres Strait Islander Perspectives in Schools*. Queensland Government.

Gramberger, M (2001). *Citizens as Partners. OECD Handbook on Information, Consultation and Public Participation in Policy-Making*. Paris: Organisation for Economic Co-operation and Development (OECD).

Gerlach, AJ, Browne, AJ, & Greenwood, M (2017). Engaging Indigenous families in a community-based Indigenous early childhood programme in British Columbia, Canada: A cultural safety perspective. *Health & Social Care in the Community*, 25(6), 1763–1773.

Hadley, F, Harrison, L, Lavina, L, Barblett, L, Irvine, S, Bobongie-Harris, F, & Cartmel, J (under review). Engaging stakeholders to inform policy developments in early childhood education and outside school hours care. *Frontiers in Education. Educational Psychology.*

Hadley, F, Harrison, L, Irvine, S, Barblett, L, Cartmel, J, & Bobongie-Harris, F (2021). *Families & Communities: Abridged version of the Discussion Paper.* ACECQA. Retrieved from: https://www.mq.edu.au/__data/assets/pdf_file/0008/1183049/ALFs-Update_Discussion-Paper_Abridged.pdf

Hadley, F, & Rouse, E (2018). The family–centre partnership disconnect: Creating reciprocity. *Contemporary Issues in Early Childhood, 19*(1), 48–62. https://doi.org/10.1177/1463949118762148

Keary, A, Garvis, S, Zheng, H, & Walsh, L (2020). 'I'm learning how to do it': Reflecting on the implementation of a new assessment tool in an Australian early childhood. *International Journal of Inclusive Education.* Advance Online Publication. https://doi.org/10.1080/13603116.2020.1803428

Krieg, S (2011). The Australian Early Years Learning Framework: Learning what? *Contemporary Issues in Early Childhood, 12*(1), 46–55. https://doi.org/10.2304/ciec.2011.12.1.46

Leggett, N, & Ford, M (2013). A fine balance: Understanding the roles educators and children play as intentional teachers and intentional learners within the Early Years Learning Framework. *Australasian Journal of Early Childhood, 38*(4), 42–50. https://doi.org/10.1177/183693911303800406

Marwick, H (2017). Supporting concordant intersubjectivity and sense of 'belonging' for under three-year-olds in early years settings. In E.J. White & C. Dalli (Eds.), *Under-Three-Year-Olds in Policy and Practice* (pp. 101–112). Springer.

McLean, K, Lake, G, Wild, M, & Licandro, U (2023). Perspectives of play and play-based learning: What do adults think play is? *Australasian Journal of Early Childhood, 48*(1), 5–17. https://doi.org/simsrad.net.ocs.mq.edu.au/10.1177/18369391221130790

OECD (2016). *Starting Strong IV. Monitoring Quality in Early Childhood Education and Care Country Note.* Finland: OECD Publication. Retrieved from: https://www.oecd.org/education/school/ECECMN-Finland.pdf

Solomon, J (2016). Gender identity and expression in the early childhood classroom. *Young Children, 71*(3), 61–72.

Vandenbroeck, M (2023). Foreword: For a re-socialisation and re-politicisation of the parent-professional relationship. In J. Lehrer, F. Hadley, K. Van Laere, & E. Rouse (Eds.), *Relationships with Families in Early Childhood Education and Care: Beyond Instrumentalization in International Contexts of Diversity and Social Inequality* (pp. xvii–xxi). Routledge.

Victorian Government (2008). *Aboriginal Cultural Competence Framework.* Victorian Government Department of Human Services: Victorian Aboriginal Child Care Agency (VACCA). Retrieved from: https://www.childabuseroyalcommission.gov.au/sites/default/files/VAC.0001.002.0001.pdf

PART III

Alternative Pedagogies and Practices

12

EMBRACING DIVERSITY AND INCLUSION

Ute Ward

This section offers five chapters which are more directly related to children and looks at different aspects of pedagogy and approaches that ensure the inclusion of all children. For many years now, numerous countries have followed curricula based on neoliberal principles. These often include clearly definite learning outcomes, reflecting the assumption that children's development is linear and universal, meaning that all children progress along the same trajectory. Children are regularly assessed against narrow outcomes, which, for some, leads to being labelled as 'falling behind' and, for many, completely ignores their family and community context. The responsibility for achieving the learning outcomes leads to ever-increasing accountability for ECEC practitioners. Consequently, they spend much time on observing and recording rather than on direct engagement with the children and their play. Governments' motivation for neoliberal practices in ECEC is twofold: Firstly, it is driven by the aim to turn children into future productive, economic beings who contribute to the wealth of the nation. Secondly, adequate childcare enables parents (and predominantly, mothers) to return to employment and resume economic productivity.

When the pandemic led to lockdowns and closures of ECEC settings, many children lost their interactions with friends and playmates as well as with their educators and teachers. The experiences of individual children during this time varied greatly, often in relation to their parents' socio-economic status. In wealthier families, young children were more likely to have access to digital tools to stay in touch with their nurseries, and middle-class parents were in general more aware of and able to support their learning at home (Spiteri, 2021). However, in many other, less well-off families, several children had to

DOI: 10.4324/9781003471172-15

share laptops; parents had less time and energy to support their children's learning; and stress levels were high due to financial pressures. Many nurseries worked hard to maintain contact with families and make activities available to them. However, this often reinforced the schoolification of ECEC (with the heavy use of work sheets, the request for parents to send evidence of the activities back and so on) and inadvertently also drove the schoolification of parents, who were expected to act as educators or teachers (Formosinho, 2021).

For many children and adults, the pandemic enhanced the levels of anxiety and stress that were already prevalent in many societies. A recent report by the German Leibniz-Institute talks about 'Dauerstress' (enduring stress) as one crisis is piled onto the next (for example, armed conflict in many countries, increasing numbers of refugees, climate change and ensuing drought, poor harvests and bushfires, poverty and precarious employment) (Frahm, 2023). Consequently, returning to 'normal' after the pandemic does not seem a desirable option. However, this seems to have happened in many countries. The ECEC curricula still stress predetermined outcomes, testing and assessment regimes continue, and educators' work remains poorly paid and undervalued (for example, in Croatia; see Chapter 7).

There seem to be two further reasons why we should not return to 'normal'. Firstly, at this point and for years to come, the children experiencing 'Dauerstress' will need support for their emotional and social development and well-being. Only when their stress levels are reduced will they be able to engage in meaningful and lasting learning that will help them to operate as effective and competent members of their families and communities (Gerhardt, 2004). Secondly, many existing national ECEC guidelines or curricula understand raising children as a simple cause–effect equation and, as mentioned above, enforce predetermined outcomes. However, such a narrow approach to what it means to prepare for the future will only give us 'more of the same'. Gopnik (2016) identifies this as the 'carpenter approach' to raising children. It works on the basis of a predetermined vision of what a chair looks like/what is needed in the future and produces mirror images of what we already have. Instead, she advocates the 'gardener approach' to raising children. This advocates that children are nurtured in their individuality; that a wide range of skills, aptitudes and interests is welcome; and that the uncertainty of the exact outcome for the mature plant/person is acceptable, even desirable. Thinking at societal level, nurturing a broad spectrum of skills, ability and interests makes it more likely that we will be able to generate novel ways of thinking and doing that will enable us to respond effectively to the unknown challenges to come. Importantly, this means all children should be nurtured and included in ECEC, regardless of disadvantage, neurodiversity, migration status, ethnicity and so on. It is the ensuing diversity in thinking that will help societies to generate new ideas and ways of being that will ensure prosperity and well-being.

Following the premise that we should not return to normal, the chapters in this section present some suggestions for changes to pedagogy with a particular view to including all children. In the first contribution, Sharon Skehill provides a link to the continuous professional development considerations from the previous section. She reports on the Irish Leadership for Inclusion in the Early Years programme, including an exploration of Heidegger's phenomenology and the need for inclusive cultures in ECEC. Here, practitioner identity is an important consideration again, and it is noteworthy that one of the main barriers for practitioners to integrate new learning into practice is the attitude of colleagues and managers. Building on her insights from her doctoral thesis, the author presents a framework for staff learning and development which acknowledges the lived experiences and life world contexts of practitioners, indicating that the one-size-fits-all approach is not helpful in either adults' or children's learning.

The foci in the following two chapters are the use of arts, creativity and imagination, and their integration into early childhood curricula. Silvia Blanch Gelabert and Gemma París-Romia from Spain present some of the findings from the international project 'Interstice: Encounters between Artists, Children, and Educators'. The project had two aims: Firstly, it wanted to bring performative and visual arts into nurseries and schools. This included, amongst a range of strategies, introducing artists-in-residence into education settings to work alongside children and teachers. Secondly, the project was designed to enable children from diverse social, cultural and economic backgrounds to gain access to art and high-level culture, from which they are often excluded.

Sue Nimmo's chapter turns our attention to the central role of imagination in children's learning. Building on historical and present-day theories, she explains the impact of imagination and argues that imagination is fundamental to problem-solving, thinking creatively, communicating effectively and collaborating with others. Consequently, it should be firmly embedded in early childhood curricula. In English Early Years Foundation Stage (Department for Education, 2013), this is not currently the case, and she presents several strategies on how practitioners could adapt their practice to help children develop their imagination.

The next chapter returns to inclusion issues but in a different context and from a different perspective. Mabel Giraldo considers up to which extent children with special educational needs or disabilities are considered in disaster planning. As she highlights, disasters were until fairly recently related to armed conflict and war, but what we understand a disaster to be has changed and now includes events in nature, like bushfires and floods, as well as man-made disasters, like terrorist attacks and industrial accidents. In disaster planning at national, regional and local levels, children are often an afterthought, and the chapter argues that particularly young children and children with special educational needs or disabilities should be given a voice in planning for responses to such events.

The final chapter in this section showcases how a literacy programme originally designed in Australia was adapted and then introduced in Israel. The chapter addresses pedagogical issues regarding literacy while also narrating how a change project can be planned, trialled and implemented. Sigal Tish and her colleagues conducted their project in the first year of formal schooling and highlighted some of the cultural differences that needed to be overcome for successful implementation. Embedded in their thinking is an image of the child as an active and competent participant in their learning and not as a vessel to be filled through knowledge transfer from teacher or parent to child, therefore envisaging and enacting a pedagogy beyond many neoliberal curricula.

References

Department for Education (2013). *The National Curriculum in England: key stages 1 and 2 framework document.* Retrieved from: https://www.gov.uk/government/publications/national-curriculum-in-england-primary-curriculum

Formosinho, J (2021). 'From schoolification of children to schoolification of parents? – educational policies in COVID times'. In *European Early Childhood Education Research Journal, 29*(1), 141–152.

Frahm, C (2023, September 9). *Die Welt im Dauerstress.* Tagesschau Deutschland. Retrieved from: https://www.tagesschau.de/wissen/krieg-frieden-leibnitz-institut-konfliktforschung-ukraine-100.html

Gerhardt, S (2004). *Why Love Matters.* Hove: Routledge.

Gopnik, A (2016). *The Gardener and the Carpenter: What the New Science of Child Development Tells Us About the Relationship Between Parents and Children.* New York: Farrar, Straus and Giroux.

Spiteri, J (2021). 'Quality early childhood education for all and the Covid-19 crisis: A viewpoint'. In *Prospects, 51,* 143–148. https://doi.org/10.1007/s11125-020-09528-4

13

THE QUIDDITY OF INCLUSION

Knowing what matters in early childhood settings

Sharon Skehill

Introduction

Based on a hermeneutic phenomenological doctoral study, this chapter discusses the 'whatness' of inclusion in considering what it means to ensure equity for all children in early years settings. In examining the influence of a continuing professional development (CPD) programme on educators' perceptions and understandings of inclusion in their working role, there are interesting findings pertaining to the factors which influence educators' engagement with learning opportunities to develop their professional practice. Research was carried out with educators prior to engaging with the LINC (Leadership for Inclusion in the Early Years) programme, and again on completion of the course using interviews, field visits and conversations with children to gather data on this experience. With initial discussion around the philosophical concepts guiding understanding of inclusion, this chapter will present some of the findings under the following key messages before outlining a Framework for Learning and Development to support educators develop their pedagogical practice:

- Inclusive culture in the early years.
- Collaboration with parents, families and other agencies.
- Professional identity and CPD experiences.

Hermeneutic Phenomenology and Pedagogical Practice

In considering the influence of theory on pedagogical practice, the research study reported on in this chapter is underpinned by the philosophy of

DOI: 10.4324/9781003471172-16

130 Sharon Skehill

Michael Heidegger (1929). While phenomenology in itself is about understanding the concept of 'Being' and what it is to exist as a person, Heidegger's (1929) hermeneutic phenomenology incorporates an interpretative stance. He asserts that a phenomenon can only be fully understood through 'Dasein'. This philosophical concept of 'Dasein' is related to humans and their individual and distinct life experiences. He emphasises the social dimensions of 'Dasein' insofar as how one perceives oneself within society, and how in turn, this perception of the self has an impact on a phenomenon. This draws an immediate connection with the role of the early years' educator and the ongoing quest for professional and societal recognition of this role working with babies, toddlers and young children. Heidegger discusses the importance of moods in our existence and the potential of our emotions to influence and alter life experiences. He also considers how the 'big' question of life and death, and one's willingness to face challenges and obstacles might influence how one approaches different experiences or phenomena in life. From this philosophical approach, understanding of the phenomenon is built through the investigation of the participants' lived experiences of engagement with the CPD programme to determine if and how it influenced their perceptions and practices of inclusion. The LINC programme is a one-year blended learning programme designed to equip the learner with the knowledge and skills to lead inclusive practice in their early years setting and is awarded a qualification in leadership as an Inclusion Coordinator (INCO).

Schutz (1932/1976, p. 24) theorises that the lived experience of research participants, which he considers to be the 'first order constructs' of the phenomenon, finds meaning through the 'second order constructs' of the researcher who connects the common-sense world with the academic world of theories. By investigating educators' perceptions and practices of inclusion, there is an understanding that these can only truly be captured through the lived experiences of those working in the early years' sector. It is through conversation and questioning that the essence of these experiences can be explained effectively to determine what constitutes inclusive practice for each of the participants. Hermeneutic phenomenology relies on the researcher to interpret and explore participants' experiences, using that awareness of 'Dasein' to guide interpretation (Hall et al., 2016). This philosophical awareness creates an understanding of the societal context of the phenomenon, the moods that may impact the experience as well as one's life attitude, thereby bridging participants' and researcher's horizons of significance to create new understandings (Gadamer, 2004; Frechette et al., 2020). As an early years' educator and a content developer on the CPD programme under discussion, incorporating a reflexive lens is embedded in the methodology of the study.

Creating an Inclusive Culture

Heidegger (1929) describes the starting point in attempting to uncover people's realities of a phenomenon as having to make a 'leap' into the data. How can the influence of CPD on participants' perceptions and practices of inclusion be understood in the context of their varied life experiences? Guskey's (2002) assessment of educational CPD recognises the challenges of embedding new learning into organisational culture to create a real impact on pedagogical practice. However, out of the depth of analysis of conversations and reflections, grew the recognition that inclusion is embedded and founded on intentional relational pedagogy. Ljungblad (2019) identifies relational pedagogy as that trusting and respectful 'in-between space' between the educator and the child where the child can flourish and grow. An inclusive culture is about developing and maintaining this relationship which is presented as central to each child's sense of security and well-being, setting the foundation for their overall positive development.

Relational pedagogy is embedded in a respectful image of the child as competent, confident and agentic. For educators, there is a pronounced need for reflection on what our image of the child looks like. Heidegger and his student, Gadamer (2004), talk about the different horizons on which we view life situations. He explains how some individuals may have a limited horizon, meaning that their point of view may not enable them to 'see' far enough, leading to an over-emphasis on what is nearest to them. The same is true of one who may stand on a high vantage point and forget to 'see' things that are close and familiar. Aligning with this insight, O'Leary and Moloney (2020) emphasise the importance of our awareness of the 'values, beliefs and narratives' that guide our interactions with children. Aistear: the early childhood curriculum in Ireland (NCCA, 2009/2023) embraces Sorin's concept of the 'agentic child' (2005) which challenges the notion of the innocent and powerless child, instead seeing children as partners in the educational environment. If the educator can truly appreciate the confident and competent child (NCCA, 2009/2023), seeing what the child 'can do' in a strengths-based approach, they set the foundation for all other elements of practice in the early years' environment.

Nutbrown and Clough (2013) offer a simplified concept of inclusion stating that it is 'ultimately about how people treat each other' (p. 4) and it rests with each educator to reflect on how we respond to individual children, ensuring their rights are being met in the setting. A helpful model by Lundy (2007) provides a guide for the practical conceptualisation of Article 12 of the United Nations Convention on the Rights of the Child (UNCRC) (1992) through the chronological implementation of the elements of space, voice, audience and influence, with reflective prompts to support those working with children in educational settings. Lundy's voice model checklist was adapted as the foundation for policy development in the Irish context in supporting children's rights (Department of Children and Youth Affairs, 2015). It places the child at the centre of all decision-making that affects them, recognising that it is our responsibility as duty-bearers in our respective societal roles to support this. Interpretation of child 'voice' in the early years requires that reflection on practice in considering how we understand and communicate what children are trying to tell us. 'Voice' may not be verbally communicated. Feelings and emotions may not be articulated. Behaviours, actions, gestures and utterances are a means of communication, and an inclusive culture is about empowering babies, toddlers and young children and noticing all the different ways in which they tell us things.

Aligning with that respectful image of the competent child, another key feature of the inclusive early years setting is the accessible and aesthetic learning environment where a play-based curriculum, incorporating effective strategies and resources, is central to practice. Lundy (2019) posits play as a rights-based issue arguing that there is not enough emphasis on Article 29 of the UNCRC, which she sees as more aspirational in its insinuation of the value of play in a more child-centred and empowering interpretation. The concept of the emergent curriculum in many ways fits the criteria of Lundy's (2019) interpretation of Article 29 in terms of basing a curriculum around children's individual interests and needs, in an environment that reflects these interests and supports their belonging (NCCA, 2009; Kelleher and Fenlon 2021). Using Lundy's model (2007) as a framework for discussion, Skehill (2021a) explains how provocations for play, set out within the early years' environment, provides opportunity for choice and engagement for all children, while simultaneously empowering the educator to guide and scaffold children's participation. A play-based curriculum provides opportunity to level the playing field for all children and ensures that everyone in the group can participate at their own stage of development in accordance with their strengths and interests (CECDE 2006; Blake, Sexton, Lynch, Moore and Coughlan, 2018). Malaguzzi (1993) depicts the environment as the third teacher, whereby children are empowered to take the lead in their own learning and educators are posited to support and facilitate meaningful participation. Crucially, the need to listen and respond to babies, toddlers and children in their assessment of the environment is an important feature of an inclusive culture. Clark (2023) advocates the need to slow down in our interactions with children, aligning with an understanding of Lundy's (2007) model of creating the space for children to 'voice' their views. In our role as the 'audience' in this model, educators notice, observe and interpret child voice. And therein lies the question – who is in the position to respond to and take action for children's expressed views? Guskey (2002) draws attention to the complexities of evaluation of CPD noting that although learning outcomes might have been achieved, it does not necessarily imply that the organisational culture facilitates change or empowers educators to implement that change.

Collaborative Practice in the Inclusive Early Years Setting

McKernan et al. (2011) define collaborative practice as central to inclusive education as a process to guide the work of relevant professionals to support children and their families to ensure access to supports and resources for the child's holistic development. In considering the influence of the LINC programme on perceptions of inclusion, one must ask how inclusion is facilitated beyond the relationship between the educator and the child and acknowledge the importance of seeking out and developing positive relationships with other important people in the child's life. Effective communication, and the confidence to initiate such communication, is a key responsibility of the educator to support children's participation. Skilled and experienced educators hold a very important role in supporting children and their families. The value of cultivating positive relationships with parents in the early years setting has been recognised as a key feature of inclusive and quality education (Graham 2017; Barr and Hilliard 2021). Most participants in this study discussed working with parents and described varying degrees of communication and interactions. Heidegger (1929) philosophises that one's moods, as well as one's response to opportunities and threats such as those interactions with parents, have a direct impact on how one experiences different situations. The lived experiences of the participants in relation to engagement with parents and families are underpinned by this philosophical principle that any act of interpretation is always informed by a fore-structure of understanding (Horrigan-Kelly et al., 2016). When one understands the nurturing and relational pedagogy that underpins quality and inclusive practice, there is also a need for a similar respectful and considered engagement with children's families. Developing, maintaining and respecting this relationship between the educator and the parent, is key to inclusive practice, yet is dependent on a number of factors. One's perception of the other is evidenced to have an influence on the level of parental involvement in supporting the child within some of the services in this study. There is a pronounced emphasis on educator assumptions of parents' perspectives of the educator's role and a perceived undermining of early years education in comparison to that within the primary school sector. In the contextual lived experiences of participants, this assumption is founded on historic issues within the early years sector, underpinned by a sense of powerlessness within the system. Supporting each child's right to participate in the early years programme requires a shift away from the self and to consider the hermeneutic principle of seeing life from the perspective of others. If there is an over-emphasis on perceptions of one's societal role as a parent or as an educator, there is a risk of the rights of the child getting lost in the process. Lundy (2019) reminds us that children's rights are not about pity or charity; they are not a gift or a favour. It is something that can be demanded and insisted upon. There is a delicate process of interpreting the voice of the child in the education system, particularly in relation to those who are more vulnerable to exclusion. Children need those who know them best to facilitate, interpret and respond to their voice. A child-centred approach necessitates engagement with their families, and it takes a strong leader within the setting to be that 'voice' to offer another perspective (O'Leary and Moloney 2020; Skehill 2021a).

Within the busy early years settings, challenges have been identified in promoting and facilitating effective communication. Engagement with parents is very dependent on one's role in the setting and the processes established to enable the educator to share information effectively. The LINC programme provided different strategies for such engagement in the module content, but the question arises of the authority of the educator to develop and implement these strategies. However, if settings could engage more effectively in partnership with parents through ongoing communication, then this may have an impact on parents' perspective of the role of the educator and the work that is done in the early years setting. This may result in a fusion of horizons whereby parents and educators have a shared understanding of each other's perspectives (Heidegger 1929; Gadamer 2004).

Supporting transitions from the preschool to the primary school sector is a key element of quality and inclusive practice (Government of Ireland, 2018) and collaboration with teachers in the school is an essential part of that process. However, this study found that there was a gap between the learning from the LINC programme and implementation of recommended strategies from the CPD experience. Policy (CECDE 2006; NCCA, 2023) reminds us that transitions to primary school are not about an 'ending' of one stage and the 'beginning' of another, but rather that it is a process that takes place over an extended period of time to support the child's move from one environment to the other. The findings from this research study indicate that, despite the wealth of literature specifying the need for collaboration between the pre-school and the primary school (Daly et al. 2015; O' Kane and Murphy 2016), there is a lack of cohesive planning and consistency in approach to supporting children's transitions. While there are some positive examples of supporting transition within the setting, such as having school uniforms in the dress-up areas and social stories about school, these were stand-alone activities without coordination with local schools. Educators expressed frustration at the absence of communication and collaboration with local schools, attributing this to the lack of regard for their role within the educational system. Being mindful of the contextual realities of the role of the educator, this may have an element of truth in it and might also be attributed to the attitudes of individual primary school teachers and principals. However, one might also consider to what extent the participants are advocating on behalf of the children and including their voice in this transition process. Confidence in one's professional role has a real impact on the participants' engagement with the school and also raises a potential ethical dilemma of being part of a hindrance to a child's development if faced with challenges making connections with the primary teacher. This lack of collaboration has been noted by the Department of Education and Skills (2018) whereby such collaborative relationships with the local school had either not been established or were not working effectively to support the children's transitions.

Liaising with other professionals to support children's participation and engagement is reflective of Bronfenbrenner's (1979) ecological systems model which evidences the need to share information and resources between all stakeholders. One of the important messages from the study highlighted the challenges in finding the time to have those meaningful conversations with the different therapists, support workers, families and educators. Inclusion requires collaboration or there is a risk of tokenistic integration without the knowledge, support and resources to empower the participation of babies, toddlers and young children.

Professional Identity and the CPD Experience

Professional identity is presented as a contextual understanding of one's 'Dasein'. Consequently, this study demonstrates how one's horizon of understanding – what one knows and has experienced – informs the interpretation of new knowledge and experience. By acknowledging the lifeworld of educators, there is an opportunity to support the fusion of horizons (Gadamer 2004) thereby creating a space where the educator is more open to the potential learning from CPD experiences. This in turn has the capacity to extend their professional knowledge, skills and ability to reflect on their life experiences, which will enhance their capabilities and enthusiasm for their work with children.

Nonetheless, the capacity to lead inclusive practice, as manager, or as Inclusion Coordinator (INCO), is dependent on a number of factors within the setting (Moloney and Pettersen, 2017; Skehill, 2022). The knowledge, skills and values of the leader in the setting is key to quality provision (European Union, 2021; Skehill, 2021b) and this is embedded in the professional qualifications of the leader. While those who engaged with the LINC programme were confident of their learning around inclusion, the capacity to implement the learning from the CPD experience rested on one's position within the organisation and the relationship with management to make changes as recommended in the LINC modules. Those participants who are already in a supervisory or leadership role had the freedom to implement changes as they decided, having the established authority to do so. However, educators who were not in an existing leadership role faced challenges in engaging with the learning from the LINC programme on a practice level. Although module 5, Leadership for Inclusion in the Early Years, was commended in the review of the programme (see Ring et al., 2018) for its quality of information and learning by participants and the wider LINC student body, this learning remained 'academic' if the educator has no authority to lead the team and make changes. This leadership position is dependent on the setting manager formalising and authorising the INCO to lead colleagues in inclusive practice. This aligns with Guskey's (2002) levels of engagement with CPD in education in recognising the complexity of incorporating new learning into the culture of a setting or school.

Conclusion

Research has consistently highlighted that the highest indicator of quality in the early years setting is the qualifications of the adults working with the children. Guskey (2002) argues that the learning outcomes of CPD can only be determined by measuring its success in multiple ways. In considering the learning outcomes of the LINC programme on professional practice, while assessment is one constant, there is a need for ongoing reflection and adaptation with each new group of children to the setting. There are many features that can support or inhibit an inclusive education system but the skills and education of educators create the foundation for the implementation of equitable and inclusive practices (UNESCO 2017; European Union 2021).

A key finding from this research study is the value of the methodology chosen to examine the experiences of educators to ascertain how to support and extend inclusive learning experiences for all children. In consideration of the fundamental right of all children to access quality and meaningful educational experiences at all levels, the reflexive and interpretative nature of this study guides the Framework for Learning and Development (see Figure 13.1). This

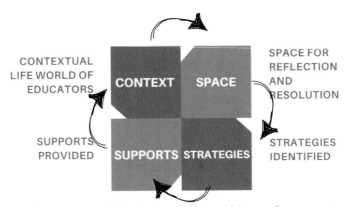

FIGURE 13.1 Framework for Learning and Development (designed by Sharon Skehill).

Framework illustrates how quality inclusive practice begins with an acknowledgement of the contextual life world of the educator. This might include a consideration of their qualifications, children in their group, the type of setting they work in, resources available and the colleagues they work alongside. It also considers the different lens through which we view life experiences – as a graduate, a parent, an advocate, a survivor. It is about recognising the unique life story of different educators, in different settings and their work with different groups of children.

The next step is consideration of how a space can be created for reflection on 'Dasein' in order to respond to the responsibilities of one's role of educator to ensure that they are leading inclusion in their setting. Communicative spaces must be identified in the routines and rituals of the day. Practical strategies should be devised through collaboration with children, families, colleagues and other stakeholders. Research, reflection and action, informed by the realities of working with babies, toddlers and young children, empower all parties to give voice to their horizons of significance (Gadamer 2004) so there is a shared understanding of inclusive pedagogical practice. The next step is to identify what supports are required, both on a broader societal level, as well as relevant to individual local cases, whether this is in the form of CPD, additional resources or mentoring sessions.

The cyclical process of the Framework creates a new platform of context for the educator, whose perspective is altered with each new experience, adapting one's perceptions and seeing other ways and possibilities for action and change. Applying this framework in practice will support educators to develop an inclusive culture and pedagogy that is relevant and meaningful for them and the children they care for and educate. Inclusion is about creating a space and a place where all babies, toddlers and young children can thrive, feel a sense of belonging and be empowered to reach their potential – for this indeed is what matters.

References

Barr, A, & Hilliard, P (2021). Realising and building partnerships with parents and families. In Ring, E., O'Sullivan, L., Ryan, M., & Daly, P., eds., *Leading Inclusion from the Inside Out: A Handbook for Parents and Early Childhood Teachers in Early Learning and Care, Primary and Special School Settings*, Oxford: Peter Lang, pp. 123–150.

Blake, A, Sexton, J, Lynch, H, Moore, A, & Coughlan, M (2018). An exploration of the outdoor play experiences of preschool children with autism spectrum disorder in an Irish preschool setting. *Today's Children, Tomorrow's Parents: An Interdisciplinary Journal*, 47–48, available: https://www.ludinetwork.eu/wp-content/uploads/2019/03/TCTP-LUDI.pdf

Bronfenbrenner, U (1979). *The Ecology of Human Development*, Cambridge, MA: Harvard University Press.

138 Sharon Skehill

Centre for Early Childhood Development and Education (CECDE) (2006). *Siolta: The national quality framework for early childhood care and education*, Dublin: CECDE. Retrieved from: http://siolta.ie/

Clark, A (2023). *Slow Knowledge and the Unhurried Child: Time for Slow Pedagogies in Early Childhood Education*. Abingdon: Routledge.

Daly, P, Ring, E, Egan, M, Fitzgerald, J, Griffin, C, Long, S, McCarthy, E, Moloney, M, O'Brien, T, O'Byrne, A, O'Sullivan, S, Ryan, M, Wall, E, & Madden, R (2015). *An Evaluation of Education Provision for Children with Autistic Spectrum Disorder in the Republic of Ireland*, Trim: National Council for Special Education.

Department of Children and Youth Affairs (2015). *National strategy on children and young people's participation in decision-making 2015-2020*. Retrieved from: http://dcya.gov.ie/documents/playandrec/20150617NatStratParticipationReport.pdf

Department of Education and Skills (2018). *A review of early–years education-focused inspection: April 2016–June 2017: Insights and future developments*. Retrieved from: https://assets.gov.ie/25246/9d33fa1d458644c98dde7069477a1351.pdf

European Union (2021). *Toolkit for inclusive early childhood education and care (ECEC): Providing high quality education and care to all young children*, Luxembourg: Publications Office of the European Union. Retrieved from: Toolkit for inclusive early childhood education and care - Publications Office of the EU (europa.eu)

Frechette, J, Bitzas, V, Aubry, M, Kilpatrick, K, & Lavoie-Tremblay, M (2020). Capturing lived experience: Methodological considerations for interpretive phenomenological inquiry. *International Journal of Qualitative Methods*, *19*, 1–12, http://doi.org/10.1177/1609406920907254

Gadamer, HG (2004). *Truth and Method*. New York: Continuum Publishing Group.

Government of Ireland (GoI) (2018). *First Five: A whole of government strategy for babies, young children and their families 2019-2028*, Dublin: Government Publications Office. Retrieved from: https://assets.gov.ie/31184/62acc54f4bdf4405b74e53a4afb8e71b.pdf

Graham, I (2017). *Realising Potential: Equality, Diversity and Inclusive Practice in Early Years*, Dublin: Barnardos.

Guskey, TR (2002). Does it make a difference? Evaluating professional development. *Educational, School, and Counselling Psychology Faculty Publications (7)*. Retrieved from: https://uknowledge.uky.edu/edp_facpub/7

Hall, E, Chai, W, & Albrecht, J (2016). A qualitative phenomenological exploration of teachers' experience with nutrition education. *American Journal of Health Education*, *47*(3), 136–148, http://doi.org/10.1080/19325037.2016.1157532

Heidegger, M (1929/1962). *Being and Time*, New York: Harper and Row.

Horrigan-Kelly, M, Millar, M, & Dowling, M (2016). Understanding the key tenets of Heidegger's philosophy for interpretive phenomenological research. *International Journal of Qualitative Methods*, 1–8, http://doi.org/10.1177/1609406916680634

Kelleher, S, & Fenlon, E (2021). Making the environment the third teacher. In Ring, E., O'Sullivan, L., Ryan, M., & Daly, P., eds., *Leading Inclusion from the Inside Out: A Handbook for Parents and Early Childhood Teachers in Early Learning and Care, Primary and Special School Settings*, Oxford: Peter Lang, pp. 211–228.

Ring, E., Daly, P. and Wall, E. eds. (2018) *Autism from the inside out: handbook for parents, early years', primary, post-primary and special school settings*. Oxford: Peter Lang.

Ljungblad, AL (2019). Pedagogical relational teachership (PeRT) – a multi-relational perspective. *International Journal of Inclusive Education*. http://doi.org/10.1080/13603116.2019.1581280

Lundy, L (2007). "Voice" is not enough: conceptualising Article 12 of the United Nations Convention on the Rights of the Child. *British Educational Research Journal*, 33(6), 927–942. http://doi.org/10.1080/01411920701657033

Lundy, L (2019). A lexicon for research on international children's rights in troubled times, *The International Journal of Children's Rights*, 27(4). http://doi.org/10.1163/15718182-02704013

Malaguzzi, L (1993). For an education based on relationships. *Young Children*, November, 9–13. Retrieved from: https://www.reggioalliance.org/downloads/malaguzziyoungchildren.pdf

McKernan, M, Church, C, & Taylor, J (2011). *Victoria Early Years Learning and Development Framework: Partnerships with Professionals*. Victoria: University of Melbourne.

Moloney, M & Pettersen, J (2017). *Early Childhood Education Management: Insights into Business Practice and Leadership*. New York: Routledge.

National Council for Curriculum and Assessment (NCCA) (2009/2023). *Aistear: The early childhood curriculum framework*, Dublin: NCCA. Retrieved from: Consultation | NCCA.

Nutbrown, C, & Clough, P (2013). *Inclusion in the Early Years*. London: Sage.

O'Kane, M, & Murphy, R (2016). *Transition from Preschool to Primary School in Ireland: Audit of Transfer Documentation in Ireland*. Dublin: National Council for Curriculum and Assessment.

O'Leary, S, & Moloney, M (2020). Understanding the experiences of young children on the autism spectrums as they navigate the Irish early years' education system: Valuing voices in child-centered narratives. *International Journal of Qualitative Methods*, 19, 1–11, https://doi.org/10.1177/1609406920914696

Schutz, A (1932/1976). *The Phenomenology of the Social World*. London: Routledge and Kegan Paul.

Skehill, S (2021a). Leadership in the early learning and care setting. In Ring, E., O'Sullivan, L., Ryan, M., & Daly, P. (eds.), *Leading Inclusion from the Inside Out: A Handbook for Parents and Early Childhood Teachers in Early Learning and Care, Primary and Special School Settings* (pp. 229–254). Oxford: Peter Lang.

Skehill, S (2021b). An action research project based on teacher reflections on their pedagogical practice in a nature preschool in the West of Ireland during COVID-19. *Sakarya University Journal of Education Faculty*, 21(1), 1–12.

Skehill, S (2022). Fusing the horizons between aspirations of continuing professional development and the realities of educators' experiences in practice: Interpretative hermeneutic phenomenology in early childhood education. *Indo-Pacific Journal of Phenomenology*, 22(1), http://doi.org/10.1080/20797222.2022.2157221

Sorin, R (2005). Changing images of childhood: Reconceptualising early childhood practice. *International Journal of Transitions in Childhood*, 1.

UNESCO (2017). *A Guide for Ensuring Inclusion and Equity in Education*. Paris: UNESCO.

14

PROMOTING INCLUSIVITY THROUGH EMBEDDING ART INTO DAILY PRACTICE

Silvia Blanch-Gelabert and Gemma París-Romia

Introduction

Art is a discipline that holds great potential for education (Camnitzer, 2015) because it provides a pathway to knowledge, offering people the opportunity to develop their own ideas and reshape the world creatively. It allows individuals to use their creativity to envision a better place to share with others. One effective method of introducing art into educational settings is by inviting artists to develop their projects within schools involving both children and teachers. Moreover, the presence of artists in schools can lead to personal, developmental, and social changes (París-Romia, 2019a). Additionally, evidence from neuroscience emphasizes that the arts should be central to any early childhood education initiative. Engaging with the arts stimulates children's neural connections more intensely, enabling them to acquire learning across various knowledge areas in a holistic manner (Bueno, 2019). Unfortunately, many schools continue to marginalize the arts, considering them as secondary, manual, and low-conceptual-intensity occupations (Acaso & Megías, 2017). Therefore, it is important to create shared scenarios between children, artists, and teachers to promote learning encounters within schools.

In this chapter, we present some of the results of the collaborative international project "Interstice: Encounters between Artists, Children, and Educators," co-funded by the Erasmus+ Programme (KA203) of the European Union. The project aims to promote performative and visual arts in the education system by creating collaborative spaces and facilitating various tools and strategies to support teachers, artists, and children in nurseries, preschools, primary schools, and with young people at universities. The goal is to

DOI: 10.4324/9781003471172-17

introduce art thinking in schools and other educational settings. The project also aims to promote opportunities for participation in cultural experiences, reducing inequalities in access, based on three principles: interaction, participation, and democracy in educational contexts. In that sense, art should have an impact throughout the curriculum to involve all children in quality artistic experiences, especially those who, due to their social, cultural, or economic context, do not have many opportunities to access high-quality culture. In this chapter, we will introduce the Interstice project and then focus on two elements, namely the peer learning methodologies for nursery teachers and the impact of having an artist in residence.

The Interstice Project: encounters between artists, children, and educators

This project is being developed by universities, artists, and cultural settings from different European countries: Catalonia, the United Kingdom, Italy, and Norway. Its goal is to promote spaces of encounter between teachers, artists, and children to enhance learning processes through the arts and build a pedagogy of co-creation between art and education. The incorporation of the arts in a transversal way, with the involvement of cultural entities in the community, facilitates the improvement of various key competences, both individual and collective, such as the construction of creative identities, the development of a critical spirit, and collaborative work (París and Hay, 2019). In this chapter, we will focus on two of the results of the project:

1 Results of the research on a peer learning methodology developed by scenic artists with teachers of three nurseries in Sabadell (Catalonia)
2 The outcomes of having an artist resident in a preschool and primary school (espais c, Escola Sagarra, Barcelona, Spain).

Inclusion and Art

Inclusion is a fundamental right for every child in their daily lives, entailing the opportunity to access and fully participate in everyday, family, and social activities within various settings and contexts of their community. According to Blanch (2016), inclusive education advocates for the right of every individual to have increased opportunities for participation, taking into account their unique needs and characteristics. Inclusion revolves around valuing diversity, viewing it as a societal challenge to be achieved, fostering educational environments that facilitate the development of everyone. Therefore, inclusion is a process that involves progressing towards a more democratic and equitable society where everyone finds a place.

In this regard, children have the right to access and participate in artistic opportunities, as recognized in the Convention on the Rights of the Child (UNICEF, 1989). Two articles in this Convention advocate for this right:

Article 29.
1. States Parties agree that the education of the child shall be directed to:
a. The development of the child's personality, talents, and mental and physical abilities to their fullest potential.

Article 31.
2. States Parties recognize the right of the child to rest and leisure, to engage in play and recreational activities appropriate to their age, and to participate freely in cultural life and the arts.
3. States Parties shall respect and promote the right of the child to participate fully in cultural and artistic life and encourage the provision of appropriate and equal opportunities for cultural, artistic, recreational, and leisure activities.

(UNICEF, 1989)

Despite the convention emphasizing the right to cultural opportunities and participation in artistic experiences, a significant portion of children lack access to culture. To uphold this right, it is imperative for nurseries and preschools to provide a context for high-quality artistic experiences. For this purpose, teachers must undergo training with artists and feel sufficiently capable of promoting high-quality artistic experiences for all their students, with the presence and collaboration of artists. Out of this necessity arises the Interstices Project, aiming to create a program that provides training for both active teachers and future teacher students at the university.

To accomplish this, the project has developed and refined a training program initially created by laSala of Sabadell in May 2019, titled "Mestres que es mouen/Teachers in Movement" (Blanch et al., 2023). This peer learning program was crafted and implemented by performing artists who collaborated with nursery teachers side by side. The goal of this program is to establish connections between art and education, aiming for quality in creative processes promoted by artistic encounters for early childhood teachers. The training has been continuously monitored and improved throughout the project, incorporating feedback from participating artists, teachers, and researchers from the Universitat Autònoma de Barcelona.

Peer learning methodology with training developed by dancers in a nursery

Creating a significant training program for teachers is crucial to achieving quality and promoting artistic experiences that encourage reflection and awaken the imagination. The Interstice project includes an action research component to evaluate the peer learning methodology developed by laSala de Sabadell. The intention is to specifically understand whether the training facilitates a change in nursery teachers and, if so, which aspects are key to the change, in order to adjust the training based on the evidence obtained.

Throughout the entire process, the UAB (Universitat Autònoma de Barcelona) as the research team, artists from laSala, and two artists and professors from the University of Stavanger have collaborated, also as the trainers' team. Additionally, the needs and assessments of the involved nursery teachers from the three nurseries have been considered, involving a total of 32 early childhood teachers working with children under 3 years old. To meet its goal, the peer learning methodology aims to:

- Reflect on the relationship between equals with children, artists, teachers, and families, questioning the horizontality among them.
- Explore and experience the methodology of peer learning through the arts.
- Recognize art as a universal human quality, discovering the artistic potential of each individual as human beings, drawing inspiration from the existing artistic world.
- Create artistic encounter spaces with an open attitude, generating new ways of relating through artistic language in the school and family environment.

Initially, the training had three different activities, but through the research process to evaluate the needs of the participants, the initial proposal changed to meet the teachers' needs and the project goals. The final proposal of the training includes eight different moments throughout the school year, as depicted in the schedule (Figure 14.1).

Phases of the Teacher Training Proposal: Enhancing Artistic Experiences in Early Childhood Education

1 Artistic Experience & Workshop with Nursery Teachers in the Theatre.

The first part of the training starts giving the opportunity to nursery teachers from three different centers in Sabadell to attend the laSala theatre and participate in the Blåfugl Workshop, designed for children under three years old by Dybwikdans[1] and the University of Stavanger. A reflective conversation between teachers and artists follows the performance, focusing on the participants' bodily presence, exploring voice and body movement, and discussing the role and presence of teachers in the artistic context.

2 Artistic Encounter with Blåfugl by the company Dybwikdans with teachers, children, and families of the three nurseries.

After the initial workshop, children around two years of age, with their teachers and some families who voluntarily participated, travelled together

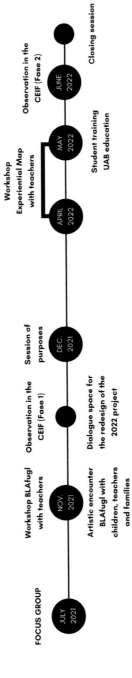

FIGURE 14.1 Diagram of the Peer learning methodology-Teachers in movement. Interstice: Artist, Children and Educators (Blanch et al., 2023).

by bus from the three nurseries to the theatre and participated in the performance. Blåfugl is an inversive show in which the public is placed inside the action, to create connections between the participants as an open artistic encounter space. For some of the families, it was their first time to have an artistic experience with their children and had a very high index of satisfaction. Also, for the teachers it was very interesting to see the families interact with their children in a different setting where all of them were equals and participated in their own way during the artistic open space. This event creates a bridge between the nursery and the laSala theatre to promote social inclusion, offering families with a high-risk index of exclusion an opportunity for their first artistic experience with children.

3 Observation 1 by Artist in the Nursery and Discussion

After the immersive artistic experience, an artist conducts an on-site observation in the nursery, focusing on peer learning methodologies and horizontal relations between teachers and children through the arts during their quotidian day. Also, an artist from laSala and the researcher from the UAB University are observing. The observations focused on the following parameters:

- Relationship and bond of the children with the space, the materials, and the teaching team.
- Individual and group dynamics related to game proposals, artistic actions, and routine operations.
- Autonomy and self-regulation of children in their relationships and learning.

After the observation, a discussion follows, highlighting artistic opportunities and challenges observed, with a report shared with the nursery, including written and photographic documentation.

4 Purpose Session

After the pilot phase, a session is conducted where each nursery reflects on their goals as professionals and as a school. The themes are presence, relational aesthetics, performing arts in practice, and spontaneity. Teachers set personal and school purposes to improve in areas related to these categories.

5 Workshop Experiential Map

Focused training is provided based on nursery-specific thematic goals, aiming to deepen the adult–childhood relationship through experiential exercises in movement, music, and emotions. Participants share challenging situations and collaboratively find solutions, with individual and collective reflection to connect with training objectives. A report is created to document and share reflections made during the workshop.

6 Time to Practice and Share

Teachers progressively incorporate and create artistic experiences for children, documenting and sharing experiences and doubts with their school team or laSala professionals.

7 Observation 2 by Artist in the Nursery and Discussion

A second observation is conducted at the end of the school year, focusing on situations recorded by teachers that reflect the purposes of the training. In addition, it was proposed to the participating centers that for three weeks the teachers of each center record on video situations experienced with the children where the purposes of the training are reflected. These could be game scenes, activities, and/or individual and group dynamics where artistic language was experimented with (voice, plastic expressions, musical games, rhythm, and movement...). A discussion follows, with teachers choosing objects representing recorded scenes, creating a mural to evaluate the positive and negative aspects of each action.

8 Closing Session

A concluding session assesses the project's impact and future. Teachers express appreciation for the training, highlighting positive changes in their vision of art and their role as mediators. Teachers share insights, emphasizing the importance of recognizing and promoting opportunities born from spontaneity and teamwork within the nursery.

Some lessons learned

Upon completing the project, educators were able to assess their experience through questionnaires and interviews. Through their voices, some changes in conceptions about art and its potential in daily daycare life became evident. Here are some of the shared conclusions expressed by the teachers from the three nurseries.

Firstly, the teachers emphasized the importance of **relational aesthetics**: art as a form of communication. Through the training, they were able to experiment and reflect on how art, with its various languages, allows for different forms of communication with children. They recognized the importance of corporality, the ability to use conscious movement, and the promotion of activities such as singing, dancing, among other forms of creativity and artistic experiences. Teachers felt more confident in their ability to communicate in ways beyond verbal expression. They also expressed how each approach can lead to different reactions from children and influence the overall atmosphere in the classroom.

On the other hand, teachers expressed the ability **to incorporate art as a fundamental aspect of their educational practices and daily activities** with children. While artistic activities were traditionally scheduled at specific times of the day or week, such as painting or singing, they now felt empowered to spontaneously integrate artistic experiences at any moment. Frequently, an experience might be initiated by a child, such as tapping an object on the floor, and the teacher becomes aware that the child is creating a rhythm. The teacher can then encourage the child to continue with this spontaneous artistic musical creation, actively participating.

In this regard, they underscored the pivotal **role of the educator**, emphasizing the need to be present and aware of the opportunities that arise in the classroom, while also being confident enough to promote or engage with them. This means not merely "letting the children be free" but also: supporting children's artistic practices; generating new artistic practices, enriching the classroom with vital experiences; and enjoying the artistic practices with the children, fostering a collaborative atmosphere where both educators and children can be artists creating together.

Finally, another critical aspect that teachers underlined was their newfound **ability to actively promote spontaneity** among children – enabling them to express emotions and improvise freely. This skill, they emphasized, is something acquired from both observing professional artists and interacting with the children themselves. In the initial stages, they admitted grappling with the challenge of incorporating unplanned artistic experiences seamlessly into their teaching practices. However, as the training progressed, they not only learned how to facilitate these spontaneous moments but also recognized the significant impact they could have on the children's development.

Moreover, teachers reported witnessing notable effects on the children in various aspects:

- Increased motivation and engagement: children demonstrated heightened enthusiasm and involvement in the proposed artistic activities, showcasing eagerness to participate.
- Improved task completion: teachers observed that children showed enhanced abilities to complete their artistic actions and projects, reflecting a positive impact on their perseverance and follow-through.
- Enhanced connection with educators: there was a noticeable improvement in the quality and depth of individual connections between children and educators, fostering more meaningful moments of interaction. This strengthened bond contributed to a more supportive and enriching learning environment.

The research provided evidence of different degrees of learning for both teachers and artists involved in the process. It highlighted the potential of artistic languages to rethink educational practices and experiences. The actual learning of artistic languages largely depends on previous experiences and starting points.

The creation of collaborative spaces for teachers and artists fostered possibilities to review teaching practices and children's activities from an external perspective using art thinking. These artistic experiences are opportunities to learn using different languages and roles, fostering learning through play in a stimulating way.

148 Silvia Blanch-Gelabert and Gemma París-Romia

The *mestres que es mouen*/peer learning training is open to anyone who wants to learn about it and adapt it to their needs. All documents can be freely downloaded from the interstice.eu website. The project has also worked on sharing different quality experiences from each country to create a document that facilitates others in promoting inclusivity through embedding art into daily practice. Six key aspects shared by all projects have been highlighted. In the next section, they will be shared using the *espais c* program as a concrete example to inspire others.

espais c. Children learning at school with an artist in residence

The espais c (space c, were "c" stands for creativity) is a program linked to the Interstice project that invites contemporary artists to do a long residency in a school, developing their own work at the atelier inside the educational setting, sharing their own processes with the children and some educators. The espais c program was initiated by the Consorci d'Educació de Barcelona, the Institut de Cultura de Barcelona (ICUB), and the Universitat Autònoma de Barcelona. Approaching art as a 'space of encounter' (Bourriaud, 2002), the espais c project invites contemporary artists to engage in residencies in primary schools in Barcelona. Each artist is chosen by a cultural center of the city (galleries, museums, or artistic centers of production), and this cultural institution works as mediator between the artist and the school, under the coordination from the artistic association EART. Cultural settings like Fundació Tàpies, La Capella, Hangar, Fundació Suñol, the gallery Chiquita Room are partners of this experience, and their professionals are working permanently with artists and also with teachers to build this space of creation inside the schools. The goal is to embed art in the school and to create synergies between education and art, fostering educational transformation and inclusion. The project enhances the continual presence of artistic creation processes in schools by establishing a space for creation and interrelation between children, educators, and artists. The atelier functions as a space for co-creation through various artistic languages, where decisions are made collectively and horizontally among children and artists, in coordination with the designated teacher from espais c.

The espais c are created in a space within the school, typically a classroom specially designated for this purpose, allowing the artist to work with flexibility and enabling children to participate in small groups. In this program the artist doesn't conduct classes or workshops at the school, but uses the provided room as their atelier for a year. They make themselves present at the center sharing the space with children who come to develop their own projects and can see how the artist works. This involves engaging in conversations, providing guidance, and sharing mutual strategies and knowledge.

The space, functioning as a shared atelier for a few hours, is managed by the espais c committee, consisting of student representatives, a representative of the teaching staff, the artist, and the program mediation team. This committee

Embedding art into daily practice **149**

oversees the regulation of employment, conditions of use, cleaning tasks, order, material management, and the identification of needs, budgeting, and the administration of learning experiences.

The creative processes undertaken in espais c, both by the artist and the participating students, are visible within the educational center and contribute to the artistic and cultural fabric of the city. In this program, cultural centers operate within the school premises: each artistic institution conducts meetings with teachers, children, and artists inside the espais c, collaborating on the next steps for joint development and addressing the needs of each participant. While schools often visit museums to explore exhibitions, it is uncommon for cultural institutions to directly engage with children and their teachers within school settings.

To share how we can create these artistic spaces of encounter, we are going to give examples based on the Interstice project and the key elements that all the partners agreed that are present in their artistic experiences developed in educational settings (París-Romia et al., 2023). The five elements will be defined as they were in the project publication with an example of the espais c program.

Creativity

FIGURE 14.2 espai c, Miralletes school. Artist: Laura Zuccaro, gallery Chiquita room, Barcelona. Photo: Laura Zuccaro.

We understand creativity as the highest form of intelligence, that is necessary to pursue something new, to generate and create ideas and solutions, alternatives and possibilities. Creativity is multidimensional and interdisciplinary. Creativity, critical thinking and complex problem-solving are identified as three key skills for future society.

París-Romia et al., 2023, p.43

The espais c program is grounded in the concept of creativity, as artists collaborate with children to construct a creative space, foster creative relationships, and cultivate creative thinking on a daily basis. Within the school, children share a studio with a professional artist, observing the artist as they develop their own creative processes. The program also facilitates time and space for children to actively engage in their own creative processes. In this studio, children have access to various artistic materials and influences that stimulate different modes of thinking, enabling them to address and overcome challenges that arise in their own creative endeavours.

Critical thinking

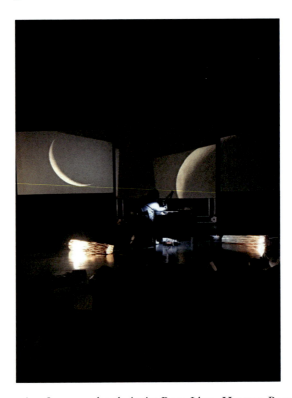

FIGURE 14.3   espai c, Sagarra school. Artist Rosa Llop. Hangar, Barcelona. Photo: Núria Grau.

Critical thinking is a complex skill that implies different cognitive processes such as conceptualizing, applying, analysing, synthesizing, interpreting, reflecting and evaluating to facilitate reflecting critically on ideas, actions, and outcomes (Craft et al., 2016).

Critical thinking is a way of approaching ideas with the aim of understanding their essence, beyond the surface. In learning processes in which critical thinking is stimulated, interactive thinking processes are created, in which a climate of trust is created where all participants, whether students or teachers, can show their ideas. Indeed, as bell hooks says, the most stimulating aspect of critical thinking in the classroom is that it appeals to everyone's initiative and actively invites students to think passionately and share ideas with an open mind (Hooks, 2022).

Parfs-Romia et al., 2023, p.63

The resident artist is someone who establishes a unique relationship with the boys and girls, as they are not required to perform specific evaluative functions. The artist encourages in children a sense of responsibility for their own learning, autonomy, teamwork, and, above all, a critical spirit that allows them to develop their own identity and build a space of shared culture within the school.

Artistic languages

It is important that children are invited to explore their ideas in different modalities – to experiment, to play, to create and share their learning through visual and performative modes of expression - through images, their movement and dance, musical or poetic languages. Every language of expression has its own integrity and form of expressive potential. Artistic languages and aesthetic experience are a form of encounter, exploration, contemplation and expression.

Parfs-Romia et al., 2023, p.76

An artist with a residence in an educational context develops a role model completely different to the teacher's; they organize the space according to their artistic process and provide technical, conceptual, and strategic knowledge in a different manner than the teacher may offer. The workspaces shared between artist and children tend to be full of different materials, such as brushes, wool, tapes, cables, boxes, paint, etc. that enable them to express their thoughts and ideas in various artistic languages and to share them.

FIGURE 14.4   espai c, Eixample school. Artist: Gina Gimenez. Fundació Tàpies, Barcelona. Photo: Maria Sellarès.

In the studio, discourse is not solely conceived and constructed through verbal language. Instead, works and creative processes are primarily shaped through other languages, specifically visual and performative ones. These languages, historically relegated to a secondary status both within and outside of school, enable individuals to give form to complex and subtle thoughts – ideas that might otherwise remain undeveloped (Eisner, 2004, cited by París-Romia, 2019b).

Co-creation

> To develop creativity and critical thinking through the art in learning spaces it is necessary to co-design spaces and places for children to explore their imagination alongside artists, educators, and cultural professionals.
>
> *París-Romia et al., 2023, p.101*

The espai c is a shared learning environment where the resident artist is not the owner of creativity; all the participants can work in a collaborative manner

Embedding art into daily practice 153

FIGURE 14.5   espai c, Arts school. Artist: Neus Frigola. Fundació Suñol, Barcelona Photo: Neus Frigola.

with different creative actions. Children are co-participants, and they share processes, responsibilities, and needs along with the artist. Therefore, the artist does not decide for the children and doesn't teach or evaluate them. During their time together, children and artist are focused on their own research, but both can be inspired and learn from each other, so the atelier appears to be a democratic space for co-creation were at some moments there is a shared decision-making. The continuous contact among artist and children facilitates a vision of fantasy and imagination that is shaking and questioning their methodological and conceptual approaches to their artistic work.

Inclusive spaces of encounter

FIGURE 14.6   espai c, Encants school. Artist: Urgell, Barcelona. Photo: Gemma París.

Every educational encounter is an invitation to explore ideas, thoughts, and feelings together and express them in many different ways, and through co-participation, where everyone is welcome, and every child is equal. In making learning processes through the arts in inclusive spaces of encounter can explore the space between children, art, artists, and educators. Through an open space of dialogue and expression there is more emphasis on the possibility of relational and collaborative artmaking rather than purely individual expression. Art is an inclusive space of encounter, a meeting place for ideas and expressions and where difference is valued. This 'public pedagogy' is art as pedagogy.

París-Romia et al., 2023, p.119

The schools who have an espai c want to facilitate a space to create a shared artistic workshop managed by the artists and the children, where learning occurs without limits within relational processes shared by the people in this space. That way of understanding artistic experiences where all the participants have the same status facilitates and promotes the inclusion of different identities, abilities, knowledge, preferences where there are no judgemental qualifications nor the need to produce a final product in a certain manner, the value is to be there and be accepted as one is, with their own singularities.

Aesthetic environments

FIGURE 14.7 espai c, Encants school. Artists: Judith Cuadros & Dave. Barcelona Photo: Gemma París.

If we understand the place as the possibility of encounter and learning it is important to create an environment that optimizes creative learning through all the senses. Aesthetic environments invite, nurture, and develop aesthetic sensibilities as an important part of being human, learning in and through the arts, and prioritizing thought and feeling rather than mere technique and practice.

París-Romia et al., 2023, p.135

The school with a resident artist provides a new way of looking at the reality, different creative relationships to the world with different artistic languages. Artists have a way of questioning and expressing that helps to open new ways of thinking and opening the mind. Also, the artist creates a safe place for the children where they together develop thinking on other aesthetic environments.

Conclusion

The Teacher Training Proposal outlined above aims to empower professionals in creating inclusive opportunities for artistic experiences in early childhood education, fostering holistic learning, and stimulating children's creativity. The accumulated experiences and reflections throughout the training contribute to a transformative and inclusive approach to arts education in nurseries. Both examples of the project, encompassing peer learning training and the resident artist in the *espais c*, have unequivocally validated the empowerment that children undergo through their exposure to the arts. This empowerment is evident in their direct engagement with professional artists, whether in the *espais c* program (Barcelona) or the *Mestres que es mouen* program (Sabadell).

The evaluation and research conducted by the UAB provide substantial evidence of the enrichment that the infusion of professional art brings to educational spaces. This integration not only enables all children to develop their creative capacity but also serves as a means for them to empower themselves as individuals. The project results have been intentionally crafted to remain open, with the overarching goal of allowing educators and artists to draw inspiration from these educational materials. This, in turn, encourages active participation in the transformative journey of education through the arts for a more inclusive and creative education for all.

Note

1 https://dybwikdans.com/.

References

Acaso, M, & Megías, C (2017). *Art Thinking*. Ediciones Paidós: *Cómo el arte puede transformar la educación.*

Blanch, S (2016). L'educació Inclusiva. A L. Martin i D. Vilalta (Coord), *L'Educació Infantil avui: reptes i propostes* (pp. 24–32) Bellaterra: ICE UAB. https://www.uab.cat/doc/Educacio_Infantil_Avui_Reptes_Propostes

Blanch, S, París, G, Cabo, H, Ciraso Cali, A, Halle, K, & Ribera, E (Coords.) (2023). *INTERSTICE: Artists, Children and Educators. Teachers in moviment. Peer learning methodology*. Retrieved from: https://ddd.uab.cat/record/275924

Bourriaud, N (2002). *Esthétique relationelle*. Les presses du réel.

Bueno, D (2019). *Neurociencia aplicada a la educación*. Ediciones Síntesis.

Camnitzer, L (2015). Thinking about art thinking. *e-flux Journal*, 65. Retrieved from: https://www.e-flux.com/journal/65/336660/thinkingabout-art-thinking/

Craft, A, McConnon, L, & Matthews, A (2016). Child-initiated play and professional creativity: Enabling four-year-olds' possibility thinking. *Thinking Skills and Creativity*, *7*, 48–61. https://dx.doi.org/10.1016/j.tsc.2011.11.005

Hooks, B (2022). *Enseñar pensamiento crítico*. Rayo Verde Editorial

París-Romia, G (2019a). El arte como espacio de reencuentro: influencias rizomáticas entre infancia y artistas residentes en la escuela, en *Arteterapia. Papeles de arteterapia y educación para inclusión social*, *14*, 55–73. https://dx.doi.org/10.5209/arte.62570

París-Romia, G (2019b). El artista residente en la escuela como agente de cambio en las estrategias de aprendizaje. *Arte, Individuo y Sociedad*, *31*(4), 951–968. https://doi.org/10.5209/aris.62384

París-Romia, G, Blanch Gelabert, S, & Hay, P (2023) (Eds.). *INTERSTICE. Encounters between artists, children and educators. Thoughts in-between the arts and education.* Retrieved from: https://ddd.uab.cat/record/275922

París, G, & Hay, P (2019). 5x5x5=Creativity: Art as a Transformative Practice. *International Journal of Art & Design Education*, *39*(1), 69–84. https://doi.org/10.1111/jade.12229

UNICEF (1989). *United Nations Convention on the Rights of the Child*, A/RES/44/25 of 20 November 1989, 1577 UNTS 3. Retrieved from: https://www.unicef.org.uk/wp-content/uploads/2016/08/unicef-convention-rights-child-uncrc.pdf

15

IMAGINATION

The missing element of Early Childhood Education?

Sue Nimmo

> Imagination, as the basis of all creative activity, is an important component of absolutely all aspects of cultural life, enabling artistic, scientific, and technical creation alike. In this sense, absolutely everything around us that was created by the hand of man, the entire world of human culture, as distinct from the world of nature, all this is the product of human imagination and of creation based on this imagination.
>
> (Vygotsky, 1978, p. 3)

Vygotsky's words are a powerful reminder that we do not fully understand the complexities of imagination or its place within learning. If imagination is truly the basis for all creative activity and a part of everyday life, then our understanding of it within education needs to be reflected on, reviewed, and revised. Take a moment to look around you, consider your current environment, what is manmade? What is natural? You are surrounded by the ideas of others, innovations and problems that have been solved through imaginative thinking. If imaginative thinking is so powerful to alter the world we live in and to enable us to understand others, could its importance be a missing element in Early Childhood Education (ECE)? This chapter will enable you to critically reflect on what you understand about imagination, from its definition to its importance in early childhood development and learning in and beyond the Early Years curriculum. A review of how imagination is viewed in Early Years Education will aim to encourage you to reflect on your own practice and the possibility of developing a pedagogy that values imagination.

DOI: 10.4324/9781003471172-18

Defining Imagination

Imagination is a fascinating and often misunderstood aspect of education. It has been debated for centuries; for example, the Greek philosopher Plato gave us an insight into what imagination was when he described it as the ability to form a mental representation, a picture within the mind. This mental image has the potential to see beyond current reality, to see the future, the past and endless possibilities. Imagination gives us the capacity to see an object differently and to use it differently, to offer an alternative perspective or to understand others' intentions, ideas, values or views of the world. This mental representation can also give voice to our expressions, thoughts, memories and perception of time. This is a complex definition and yet it has been the basis for all other definitions such as 'Imagination: the ability to represent possibilities that are not present' (Gilbert and Wilson, 2007, p. 1351). This is essentially a historical perception of imagination, which has throughout time been synonymously linked with the Arts, which involve painting, music, and the performing arts.

Other philosophers have deliberated that imagination is a definitive part of human nature, even though it is an abstract concept, and consequently, can be perceived, promoted and playful. Immanuel Kant's reflections on imagination considered a different perspective as he proposed that imagination could also involve elements of intuition and experience, that imagination was a part of our own perceptions and realities, and how this can affect our decisions, beliefs and reasoning. Kant also contemplated the irony that to understand imagination, we use imaginative thinking (Furlong, 2014).

Hume's work on imagination considered that imaginative thinking has the possibility to generate social understanding, to establish emotional intelligence and to aid learning. Although Hume does not give a clear definition of imaginative thinking, he considered that we should not neglect the power and intensity of mental imagery. He argued that when we are imagining, we use our experiences and metaphysical perceptions, a branch of philosophy that examines the fundamental nature of reality, including the relationship between mind and matter. Hume believes we construct our conceptions of the world through imaginative thinking which allows us the potential to see beyond our current reality and situation (Costelloe, 2018).

This ability to see beyond our own reality is, according to Jackson, Oliver, Shaw and Wisdom (2007), a fundamental human asset explaining that we need imagination to innovate, solve problems, connect with the world and ultimately survive. Harris (2000) suggests that imagination is an intrinsic part of being human and argues that imagination and imaginative thinking became a part of our cognitive thinking process when we started to create cave paintings, as this was the first time, we used our thought processes to communicate a different perception of reality and to create a symbolic representation of the image we create with our minds. This ability to share knowledge, ideas and a sense of time which goes beyond our current reality is the very reason we are able to survive.

Imagination is without doubt a complex phenomenon, which is widely debated and discussed. Although ambiguous in nature, many of these theories and ideas about imagination agree on two aspects, namely, that imagination exists and that we use it in differing ways in different situations. There are commonalities between the different views on imagination, such as how, when and why we use imagination in a real-world context (Gendler, 2003). However, Kind (2013) reminds us that there can never be one true definition of imagination because of complex roles, cognitive thought patterns and our individual perceptions of the world. In addition to the fact that it is difficult to conclusively define imagination, there are also questions around our individual understanding of imagination. In our thinking processes, are we aware when we are imagining something? And could we ever be fully aware of what imagination means to us? As early childhood practitioners we also have to examine the role and relevance of imagination in children's development and learning.

Imagination: An Alternative perspective

Having considered the historic and philosophical viewpoints, there is a need to consider how imagination is viewed in the 21st century as well. Imagination has without doubt a synonymous link with creativity. The idea that imagination is a vital aspect of creative thinking is not contested here. However, there is a need to think critically about how we understand both creativity and imagination in the early childhood context.

An important aspect to consider is the development of neuroscience and its ability to allow imaginative thinking to be made visible. Vyshedskiy (2019) explains that imaginative thinking is a sophisticated and complex process of the brain. It is like a sea of electrical impulses of information that come together at exactly the right time to form a mental image. These constituent pieces of imagination come from our experiences, knowledge and intuition to make new connections, which can be fantastical and diverse, transcending time and space. The Hebbian principle in neuroscience demonstrates the ability of neurons to link together and remain wired together to create an ensemble of neural connections (Vyshedskiy, 2019). Each object, experience or idea has a different ensemble, similar to Piaget's (1929) schematics theory.

The ability to create an image within the mind is made possible by the synthesis of these ensembles of information. This process is described by Mental Synthesis Theory, which can be demonstrated with the example of a dolphin balancing a pineapple: This image consists of two different ensembles, one for a pineapple, the other for a dolphin. To create the complete image, these two pieces of neural information need to come together at exactly the same time. Research suggests that in order to enable these complex neuron ensembles to connect at exactly the same time, the brain needs to purposefully coordinate and synchronise its cognitive functions. This is done through neural fibres which reach from the prefrontal cortex at the front of the brain to the posterior cortex at the back of the brain where these ensembles of information are stored. The brain then sends a signal to stimulate these ensembles to race to the front of the brain to connect simultaneously, creating the image of a dolphin balancing a pineapple (Vyshedskiy, 2019).

One of the issues the brain has with this complex process is that ensembles of information are located at varying distances from the prefrontal cortex, so if the ensembles travelled down the neural fibres at the same time, they may not arrive in sync, and the image would not appear. The brain counteracts this problem by laying down layers of myelin along the outside of the neural fibres. This fatty substance of myelin acts as an insulator and enables the electrical signals to move at different speeds along the neural fibres allowing the ensembles of information to arrive simultaneously to create that mental image in the mind, to think imaginatively. Early childhood is the time when these neural fibres develop, and the layers of myelin are added. Opportunities to think imaginatively offer the brain the chance to add myelin layers to these neural fibres, building up the myelination around each fibre. This then allows the neural signals to move up to 100 times faster than before. Allowing children to develop their capacity to be imaginative, to problem solve and to think fantastically equips them with strong cognitive processes by which they can create mental images (Vyshedskiy, 2019).

Galton's (1880) original work on imagination stimulated a number of theories relating to imagination linking it to mental imagery, and neuroscience has now started to unpick the complexities of what imagination is and how it relates to learning. However, what happens if you cannot create a mental image? Galton's work first introduced the idea that there are individuals who cannot form mental images. If this is so, then it brings into question the very definition of imagination, to form a mental image as proposed by Plato. Galton coined the phrase Aphantasia, denoting those individuals, who for whatever reason cannot create a visual image in the mind. This presents an interesting alternative perspective and raises the question of whether someone who cannot form an image in the mind can be imaginative. Watkins (2018) offers a biographical perspective on Aphantasia as he considers himself to be imaginative but through a different way. He uses his other senses to create an imaginative representation through smell, touch or taste to invoke the same imaginative cognitive response within the mind.

O'Donnell, Di Simplicio, Brown, Holmes and Heyes (2018) provide an insight into how imaginative thinking can be affected by our mood and social status at any one time. The ability to be imaginative relies not only on the environment and the stimulus we are interacting with, but it is also linked to our emotional responses. O'Donnell et al. (2018) explain that the neurological pathways or neural fibres the brain uses can differ between individuals. This links directly to the ideas of Pearson (2019), whose recent work concludes that there is a spectrum of imagery vividness from Aphantasia to Hyperphantasia suggesting that the ability to form an image can vary in its strength depending on the individual.

The understanding we gain from neuroscience is that there is a need to support, promote and offer opportunities for young children to build up their myelination and therefore the potential strength of the neural fibres required for mental imagery and imaginative thinking to occur. Interestingly O'Donnell et al.'s work (2018) reiterates that imagination is extremely complicated and adds that it is linked to social status and how we value imagination. This can impact on whether we choose to share those ideas and whether they are valued by others. The confidence we have to share our imaginative thinking in varying situations is influenced by the environment and our emotional responses at any given time. Reflecting on the neuroscience of imagination and the cognitive processes required, it is imperative that we offer young children the chance to be imaginative through as many varied and sensory experiences as possible.

Some educationalists, such as Jackson et al. (2007) and James and Brookfield (2014), consider that imagination is more important than creativity. These theorists believe that imagination is an essential element of learning. They see imagination as a separate entity to creativity. The National Advisory Committee of Creative and Cultural Education (1999: p. 6) defines creativity as 'Imaginative activity fashioned so as to produce outcomes that are both original and of value'. This definition implies that there is a direct need to use creative thinking to produce a solution, that the process is both purposeful and directed. Whereas imaginative thinking, the process as described by Vyshedskiy (2019), is the capacity to think fantastically, freely and without direct purpose, which allows the mind to generate numerous ideas through experiences, sensory stimulation and emotional connections. Therefore Jackson (2007) and James and Brookfield (2014) argue that to be creative, you require imagination, and therefore it is a vital aspect of development that should not be seen merely as a part of the creative process.

Imagination is a key element when young children are developing as it enables them to think divergently, to imagine numerous ideas and think convergently, and to discard ideas that cannot work until a solution is found (Guilford, 1957), which is required for problem-solving. Equally, imagination enables children to develop a 'theory of mind', that is to say, an understanding of the thought, feelings and actions of others, to become socially aware and to predict outcomes and events (Wellman and Phillips, 2000). This self-awareness enables young children to acquire emotional intelligence (Goleman, 2011), to position themselves in the world and to understand it. Consequently, there is a need to understand the impact imagination can have on learning.

James and Brookfield (2014) propose that imagination is the 'key' to human thinking processes. This echoes the previous philosophical ideas of Hume and Kant in relation to imagination being an integral aspect of what defines us as human beings, the perspectives we hold, and our interactions with others and the world. James and Brookfield's theory (2014) aims to engage and inspire practitioners and teachers to blend creativity, reflection and imagination into playful situations. For imagination to flourish, they endorse three pedagogical axioms:

> Axiom 1
> **Deep**: encourages imaginative thinking that is directly linked to personal connections; offers the opportunity for young children to play with unexpected patterns, solve problems and generate new questions.

> Axiom 2
> **Sticks**: encourages imaginative thinking to enable learning to be memorable, easy to recall and tapped into in a variety of situations.

> Axiom 3
> **Challenge**: requires learning opportunities that are unexpected, unique, and playful. The opportunity to challenge your own ideas and perspectives, to come to new learning in a new and natural way.
>
> *(James & Brookfield, 2014)*

These axioms are an interesting perspective on the imaginative thinking and cognitive thought processes we as humans engage in. These axioms can be seen within early years learning and teaching:

- 'Deep' can be seen as new experiences, exploration of self-identity and the opportunity to explore abstract concepts, practise physical skills and develop cognitive connections.
- 'Sticks' are those 'wow' moments we see when children demonstrate their knowledge and the ability to offer children different learning opportunities within play.
- 'Challenge' can be the understanding a child develops about the world and their place within it.

These axioms offer a way to see imaginative thinking at work and to understand how it can enable children to develop numerous areas of learning (Kaufman and Beghetto, 2009).

Is imagination more important than creativity, if it is a key component of being human as suggested by Jackson and Harris? If so, should imagination in early childhood be recognised as an essential element of learning that requires specific promotion to enable young children to have opportunities to be imaginative? If so, then the ideas developed by Vyshedskiy (2019) in relation to

Missing element of Early Childhood Education

neuroscience need to be very carefully considered and also the possibility that there may be children who have Aphantasia and therefore require an even more varied environment in which to be imaginative.

Imagination and the Early Years Curriculum

After contemplating how imagination is viewed historically, by philosophers and 21st-century theorists alike, it is vital that we consider how imagination is currently viewed within education and in the current English Early Years curriculum. Imagination, in educational terms, does not appear to be important as the UK National Curriculum guidance only mentions it within creative writing (Department for Education (DfE), 2013). This view of imagination holds on to the notion that it is only a part of creativity. There is no consideration of imagination as a means to explore abstract concepts, become socially aware or develop our own perceptions, opinions and values.

Early years policy holds imagination in a little more regard in relation to the 'Characteristics of Effective Teaching and Learning' (DFE, 2021, p. 16) which asserts that creating and thinking critically can enable children to develop their own ideas. However, it does not specify how children do this. There appears to be an assumption within the Statutory Framework for the Early Years Foundation Stage (DfE, 2021) that children have an innate skill to think imaginatively and that there is no need to promote this type of thinking.

The Statutory Framework only uses the word imagination twice and links it directly to the specific early learning goal of Being Imaginative and Expressive (DFE, 2021), which relates explicitly to the Expressive Art and Design area of learning for young children. This developmental area relates to the child's skill of being able to invent, understand and recount narrative, to be able to sing rhymes and songs, and to move to music. Consequently, the English Early Years curriculum still holds to the adage that imagination is only linked to creative thinking. This is a historical concept that associates imagination and creativity as being directly connected to the 'Arts' such as painting, sculpture, music, literature, or theatre and performing arts.

There is clearly an unequivocal link to societal and historical expectations of what creativity and imagination are used for within learning. The English early years curriculum is based on neoliberal approaches to education and by its very nature requires the teacher or practitioner to assess a child's learning in relation to its contents. Perhaps it is the inability to assess imagination that makes it potentially problematic and reduces imagination to being a necessary conduit for creativity, however, it is not seen as a separate and important aspect of development and educational practice. This consideration of the current UK curriculum leads to the question of what is more important for young children's development and learning. Are we marginalising the experiences and potential of young children if imagination is only promoted as a conduit for creative thinking based on historical perspectives and related only to specific areas such as art, music and drama? Should imagination be used by children to understand the world beyond a curriculum? Is imagination an essential asset to developing life skills for survival?

Imagination: A skill for life

The Institute of Imagination (IoI) (2023) endorses that imagination is humanity's greatest faculty, that it enables us to navigate the ever-changing world and our part in it. They also believe that imagination in education and life in general is undervalued. To understand how vital imagination is to children's development, it is necessary to explore how others have viewed imagination in their research within education and early childhood development.

Goleman's (2011) work on emotional intelligence is significant as an underpinning theory which links emotional intelligence to imaginative thinking. Goleman explores the ability of humans to be self-aware and holds that we have developed the ability to read other's emotions. This intelligence enables people to become more acutely aware of how others can react and how they themselves respond to a situation or problem. This emotional intelligence also enables organisational functioning, citizenship and social interactions.

This relates precisely to Wellman and Phillips's (2000) 'A theory of Mind' which enables children to develop empathy and sympathy, and to express kindness, caring and compassion for others. Ledoux's (2000) theory incorporates the idea that imaginative thinking and emotional responses are inextricably linked clearly showing a need for imaginative thinking to be promoted, explored and utilised in young children's play.

Siraj-Blatchford's (2009) theory of 'Sustained shared thinking' explores the social interaction of working together with others as a group and sharing in having a common goal. This demonstrates how important imagination is as a skill to enable young children to develop their abilities to understand how another's ideas, thoughts and feelings can offer an alternative perspective on our world. Without these life skills that imagination can develop, children may find it difficult to interact and express their own ideas, thoughts and feelings.

In addition, young children require imagination to begin to understand complex and abstract concepts that enable them to comprehend and interact in the world in a meaningful way. These abstract concepts can include some of the fundamental underpinning skills for learning such as generalisation or the ability to apply rules of always, sometime, never. Other important concepts include the understanding of how to apply these rules and support the development of schematic thought processes which are required to identify, categorise and develop specific strategies for ordering, sorting and connecting. A child's ability to understand the abstract concepts associated with pattern, for example, the notion of 'next' or 'between' is imperative for understanding number and values (Montague-Smith & Price, 2012).

Young children need to be able to engage with representation which is based in the understanding that we can express meaning in many forms and which links directly to Goleman's and Blatchford's theories of social integration (2009 and 2011 respectively). A child's ability to explore and utilise representation and pattern is an essential process for the development of linguistic skills (Neaum, 2017). This ability to understand that a letter is representational of sound is required to develop phonic knowledge. The development of imaginative thinking processes, to represent possibilities that are not present, is the skill required to understand and develop mathematical thinking and the ability to read and write (Gilbert and Wilson, 2007). Without these essential skills, navigating the world and understanding their place in it would be extremely difficult for children. Imaginative thinking enables us to comprehend our own realities, to socially engage and to express our own ideas and opinions as well as to effectually write our own narrative and to become innovative thinkers and survivors (Harris 2000).

In light of this reflection on how important imagination is in developing emotional intelligence and the underpinning skills of generalisation and representation, it is evident that imagination is required for more than just creative thinking; it is a means of understanding social integration and expressing ideas within a social context. Therefore, there is a need to rethink how we promote imagination in young children's learning. Although we do need to promote imaginative thinking in relation to creative thinking and its links to the arts, music and drama, we need to venture beyond that perspective to truly make a significant impact on children's learning and development and to start to question what value we as practitioners place on imagination in education.

Towards a pedagogy of imagination

Imagination is vital and yet so complex that it can be difficult to interweave into everyday practice. Developing your own knowledge of imagination and how it supports learning is the first step to valuing imagination within your own pedagogy. The following theories offer ways to integrate imagination into playful situations and learning opportunities.

Craft (2003) offers a unique theory of 'possibility thinking'. This theory encourages children to generate 'what if' questions, instigating imaginative thinking, where children can express their unique ideas in relation to objects, resources, and situations. To utilise these resources by thinking 'what can I do with these', beyond the obvious or an adult's direction, for example, turning a bucket and spade into a time machine or a superhero gadget. The opportunities for young children to think 'what if I do this or that' can give them the opportunity to think divergently and fantastical, leading to innovation, a new understanding or alternative perspective (Guilford, 1957).

Invoking curiosity in young children is a simple and yet effective way to encourage imaginative thinking. Curiosity enables children to move beyond their present situation, and they are freed from immediate sensations and distractions. Curiosity allows a child to actively seek out new learning and experiences, to think in a fantastical way, to become engrossed in their own ideas and to share those ideas with others (Duffy, 2006). Simple activities such as 'what's in the box?' or placing footprints around a room, can invoke a child to consider what made the footprints, why they are there or whether they left anything behind? These types of simple activities offer open-ended opportunities to socially engage, communicate ideas, work collaboratively and problem solve, all of which are skills children need beyond a curriculum.

Offering open resources which engage 'what if' questions and promote curiosity is a first step to enacting pedagogical change. Allowing children the time to explore and express their ideas and perceptions is a key aspect of a pedagogy that truly values imaginative thinking.

Freedom to explore beyond the constraints of routine and curriculum is vital, and it requires practitioners to be flexible, thoughtful and willing to embrace the child's perspective of the world, including their sense of time. Offering problems that involve risk or challenge, teamwork and collaboration can also elicit imaginative opportunities, as can activities such as den building, map making and treasure hunting or introducing a character that requires the children's help or needs to be cared for, which could be a teddy, an alien or even a rock (Thornton and Brunton, 2005).

Ken Robinson (2011), who is the founder of the Institute of Imagination, truly believes that imagination and its promotion in education can enable children's learning to flourish and that pedagogical change is necessary to resolve issues in education relating to children's willingness to learn, engage and reflect. By offering children the possibility to be imaginative, practitioners can unleash children's ideas, experiences, opinions and perceptions of the world.

Now you have developed a better understanding of the complexities of imagination and imaginative thinking, the question is: Can you imagine changing your pedagogy to value imagination in your daily practice?

References

Costelloe, TM (2018). *The Imagination in Hume's Philosophy: The Canvas of the Mind.* Edinburgh University Press.

Craft, A (2003). The limits of creativity in education: Dilemmas for the educator. *British Journal of Educational Studies, 51*(2), 9113–9127.

Department for Education (2021). *Statutory Framework for the Early Years Foundation Stage.* Retrieved from: https://www.gov.uk/government/publications/early-years-foundation-stage-framework--2

Department for Education (2013) *The National Curriculum in England: key stages 1 and 2 framework document*. Retrieved from: https://www.gov.uk/government/publications/national-curriculum-in-england-primary-curriculum

Duffy, B (2006). *Supporting Creativity and Imagination in the Early Years* (2nd edn.). Maidenhead: Open University Press.

Furlong, EJ (2014). *Imagination*. Routledge.

Galton, F (1880). Statistics of mental imagery. *Mind, 5,* 301–318.

Gendler, T (2003). On the relation between pretence and belief, in M. Kieran and D.M. Lopes (eds.), *Imagination, Philosophy, and the Arts*, pp. 124–141. New York: Routledge,

Gilbert, DT, & Wilson, TD (2007). Prospection: Experiencing the future. *Science, 317*(5843), 1351–1354.

Goleman, D (2011). *Leadership: The Power of Emotional Intelligence*. Florence, MA: More Than Sound.

Guilford, JP (1957). Creative abilities in the arts. *Psychological Review, 64*(2), 110.

Harris, PL (2000). *The Work of the Imagination*. London: Blackwell Publishing.

Institute of Imagination (IoI) (2023). *Literature Review of Imagination in Education and Learning*. Retrieved from: Literature Review of Imagination in Education and Learning - Institute of Imagination (ioi.london).

Jackson, N, Oliver, M, Shaw, M, & Wisdom, J (2007). *Developing Creativity in Higher Education: An Imaginative Curriculum*. Hoboken. Taylor & Francis Ltd.

James, A, & Brookfield, S (2014). *Engaging Imagination*. San Francisco: John Wiley and Sons Ltd.

Kind, A (2013). The heterogeneity of the imagination. *Erkenntnis, 78*(1), 141–159. Doi:10.1007/s10670-011-9313-z

Kaufman, J, & Beghetto, R (2009). Beyond Big and Little: The Four C model of creativity. *Review of General Psychology, 13*(1), 1–12.

Ledoux, JE (2000). Emotion circuits in the brain. Annual Review. *Neuroscience, 23,* 155–184.

Montague-Smith, A, & Price, A (2012). *Mathematics in Early Years Education*. Abingdon: Routledge.

National Advisory Committee for Creative and Cultural Education (NACCCE) (1999). *All Our Futures: Creativity, Culture, Education*. Nottingham: Crown

Neaum, S (2017). *What Comes Before Phonics?* London: Sage Publications.

O'Donnell, C, Di Simplicio, M, Brown, R, Holmes, EA, & Heyes, SB (2018). The role of mental imagery in mood amplification: An investigation across subclinical features of bipolar disorders. *Cortex, 105,* 104–117.

Pearson, J (2019). The human imagination: The cognitive neuroscience of visual mental imagery. *Nature Reviews Neuroscience, 20*(10), 624–634. doi:10.1038/s41583-019-0202-9. PMID: 31384033

Piaget, J (1929/1979). *The Child's Conception of the World*. New York, NY: Harcourt, Brace.

Robinson, K (2011). *Out of our Minds: Learning to be Creative*. John Wiley & Sons.

Siraj-Blatchford, I (2009). Conceptualising progression in the pedagogy of play and sustained shared thinking in early childhood education: A Vygotskian perspective. *Educational and Child Psychology, 26*(2).

Thornton, L, & Brunton, P (2005). *Understanding the Reggio Approach*. London: David Fulton Publications

Vygotsky. LS (1978). *Mind in Society: The development of Higher Psychological Processes.* Cambridge, MA: Harvard University press.

Vyshedskiy, A (2019). Neuroscience of imagination and implications for human evolution. *Current Neurobiology, 10*(2), 89–109.

Watkins, NW (2018). (A)phantasia and SDAM: Scientific and Personal Perspectives. *Cortex, 105,* 41e52.

Wellman, HM, & Phillips, AT (2000). Young children's understanding of perception, desire and emotion. *Child Development, 71*(4), 895–912.

16

EDUCATION AT THE CROSSFIRE

A human right-based approach to support children with disabilities in disasters

Mabel Giraldo

Introduction

'Disaster' and 'childhood' are commonly intended as two oxymoronic life conditions. In a commonly used definition, disaster is 'a serious disruption of the functioning of a community or a society involving widespread human, material, economic or environmental losses and impacts, which exceeds the ability of the affected community or society to cope using its own resources' (UNISDR, 2009). For centuries crisis situations mainly concerned wars in the form of clashes between soldiers, with civilians in the role of spectators or casual victims. But this scenario has been massively extended after the Second World War. Firstly, the theatres of modern conflicts are no longer battlefields, but cities, villages, schools, and hospitals, as over 90% of the fallen in the wars were civilians, half of them children (UNICEF, 2007). Secondly, new man-made (such as industrial accidents, chemical disasters, terrorist attacks) and natural disasters (such as tsunamis, earthquakes, floods) are now regularly occurring. All these events affect the lives of millions of people worldwide, but what consequences do they have for children, their educational process, and their right to a childhood? What happens when these children have disabilities? What actions should be taken to respond to their needs and to ensure their inclusion in the disaster management process? These are the questions this chapter will address.

The impact of disasters on children with disabilities

Persons with disabilities are four times more likely to die in disasters than those without disabilities, and 6% of all disaster-affected people acquire disabilities

DOI: 10.4324/9781003471172-19

from the event (UNESCAP, 2017). This (especially) applies to children who are 'two time vulnerable'[1] (Bongo, Lunga, Van Niekerk & Musarurwa, 2019) experiencing amplified exposure due to increased psychological, physical, and educational vulnerabilities (Brittingham & Wachtendorf, 2013). Referring to the latter, several inferences can be drawn on how disasters might impact the education of children with disabilities: decreasing academic achievement; losing teachers and other personnel with expertise on disabilities; destroying school buildings or accessibility features (for example, ramps); and missing diagnostic and special educational records, also affecting the continuity of appropriate educational services (Stough, Ducy, Kang & Lee, 2020).

The children may have a pre-existing disability prior to emergencies, or they may have reported an impairment due to the disaster. Vulnerability, in both cases, is exacerbated by factors including mobility, communication, and cognitive difficulties, as well as psychological factors, medical and health conditions, social and physical environments and policies (Stough, Ducy & Kang, 2017; Boon et al., 2011). Additionally, the more pressing needs of living arrangements, food and basic healthcare in countries affected by conflicts and other disasters are (understandably) prioritised over disability. As a result, children with disabilities are overlooked in Disaster Risk Reduction (DRR) planning or emergency training (Ronoh, Gaillard & Marlowe, 2015).

In particular, the barriers faced by persons with disabilities during disaster may differ significantly depending on the type of impairment. Consequently, there is no single strategy that meets the needs of all, and incorrect or inappropriate assistance may be rendered in disaster circumstances, as responders may inaccurately identify the form of disability an individual has (Alexander, 2015; Lemyre, Gibson, Zlepnig, Meyer-Macleod & Boutette., 2009). For instance, physical and motor disabilities can limit children's effective responses to disasters (Kettaneh & Slevin, 2014). None of the 700 people with post-polio paralysis on an island of the Andaman archipelago in the Bay of Bengal survived the 2004 tsunami because they were unable to run to the surrounding hills (Alexander & Davis, 2012).

Concerning intellectual disabilities, these children may experience confusion and anxiety when making sense of their environment, changes or emergency situations occurring during a disaster. They may have limited capability, for example, to recognise nature and signs of environmental dangers, understand impending threats or gauge the level of danger or risk (Stough, 2015). These difficulties may be exacerbated by the loss of or disconnection from their support networks, including family, friends and care providers (Stough, 2015). Children with autism spectrum disorders are particularly vulnerable during emergency situations (Edmonds, 2017). Due to their high sensitivity to light, sounds, odours, tastes, and touch and their information processing difficulties, they may become agitated by the systems used to alert people, by the disaster sheltering or by the challenges they face regarding change (Peek

& Stough, 2010). Finally, it should be considered that engaging children with autism in emergency preparedness would require different approaches which are dependent on the severity of the autism and the ability of the individual to understand the different concepts.

Additionally, very few studies focus on the needs and experiences of persons with sensory impairment during the disaster cycle (Stough & Kelman, 2018). Often public warning systems do not appropriately include adaptations for this group (Alexander, 2015) and thus children with hearing difficulties are disadvantaged in recognising an (impending) disaster or in accessing emergency information when oral directions are given unaccompanied by sign language or visual hints (Boon et al., 2011). Finally, there are great difficulties concerning mental disorders diagnosed pre- or post-disasters (Roudini, Khankeh & Witruk, 2017), as only limited research has been undertaken examining the impacts that emergencies have on this group of people (Stough & Kelman, 2018).

Nevertheless, while the disaster literature highlights the overall effects of emergencies on children as a vulnerable group in society (Gaillard & Pangilinan, 2010), few studies document the experiences of children with disabilities during disasters, regardless of their type of disability (Stough & Mayhorn, 2013; Peek & Stough 2010; Boon et al., 2011). This lack reinforces the perception of children with disabilities' inherent vulnerability and increases their invisibility as well as the level of discrimination (Alexander, 2011). However, the little existing literature is concordant on some shortcomings characterising the conditions of children with disabilities in disasters.

The first shortcoming concerns the lack of reliable disaggregated data on disability, as argued by the influential UN report *Nobody Left Behind: Investigating Disaster Preparedness and Response for People with Disabilities* (UNHRW, 2022). This lack arises from the limited availability or complete absence of data and general basic information on the numbers and locations of disabled persons in a country. Furthermore, there are considerable variations in the philosophies, methodologies and datasets used by each region or organisation when collecting and assessing data. And finally, a third factor adding to the lack of data is the different cross-cultural understanding of disability (Donovan 2017; Kett & Twigg, 2007). Consequently, without accurate data and information meaningful targeted policymaking is impossible, and emergency responders cannot correctly identify, quantify and locate vulnerable populations before or during an emergency, which means it is difficult for them to allocate appropriate resources or include persons with disabilities in pre-disaster training and post-disaster response efforts (Twigg, Kett & Lovell, 2018; Smith, Levy, Hsu & Levy, 2012).

Secondly, most disaster response systems are designed for able-bodied persons, with the utilitarian view that effective support is measured by the number of people assisted. Furthermore, according to Reinhardt et al. (2011), policies for DRR presume the dependence of the person with disabilities upon a

172 Mabel Giraldo

caregiver and disregard situations in which there may not be anyone to assist the individual in question, nor do they consider a person with disability as an asset. This may be the result of the generalised view of emergency responders that persons with disabilities are likely to be put with others into the catch-all category of 'vulnerable groups', which fails to identify their specific needs (Stough, 2015; Phillips et al., 2010), especially in the early phases of emergencies (UNHCR, 2014).

With such attitudinal barriers, it is not surprising that persons with disabilities are usually seen as mere passive recipients of aid and are generally excluded from planning and implementing emergency responses (Twigg, Kett, Bottomley, Tan & Nasreddin, 2011). This third shortcoming could be directly attributable to limitations in staffing and management. According to Clive, Davis, Hansen and Mincin (2010), these arising issues lead to poor DDR planning, confusion about roles and responsibilities and misplaced assumptions among emergency managers that disability service providers can meet all needs of persons with disabilities in a crisis. As a result, persons with disabilities (especially children) remain largely invisible to emergency officials and are disregarded in most disaster response systems (Twigg et al., 2011).

A fourth shortcoming refers to some local and pre-existing social, political, cultural and educational barriers. There is plenty of evidence on the implications that countries' definition and interpretation of disability have for practice and policy responses regarding the needs of persons living with disability (Yeo & Moore 2003). The extent of considerations of disabilities varies depending on whether 'planning' is linked to DRR and/or disaster response and recovery (Bongo et al., 2019). Social distancing or stigma towards disability may further limit access to primary resources, social networks and other psychological supports, or make it difficult for a child with a disability to adjust emotionally to a new neighbourhood or community (Tierney, Petak & Hahn, 1988). In many countries, such discrimination experienced by persons with disabilities is the outcome of dominant negative attitudes, customs, cultural and religious beliefs, and governmental policies that curtail their access to educational and livelihood opportunities, social support systems, public and private workspaces, which taken collectively produce vulnerability (UNESCAP, 2017; Stough & Kang, 2015). Together, the four shortcomings call for a new framework for orienting inclusive disaster management initiatives and related targeted actions, beyond the widespread humanitarian approach.

Human rights-based model: a new approach for shifting emergencies management?

In spite of these problems and the small body of research on children with disabilities involved in disasters, several non-governmental organisations (NGOs) and many sub-institutions under the UN system work toward disability inclusion in disaster management, as well as address the needs of children with disabilities[2]. This contributes to consolidate a 'disability focus' within the humanitarian sector (Kett & van Ommeren, 2009), certainly pushed by the UN *Convention on the Right of the Persons with Disabilities* (CRPD) (United Nations, 2006) which embeds into international law, the need for measures for the 'protection and safety of persons with disabilities in situations of risk, including situations of armed conflict, humanitarian emergencies and the occurrence of natural disasters' (art. 11). These rights refer to children too and should be reinterpreted in the light of the *Convention on the Rights of the Child* (United Nations, 1989) which is an important reminder of the civil, political, economic, social, health and cultural rights of children, including, not secondarily, the right to be protected in case of war (art. 38) and to receive appropriate care and reintegration into society (art. 39).

These UN milestone documents inaugurate, also into disaster literature, the human rights-based approach to disability reflecting a paradigm shift in attitudes and focus to persons with disabilities, including children. This model moves from the treatment of persons with disabilities as objects of charity, medical treatment, and social protection (which in the context of disasters translates into the humanitarian approach), towards viewing them as people with rights who can claim these rights and make decisions for their lives based on their free and informed consent, as well as being active members of society (Njelesani, Cleaver, Tataryn & Nixon, 2012). This approach explicitly includes human rights into programs, not only providing care or first aids (food, health, etc.) and improving access to quality services, but also increasing participation in decision-making and creating public awareness and demand for better services (Klasing, Moses & Satterthwaite, 2011).

This increasing international awareness calls for guidance in meeting the needs of persons with disabilities in disasters and has inspired, over the years, some initiatives, such as *The Verona Charter on the Rescue of Persons with Disabilities in Case of Disaster* (ULSS20, 2007), the NGO *Handicap International* (2006; 2008)[3] or some manuals of best practice by the US Federal Emergency Management Agency (FEMA)[4]. More recently, the same mission is recalled by two milestone documents. The first is the *Sendai Framework* (2015), an international accord on disaster risk reduction adopted by UN Member States, which specifies the inclusion of persons with disabilities in the assessment of disaster risk, the design and implementation of plans, and the involvement in the promotion of accessible response, recovery rehabilitation, and reconstruction approaches (UNISDR, 2015). Common to these instruments and frameworks is an emphasis on equal access to information, aid, and resources, as well as the recognition of the unique insights of persons with disabilities (or their parents/caregivers in case of children) about their own needs during disasters and the importance of their inclusion in disaster planning. The second set of documents concerns the recent UN

174 Mabel Giraldo

Resolution 2475 (United Nations, 2019) and *Resolution* 76/204 (United Nations, 2022). The latter promotes an international commitment to disability-inclusive disaster risk reduction (DiDRR)[5] and urges states to:

1 prioritise the establishment and strengthening of national disaster loss databases to augment efforts to create or enhance systems for disaggregated data collection and the development of new baselines (art. 19);
2 recognise that DRR requires a systemic approach and inclusive risk-informed decision-making (art. 20);
3 promote the full, equal, and effective participation and leadership of persons with disabilities, in the design, management, resourcing and implementation of disability-inclusive disaster risk reduction policies, plans and programmes (art. 42).

Despite this increased international commitment to DiDRR, agencies that support inclusion in principle, struggle to put these statements into practice due to a lack of standards and indicators to monitor inclusion and due to a poor awareness and training at practice level (Kett & van Ommeren, 2009). It is a vicious circle within which children with disabilities usually risk being considered as mere passive recipients of aid (Twigg et al., 2011) and as helpless in the face of disaster (Smith et al., 2012). Therefore, a comprehensive rights-based reorientation in emergency planning is needed, from assisting groups of people (with disability) to providing help to single individuals that is tailored to their specific needs, as well as proposing direct and practical solutions. The next section offers tips for practitioners for putting this approach into action.

Tips for practising a (real) disability-inclusive disaster management

Below is a brief (and surely not exhaustive) guide for stakeholders to consciously incorporate the rights of persons with disabilities into the *modus operandi* of all disaster management initiatives (in particular those currently not disability focused). The strategies presented here have been designed according to the disability rights-based model and to the statements of the last UN *Resolution* 76/204 (2021). They are intended to be the starting point of a good planning process and are designed to be interrelated and applicable along the continuum of disaster management initiatives.

Employing a person-centred perspective

Effectively including persons with disabilities as part of a disaster response requires overcoming the standpoint of medical and charity models of disability (Clive et al., 2010) as well as a humanitarian approach in disasters and adopting a person-centred approach (Villeneuve, 2022; Pertiwi, Llewellyn & Villeneuve, 2019). This perspective is a mindset which involves viewing, listening to and supporting a person with a disability based on their strengths, abilities, aspirations, and preferences to make decisions which maintain a life that is meaningful to them. Applied to disability management initiatives, this approach entails starting from the identification of an individual's function-based support needs in emergencies, in personal and social areas. This identification, possibly obtained through specific models or survey tools, guides the determination of tailored objectives and interventions on a practical level, identifying priorities and strategies (also in relation to the specific disability) and considering the possibilities for action defined by the present institutional boundaries, including internal and external resources (professional, organisational, economic, etc.). In the case of children with disabilities (as they are pre-verbal or have linguistic and communication difficulties due to their disability), the parents or caregivers play a crucial role. Parents would be the people who know their young children best and may be able to or even have to speak for them to help practitioners and planners to understand what would help their children in an emergency.

Adopting a participatory risk management approach

Ensuring a response centred on the needs of persons with disabilities implies placing them at the heart of decision-making and implementation of disaster risk management activities and working together with them. This can be achieved by adopting and practising participatory approaches. Despite the divergence in conceptualisation of participation, it is generally accepted that participation is not only about 'being involved', but also 'having people's voice heard' and 'being empowered to transform their voice into actions' (which means being able to decide and act for themselves) (Ton, Gaillard, Adamson, Akgungor & Ho, 2019). Beyond the principle of 'full and effective participation and inclusion' underlined by CRPD, empirical evidence supports that including persons with disabilities (even children) in the leadership of disaster management activities reduces their vulnerability, improves the effectiveness of the initiatives, and reduces the impacts of disasters (Njelesani et al., 2012). Shier (2001) proposed five steps of related participation: listen to persons' voice; support them in expressing their views; consider their views; involve them in decision-making processes; and share power and responsibility for decision-making with them.

Working for accessibility

From the rights-based DiDRR perspective, accessibility is the facilitation and access of persons with disabilities in all phases of the management cycle and

176 Mabel Giraldo

related services (UNISDR, 2015). This involves equal physical access (buildings, routes, entrances, transports, emergency shelters or camps, health care facilities, etc.); appropriate methods of communication (visual, audio and interpreters); accessible materials and resources (school programs, educational kits, evacuation plans, manuals, technology, etc.); trained frontline workers, more attentive towards persons with disabilities and their contribution to adaptations and creative solutions.

Assuming an all-stakeholder approach

Related to disability, Jang and Ha (2021) encourage to move from an *individual-stakeholder-based* towards an *all-stakeholder approach*. While in the first perspective, each stakeholder carries out their own task, without coordinating their efforts with other stakeholders, in the all-stakeholders approach, every actor deals with disability inclusion in coordination and collaboration with other stakeholders. Assuming this second approach entails actively engaging at-risk communities (such as persons with disabilities) or their advocacy organisations in the identification, analysis, treatment, monitoring, and evaluation of disaster risks to reduce their vulnerabilities and enhance their capacities (Shaw, 2012).

Ensuring education

The 2021 UN *Resolution* reiterates the *Sendai Framework's* call for the prevention of new and the reduction of existing disaster risk through the implementation of integrated and inclusive educational measures that prevent and reduce exposure and vulnerability to disaster. This goal is generally guaranteed by governmental and non-governmental school-based interventions. As Baxter and Bethke (2009) underline, they concern 'three different types of alternative access programmes: accelerated learning, home-based or community-based schools and education programmes that are partly literacy/numeracy and part skills training' (p. 45). The educational kits for these programmes generally contain, in one easily transportable container, the basic materials (exercise book, pencil, erasers, scissors, chalkboard, chalk) (Penson & Tomlinson, 2009). Moreover, these programmes can carry 'alternative' topics like hygiene, peace education, or civic skills, and can be used in post-conflict situations as well as for educational access for otherwise marginalised children, such as child labourers, children living in remote geographical areas and very poor children. Alongside these experiences, alternative curriculum programmes are developed because the mainstream curriculum is not attempting to respond to the children's perceived needs (Baxter & Bethke, 2009). They generally include a 'preventive programme' (such as HIV and AIDS education) as well as a 'psychosocial programme' designed to 'help overcome negative consequences of conflict or disaster and associated trauma' (Baxter & Bethke, 2009, p. 33) and to modify behaviours according to modern behaviour change approaches (Grizzell, 2007).

Child-Friendly Spaces (CFS) could also play a wider role. By definition, these 'are community programmes to create larger protective environment [as they] are developed with communities to protect children during emergencies through structured learning, play, psychosocial and access to basic services' (Save the Children, 2007, p. 4). CFSs have been created as 'spaces to give children the space to be children' (Penson & Tomlinson, 2009, p. 30).

Restoring the right to play

During disasters play is often given lower priority than the provision of food, shelter, and medicines with a consequent lack of access to play resources. Different governmental institutions and NGOs try to manage this enormous educational problem proposing activities based on play or including play in some way (Giraldo, 2020). Over the years, these experiences have produced a number of materials, documents, operational and methodological proposals (mostly accessible online) aimed at ensuring that all children involved in crisis situations can fully enjoy the aforementioned right to play. Nevertheless, as Giraldo (2020) argued, within humanitarian programmes and research for children in crisis situations play is often subordinated to therapeutic-rehabilitation goals, especially those dedicated to children with disabilities. This may neglect the pure, innate, and intrinsic value of play and playfulness. Therefore, real play-based interventions are needed to ensure the right to play and to restore its intrinsic recreative, instinctive and free expressiveness.

Conclusions

At the intersection of disability and disaster, the issue of human rights becomes muddled and violated, and not enough effort is made in this area, especially regarding children. Due to the exclusion of persons with disabilities in disaster management initiatives, their rights and needs are often unmet resulting in unnecessarily high rates of mortality and morbidity, deterioration of health conditions and loss of autonomy (Njelesani et al., 2012). This tendency could be reversed through using a rights-based approach as a rationale to disaster management initiatives that are rooted in the guiding principles of the CRPD. This chapter has offered some insights into how practitioners can shift their thinking about disaster management towards inclusion and consequently support all children during and after disasters for a better future.

178 Mabel Giraldo

Notes

1 The term 'vulnerability' has been employed to refer directly to disaster. During the past few years, a considerable number of social scientists have renewed interest in the field: Gaillard, Liamzon and Villanueva (2007) and Wisner, Gaillard and Kelman (2012) believe that it is not so much the 'vulnerability of people' (or groups) – which underlines a sort of 'outsider's perspective' (Numans et al., 2021) – but rather the 'vulnerable conditions'. Studies from scholars using the social vulnerability perspective demonstrate that vulnerabilities to disasters emerge from a combination of factors (Phillips et al., 2010) and disability status appears to stretch across these other socially vulnerable categories, leading to a 'layering' of vulnerability factors (Peek & Stough, 2010).
2 For example: the UN Office for Disaster Risk Reduction (UNDRR) for disaster management, the UN Office for the Coordination of Humanitarian Affairs (OCHA) for people with disabilities, the UN Children's Fund (UNICEF) for all children, and others.
3 See: https://hi.org (retrieved: July, 2023).
4 See: https://www.fema.gov (retrieved: July, 2023).
5 DiDRR is about ensuring that persons with disability have the same opportunity to access emergency preparedness information, to participate in emergency preparedness programs in their community, and to be included as a valuable stakeholder in all phases (prevention, preparedness, response, and recovery) of local community disaster risk management (Pertiwi et al., 2019). DiDRR depends on effective cross-sector collaboration between emergency managers and community services and disability support personnel working together with persons with disability, their family, and allies.

References

Alexander, DE (2015). *Disaster and Emergency Planning for Preparedness, Response, and Recovery.* Oxford University Press.

Alexander, DE (2011). Disability and disaster. In: B. Wisner, J.C. Gaillard, I. Kelman (Eds.). *Handbook of Hazards and Disaster Risk Reduction* (pp. 384–394). London, UK: Routledge.

Alexander, DE, & Davis, I (2012). Disaster risk reduction: An alternative viewpoint. *International Journal of Disaster Risk Reduction, 2*, 1–5.

Baxter, P, & Bethke, L (2009). *Alternative Education. Filling the Gap in Emergency and Post-conflict Situations.* Paris: International Institute for Education Planning.

Bongo, PP, Lunga, W, Van Niekerk, D, & Musarurwa, C (2019). Disability and disaster risk reduction as an incongruent matrix: Lessons from rural Zimbabwe. *Jàmbá: Journal of Disaster Risk Studies, 11*(1), 1–7.

Boon, HJ, Brown, LH, Tsey, K, Speare, R, Pagliano, P, Usher, K, & Clark, B. (2011). School Disaster Planning for Children with Disabilities: A Critical Review of the Literature. *International Journal of Special Education, 26*(3), 223–237.

Brittingham, R, & Wachtendorf, T (2013). The effect of situated access on people with disabilities: An examination of sheltering and temporary housing after the 2011 Japan earthquake and tsunami. *Earthquake Spectra, 29*(1_suppl), 433–455.

Clive, A, Davis, EA, Hansen, R, & Mincin, J (2010). Disability. In: B.D. Phillips, D.S.K. Thomas, A. Fothergill, L. Blinn-Pike (Eds.). *Social Vulnerability to Disasters* (pp. 187–216). Boca Raton, FL: CRC Press.

Donovan, A (2017). Geopower: Reflections on the critical geography of disasters. *Progress in Human Geography, 41*(1), 44–67.

Edmonds, CO (2017). Designing emergency preparedness resources for children with autism. *International Journal of Disability, Development and Education, 64*(4), 404–419.

Gaillard, JC, Liamzon, CC, & Villanueva, JD (2007). 'Natural' disaster? A retrospect into the causes of the late-2004 typhoon disaster in Eastern Luzon, Philippines. *Environmental Hazards, 7*(4), 257–270.

Gaillard, JC, & Pangilinan, MLC (2010). Participatory mapping for raising disaster risk awareness among the youth. *Journal of Contingencies & Crisis Management, 18*(3), 175–179.

Giraldo, M (2020). Children with and without disabilities in disasters. A narrative overview of play-based interventions into the humanitarian programmes and research. In: Bulgarelli, D. (Ed.). *Perspectives and Research on Play for Children with Disabilities. Collected papers* (pp. 61–82). Warsaw, PL: De Gruyter.

Grizzell, J (2007). *Behavior Change Theories and Models.* Retrieved from http://www.csupomona.edu/~jvgrizzell/best_practices/bctheory.html

Jang, JH, & Ha, KM (2021). Inclusion of children with disabilities in disaster management. *Children, 8*(7), 581.

Kett, M, & Twigg, J (2007). Disability and disasters: Towards an inclusive approach. In: IFRC, *World Disasters Report. Focus on Discrimination* (pp. 86–111). Geneva, CH: IFRC. Retrieved from: http://www.ifrc.org/Global/Publications/disasters/WDR/WDR2007English.pdf

Kett, M, & van Ommeren, M (2009). Disability, conflict, and emergencies. *The Lancet, 374*(9704), 1801–1803.

Kettaneh, AA, & Slevin, JR (2014). National module for helping individuals with physical disabilities in disaster events. *Journal of Applied Rehabilitation Counseling, 45*(1), 3–10.

Klasing, AM, Moses, PS, & Satterthwaite, ML (2011). Measuring the way forward in Haiti: Grounding disaster relief in the legal framework of human rights. *Health & Hum. Rts., 13*, 15.

Lemyre, L, Gibson, S, Zlepnig, J, Meyer-Macleod, R, & Boutette, P (2009). emergency preparedness for higher risk populations: Psychosocial considerations. *Radiation Protection Dosimetry, 134*(3-4), 207–214.

Njelesani, J, Cleaver, S, Tataryn, M, & Nixon, S (2012). Using a human rights-based approach to disability in disaster management initiatives. *Natural Disasters,* 21–46.

Peek, L, & Stough, L (2010). Children with disabilities in the context of disaster: A social vulnerability perspective. *Society for Research in Child Development, 18*, 1260–1270.

Penson, J, & Tomlinson, K (2009). *Rapid Response Programming for Education Needs in Emergency.* Paris: IIEP.

Pertiwi, P, Llewellyn, G, & Villeneuve, M (2019). Persons with disabilities as key actors in community-based disaster risk reduction. *Disability & Society, 34*(9-10), 1419–1444.

Phillips, BD, Thomas, DSK, Fothergill, A, & Blinn-Pike, L (2010). *Social Vulnerability to Disasters.* Boca Raton, FL: CRC Press.

Reinhardt, JD, Li, J, Gosney, J, Rathore, FA, Haig, AJ, Marx, M, Delisa, J, & International Society of Physical and Rehabilitation Medicine's Sub-Committee on Rehabilitation Disaster Relief(2011). Disability and health-related rehabilitation in international disaster relief. *Global Health Action, 4*(1), 7191.

Ronoh, S, Gaillard, JC, & Marlowe, J (2015). Children with disabilities and disaster risk reduction: A Review. *International Journal of Disaster Risk Science*, *6*(1), 38–48.

Roudini, J, Khankeh, HR, & Witruk, E (2017). Disaster mental health preparedness in the community: A systematic review study. *Health Psychology Open*, *4*(1), 2055102917711307.

Save the Children (2007). *Child Protection in Emergency*. Retrieved from: http://www.refworld.org/docid/47fb94fe2.html

Shier, H (2001). Pathways to participation: Openings, Opportunities and Obligations. *Child. Soc.*, *15*, 107–117.

Shaw, R (Ed.). (2012). *Community Based Disaster Risk Reduction*. Emerald Group Publishing.

Smith, J, Levy, MJ, Hsu, EB, & Levy, JL (2012). Disaster curricula in medical education: Pilot survey. *Prehospital and Disaster Medicine*, *27*(5), 492–494.

Stough, LM, Ducy, EM, Kang, D, & Lee, S (2020). Disasters, schools, and children: Disability at the intersection. *International Journal Of Disaster Risk Reduction*, *45*, 101447.

Stough, LM (2015). World Report on Disability, Intellectual Disabilities, and Disaster Preparedness: Costa Rica as a Case Example. *Journal of Policy and Practice in Intellectual Disabilities*, *12*(2), 138–146.

Stough, LM, Ducy, EM, & Kang, D (2017). Addressing the needs of children with disabilities experiencing disaster or terrorism. *Current Psychiatry Reports*, *19*, 1–10.

Stough, LM, & Kelman, I (2018). People with disabilities and disasters. *Handbook of Disaster Research*, 225–242.

Stough, LM, & Mayhorn, CB (2013). Population segments with disabilities. *International Journal of Mass Emergencies & Disasters*, *31*(3), 384–402.

Stough, LM, & Kang, D (2015). The Sendai framework for disaster risk reduction and persons with disabilities. *International Journal of Disaster Risk Science*, *6*, 140–149.

Tierney, KJ, Petak, WJ, & Hahn, H (1988). *Doubled Persons and Earthquake Hazards*. Colorado, CO: University of Colorado Boulder, Institute of Behavioral Science.

Ton, KT, Gaillard, JC, Adamson, CE, Akgungor, C, & Ho, HT (2019). Expanding the capabilities of people with disabilities in disaster risk reduction. *International Journal of Disaster Risk Reduction*, *34*, 11–17.

Twigg, J, Kett, M, & Lovell, E (2018). Disability inclusion and disaster risk reduction. *Briefing Note* London: Overseas Development Institute.

Twigg, J, Kett, M, Bottomley, H, Tan, LT, & Nasreddin, H (2011). Disability and public shelter in emergencies. *Environmental Hazards*, *10*(3-4), 248–261.

ULSS20 (2007). *Verona Charter on the Rescue of Persons with Disabilities in Case of Disasters*. Retrieved from: www.eena.org/ressource/static/files/Verona%20Charter%20approved.pdf

United Nations (UN) (1989). *Declaration of the Right of the Child*. Retrieved from: http://www.ohchr.org/en/professionalinterest/pages/crc.aspx

United Nations (UN) (2006). *Convention on the Right of the Persons with Disabilities*. Retrieved from: https://www.un.org/development/desa/disabilities/convention-on-the-rights-of-persons-with-disabilities.html

United Nations (UN) (2022). *Resolution 76/204. Disaster risk reduction*. Retrieved from: https://www.undrr.org/publication/disaster-risk-reduction-A-RES-76-204

United Nations (UN) (2019). *Resolution 2475. Protection of Civilians in Armed Conflict*. Retrieved from: http://unscr.com/en/resolutions/2475

UNHRW (2022). *Leave no one behind. People with Disabilities and Older People in Climate-Related Disasters*. Retrieved from: https://www.hrw.org/sites/default/files/media_2022/11/202211drd_global_LeaveNoOneBehind.pdf

UNESCAP (2017). *Disaster resilience for sustainable development: Asia-Pacific disaster report*. Bangkok, Thailand: UNESCAP.

UNICEF (2007). *Bambini e guerra: speciale sul rapporto ONU/UNICEF*. Retrieved from: http://www.unicef.it/flex/cm/pages/ServeBLOB.php/L/IT/IDPagina/3755

UNHCR (2014). *Needs Assessment of Syrian Refugees with Disabilities in Central and West Bekaa, Lebanon*. Retrieved from: www.data.unhcr.org/syrianrefugees/download.php?id=956

UNISDR (2009). *2009 UNISDR terminology on disaster risk reduction*. Geneva: UNISDR.

UNISDR (2015). *Sendai Framework for Disaster Risk Reduction 2015–2030*. Retrieved from:https://www.undrr.org/publication/sendai-framework-disaster-risk-reduction-2015-2030

Villeneuve, M (2022). Disability-Inclusive emergency planning: Person-Centered emergency preparedness. In *Oxford Research Encyclopedia of Global Public Health*.

Wisner, B, Gaillard, JC, & Kelman, I (2012). *Handbook of Hazards and Disaster Risk Reduction*. New York, London: Routledge.

Yeo, R, & Moore, K, (2003). Including disabled people in poverty reduction work: "Nothing about us, without us". *World Development, 31*(3), 571–590.

17

'CHILDREN READING TO THEIR PARENTS' – FROM AUSTRALIA TO ISRAEL – IMPLEMENTATION AND CHALLENGES

Sigal Tish, Sivan Shatil Carmon, and Clodie Tal

Introduction

The practice of encouraging first graders to read regularly to their parents is heavily embedded in English-speaking countries. In many cases this daily literacy practice doesn't have a specific name in English, as it seems to be rooted within deeply shared norms and social behavior within the educational fields. The first researcher had the chance to familiarize herself with this practice as a parent and a teacher in her long stay in South Australia. Following this experience, she initiated the implementation of the practice in Israel. In Israel the implementation of this practice has been included in a program that received the name 'Children Read to Their Parents' (CRTP). Similar to the practice in Australia and other English-speaking countries, the CRTP defines parents' involvement in their first graders' literacy learning as listening daily to their children reading. The aim of the program, beyond promoting the quality of reading, is to promote parents' involvement in their children's learning, children's sense of competence and motivation to read, and creating a community of readers. Shifting the CRTP program from one educational system to another involves numerous challenges that are embedded in teachers' and parents' perceptions related to literacy, literacy learning, children's competencies and parents' and teachers' roles in children's learning. In this chapter, we show how the CRTP program has been gradually implemented in Israeli schools and how it is being perceived by all stakeholders: children, parents, and teachers in one school in which it has been implemented.

DOI: 10.4324/9781003471172-20

The special role of literacy in children's development

Literacy is considered as an increasingly essential condition for full participation and success of individuals in societies today (OECD, 2000). We understand literacy as a situated complex social and cultural practice (Gee, 1990; Lankshear 1994; New London Group, 1996). According to this perception, reading and writing are not 'context-neutral, value-free skills' (de Castell & Luke, 1986, p. 87) that involves only simple skills of decoding. Rather, literacy learning involves social interactions and collaborations which include dialogues and negotiations of meanings. Therefore, language and literacy education must be part of a process that allows children to fully participate in society and involve the development of literate skills of thinking, interpretation, and analysis (Warschauer, 1997).

Research highlights the critical importance of developing literacy skills from birth to the age of 6 to children's development and social mobility (ERI, 2019). According to the 'Knowledge Map'[1] this is 'critical' from birth to the age of 6, and 'very important' from the first to the third year in Elementary school in order to create conditions for children's optimal development and social mobility (ERI, 2019).

Children Agency

According to the OECD, when children play an active role in their learning, they tend to show greater motivation to learn, they are more likely to define objectives for their learning, and they are more likely to become lifelong learners (OECD, 2019). Agency is commonly understood as the capacity of an individual to choose, act, and influence matters in their everyday lives (e.g., Houen et al., 2016; James & James 2012; Mentha, Church & Page, 2015). Yet, as Sirkko, Kyrönlampi, and Puroila (2019) point out, 'children's agency cannot be explored as an inner feature of individual children because ideas about children's agency are tightly connected to moral and political ideas about what kinds of agency are appropriate for children in specific cultural contexts'. Houen et al. (2016) suggest that teachers create spaces for children's agency.

In the program CRTP, children's agency is reflected in their choice of books and in the central component of the program related to the fact that the children do the reading and the parents do the listening.

Parent involvement

The key role of parents in the literacy development of their children has long been recognized in numerous research studies in promoting children's success in school (Baker & Scher, 2002; Weigel, Martin & Bennett, 2006; OECD, 2009). In addition, it was found that parental engagement in children's

184 Sigal Tish et al.

learning at home makes the greatest difference to students' achievement (Harris & Goodall, 2008). Furthermore, in the first year of schooling, parents' involvement in reading acquisition promotes children's academic achievements and their motivation for reading (Hewison & Tizard, 1980; OECD, 2011). Research claims that children's motivation to learn is a crucial factor that affects the learning process and its outcomes (Nevo & Vaknin-Nusbaum, 2020; Tolchinsky, 2008;). Therefore, first grade becomes a critical time not only for reading acquisition but also for building motivation that contributes to reading development (Bates, D'Agostino, Gambrell & Xu, 2016).

A close relationship was found between parental involvement in literacy activities in first grade and better performance in reading tests at the age of 15. According to the OECD (2011): 'In this sense, student learning is most effective when it is the result of a partnership among the school, teachers, parents and the community' (OECD, 2012, p. 13). Nonetheless, the role of parents is a complex issue, and parents' involvement is always difficult to promote and maintain (LaRocque, Kleiman & Darling, 2011) as it is embedded in a complex web of local and global networks and is shaped by politics and power relations within the field of education. In his 'Theory of practice', Bourdieu (1991) uses the metaphor of a game to define 'field'. According to Bourdieu field is 'a kind of arena in which people play a game which has certain rules' (p. 215). Bourdieu stresses that fields are 'always sites of struggle' (Thompson, 1991, quoted in Bourdieu, 1991, p. 14) and power relations where different individuals seek to preserve the status quo or to change it, depending on where they are located in the structured positions of the specific field. According to Bourdieu's theory of practice, the social acts of parents as agents in the field of education must be viewed in relation to the context of the educational field, which is embedded in a larger field of power of a given society.

It seems that the Israeli Ministry of Education acknowledges the importance of parents' involvement as it is stated in official literacy programs: 'The parents are important and central partners in young children's learning in grades 1-2. [Therefore] It is important to engage them in their children's experiential and meaningful learning' (Ministry of Education, 2014). In addition, in the first-grade curriculum, there is a reminder of the importance of the relationship with the parents as well as a recommendation to encourage the parents to read to their children (Ministry of Education, 2019). Nevertheless, in Israel there are no official guidelines or systematic programs that guide parents' involvement in their children's learning to read.

Literacy learning in the first grade in Israel

In education systems around the world, school entry is considered a significant step, causing both stress and stimulation (Griebel & Niesel, 2006). It brings children and their families into contact with a host of new environments, demands and relationships (Duncan et al., 2007). Moreover, reading, which is formally learned from first grade, is one of the critical skills for children's success in school and life, for personal and social empowerment, and for social mobility (Dickinson, Griffith, Golinkoff & Hirsh-Pasek, 2012).

Israeli children begin school at the age of six. The children study six days a week from 8 am to 1 pm (some children also attend after-school programs). Classrooms in Israel are very crowded including approximately 30–35 children. The classes are heterogeneous in terms of children's literacy experience and proficiency in reading. There is one class teacher heading each classroom, and she holds the responsibility for the academic learning and for the emotional and social well-being of the children in her class. The main expectation is that all children will become skilled and independent readers of written texts during the first grade.

Since its inception the education system in Israel has produced programs to regulate the teaching of reading and writing in either Hebrew or Arabic. The main schooled literacy practice consists of exercise books which are based mostly on phonics-texts. Typically, children learn using these workbooks during the school day as part of the class reading program and are also given homework in these workbooks. The expectation is that children will work on their homework independently. Parents are encouraged to assist their children only if necessary and are encouraged to read to their children children's books.

'Children read to their parents' (CRTP) – The program

The practice of encouraging children to read daily to their parents is well established in many English-speaking countries and is based on a method developed in New Zealand by Marie Clay. In its current version, this practice creates a daily routine in which parents listen and scaffold their first graders reading aloud. In the CRTP program, children have a central role as active learners who learn to read by reading and building their own reading skills and stamina. They are simultaneously building their word recognition, fluency, vocabulary, and text-dependent comprehension skills.

The books included in the program engage children in experimentation of reading without having to be bound to phonological acquisition, which is supported by scaffolding using clear illustrations of newly introduced words, repetitions and more. The books deal with diverse subjects, are colorful, funny and include a developing plot which may interest the children. Reading at home as part of the implementation of the program is accompanied by a reading diary that includes both parents' and children's record of the children's daily reading.

In the CRTP program parents have to adopt a daily, structured role, and they are expected to be involved in a meaningful way in their children's literacy learning in the first year of schooling. Children are encouraged to take an active role in the program, and teachers are expected to be the administrators.

186 Sigal Tish et al.

This means that the schools become facilitators and promoters of reading routines established at home.

It is important to emphasize that such a program is new in the Israeli context both in terms of the role of parents and children, and in terms of the structure and content of the books that are given to children to read in first grade. The program brings about changes in the status quo of the Israeli field of education in relation to parents', teachers' and children's roles in learning to read. For about five years, the three authors of this chapter have been involved in the gradual implementation of the program in Israel.

Implementation of the CRTP program in Israel

Shifting educational programs from one sociocultural context to another involves numerous challenges. According to Luke (2011), implementing new policies requires deep consideration of matters of culture and ideology and coping with complexities across real and imagined borders. These are reflected also in teachers' and parents' perceptions of what reading is about and what the role of children, parents and teachers is in the process of learning to read. As mentioned before, the teaching methods of reading in the first grade in Israel are mostly focused on phonics with almost no references to the social-emotional aspect of reading and deep meaning of texts. In addition, parents are not attributed a defined role in the enhancement of reading of their first-grade children. That means that implementing the program CRTP requires changes in parents' and teachers' perceptions of literacy and of what it means to be literate, of the meaning of literacy learning, and of what parents' and teachers' roles are in its enhancement. In addition, CRTP constitutes a supplementary element included in the mainstream first-grade reading curriculum, which means an extra effort for the teachers.

Since there had not been any program of this kind in Israel before, we had to first name it. Naming the program made the practice visible in the Israeli educational field, assisted in the communication about the program and delivered the main concept of the program to all partners. The implementation process of the CRTP program in Israel includes four stages (Figure 17.1). In this chapter we will mainly focus on the first and second stages (2019–2022).

Stage 1 – Pilot Study

In the first year of the implementation of the program, we initiated a pilot that included meeting with several experts and policy-makers in order to refine and clarify how best to implement the program in Israel. The pilot study was supported by MAHUT[2], and connection was made with ERA books, an Australian publisher, who gave its permission to translate three books of the program into Hebrew for the Israeli pilot.

Children reading to their parents

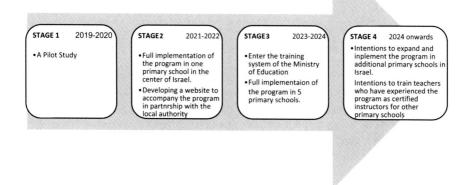

FIGURE 17.1 The sequence of the four stages of the program implementation. Image created by the authors.

As part of the pilot study, we interviewed parents and teachers of Israeli first graders and made an inquiry into their view about home literacy practices, teaching of reading, and the role of parents and teachers in the children's reading. In addition, we introduced the CRTP program to a small group of parents and teachers and asked them to share their opinion of the program and its necessity in Israel. It is important to note that the study was conducted shortly before the outbreak of the COVID-19 epidemic and its beginning stages in Israel. During this time the role of parents was shaped differently, and parents were required to be more involved in mediating learning for their children. This period challenged taken-for-granted beliefs about parents' roles in children's learning.

Data analysis showed that all parents were aware of the importance of their role in promoting their children's literacy. All parents stated that their role in their children's learning to read is 'very important' or 'important'. There were no parents who claimed that their role was not important.

A number of parents criticized the way reading is being taught in Israeli schools. For example, one of the mothers complained that schools in Israel teach reading as a technical skill as opposed to teaching reading in a way that is aligned with 21st-century skills:

> …If a child knows how to pronounce the vowels, then for the school, he probably knows how to read… Now there is no connection between all these technical functions that a school knows how to deliver, and between what we, as parents or in general as a society should expect the children to achieve… I mean, talking about the 21st century skills… Learning to read at school is very technical and very functional and that way I think they miss out.

188 Sigal Tish et al.

Overall, data analysis from the pilot study showed that there is a need for a program that motivates children to read and that includes parents as partners. In addition, we found that parents are willing to take part in their children's learning to read.

Stage 2 – Full implementation in one school

Following the pilot study, we have translated another 50 books from English into Hebrew. In addition, the program was recognized and funded by 'HAMMOP'[3]. Recognition of the program by the Research and Development Division allowed us to implement the program in one state school for two years. The implementation of the program was accompanied by evaluation research that was supported by MAHUT[4].

The main goals of the program were presented to the school principal and the four first-grade teachers of a school in a city in the center of Israel: promoting the quality of reading and reading motivation of first graders with the involvement of parents. The teachers were enthusiastic about the books included in the program but expressed concerns about the parents' reluctance to be involved, and about the children's ability to read texts containing all the vowels in the first stages of learning to read.

We began the implementation of stage 2 with all first graders in the school (120 children), their parents and the four teachers. Our main goal was to mediate the program's key principles to the parents, teachers and children: the importance of parents' role in children's learning to read; the importance of children's active role in their own learning, and understanding literacy in its wide sense. Figure 17.2 shows the activities done by the researchers throughout the school year.

The evaluation of the program was based on a mixed methods methodology. The participants were 45 parents, 30 children, and four teachers. Questionnaires were administered to all parents before and after children's participation in the program. In-depth interviews were performed with six parents and the four first-grade teachers in the school. In addition, in-depth conversations with 30 children took place at the beginning and at the end of the school year. Furthermore, occasional videos sent by parents, WhatsApp correspondence with parents and transcripts of discussions with the children were analyzed. We analyzed the data all through the first and second years of implementation and developed the program according to the findings extracted from the analysis of data. In the following section we will discuss the achievements and challenges of the program.

Achievements

During the two years of implementation, children, parents and teachers took an active role in the program. During these years a new path of connection between all partners was created related to reading and literacy. Reading took a

Children reading to their parents **189**

> **Teachers**
> - **Regular face to face meetings throughout the year-** The team have met with the teachers once every fortnight. In these meetings we discussed and specified the programs' aims, rationale and teachers' difficulties and challenges.
> - **Assistance** with challanges of individual children and parents.
> - **Special in-class literacy activities** -we have planned together with the teachers special literacy activities related to the program which took place within the classroom.

> **Parents**
> - **Meeting at the beginning of the year** -As the year began, we gathered all the first graders parents for a special meeting. In this meeting we emphasized the great importance of their role in the literacy development of their children in the first year of schooling. In addition, we introduced the new program and its rationale.
> - **Written Instructions in the reading journal** in which they write daily with their children - In the program's children reading journal we addressed the parents and outlined the rationale of the program, and recommendations for ways of working with the children.
> - **Digital messages every forthnight** -digital messages via WhatsApp were sent every fortnight to the parents with encouragements and instructions for the reading sessions with their children.
> - **Encouragement to share videos - children reading sessions at home-** In order to stay in touch with the parents we asked them to share with us short videos of the reading sessions at home. The teachers and the team received a lot of videos from the parents and we responded in encouraging and guiding the parents and the children.

> **Children**
> - **Conversations with the children** every fortnight for the first two months – The team entered the classrooms on several occasions and talked in a dialogic way with the children. The conversations focused on: the great knowledge they already have about reading and how capable they are to read independently with a little help of their parents, the importance of reading in our lives, the importance of practicing in order to be better in what we do, and ways they can use to remind themselves and their parents to read daily.
> - **Small group discussions** with the children about their experiences and challenges in reading and with relation to the program. In cases that we noticed that children experience difficulties in participating in the program we shared the information with the teacher and parents.

FIGURE 17.2   Chart of the activities included in the implementation of the program. Image created by the authors.

more central place in the classroom discourse, and a community of readers was created in which children played an active role in their learning to read. Most of the first graders borrowed the books included in the program regularly and read them at home to their parents every day. Many of the parents and children also filled reading journals daily and took part in different literacy activities.

Acknowledgment of the parents' key role in children's learning to read

Although teachers were skeptic about parents' motivation to be involved in their children's learning, we found that parents were aware of the importance of their role in nurturing their children's learning to read. Most of the parents (96%) stated in the pre- and post-questionnaire that it is important for them to assist their first graders to learn to read.

We have learned from the conversations with the children that parents had an important role in the program as they provided their children with emotional and cognitive support. For example, Alona stated: 'I learned how to read from my mother and from the teacher - the teacher taught me how to read the vowels and my mother helped me to improve'. Alona attributes her improvement in reading to her daily work with her mother. Tehal describes the emotional contribution of parents' involvement: 'My mother wrote to me in the reading journal: I'm proud of you …'.

The teachers also addressed the parents' important role in their children learning to read. For example, one of the teachers commented: 'You can't do it alone at school (teaching reading and writing). The children need that extra space at home too' (Michela). Another teacher emphasized the importance of the parents' role in addition to the teachers' work in class: 'The children loved the books; I see the program as complementary to the process done in class. It completes the whole part of the language, the experience and the pleasure of reading books'.

Increasing the children's self-confidence and sense of competence

The children's responses in the conversations with them showed that the program promoted their self-confidence and self-efficacy related to reading. For example, Yuli, felt that the books were 'easy' to read: 'The books are beautiful and easy to read'. Tahel noted that she felt how she improved as she kept reading: 'I kept getting better and better…' David argued that the books included in the program allow children to feel confident about their performance: 'tell the children: open the first page … then the child will see how smart he is and that he can read'.

From the parents' point of view, 75% of the parents stated that the program resulted in an increase in the children's motivation to read. For example: 'the program contributes to the child's confidence and to his desire to read'; 'the program made the child to devote himself to reading and to show us that he can'. As noted above, we also corresponded with parents via WhatsApp encouraging them to share with us their experiences with the program:

> Maor and Ohad are searching for books to borrow in the library and Maor says that he will try to read by himself like the books from school. This is the great influence of the project and it is great fun. Experiences of success.
>
> *(Maor's mother, 2021)*

> Noam enjoys reading and very committed to the program. There is no chance in the world that we will miss a day because it's really important to him. There is a significant improvement in reading. And most importantly, even when he brings a new book he insists on reading and has a lot of self- confidence.
>
> *(Noam's mother, 2021)*

Challenges

During the first year of implementation, we encountered a number of challenges some of which we tried to address in the second year. We identified two main general challenges: teachers' perceptions related to what it means to learn to read, and the high work load associated with the implementation of the program.

Teachers' beliefs about what promotes children's learning to read affected the success of the program. A narrow view of literacy (based primarily on phonetics) may lead teachers to focus on a 'context-neutral, value-free skills' curriculum (de Castell and Luke 1986, p. 87). This view also affects perceptions about parents' and teachers' roles in children's learning to read and leads to a perception that the work of teaching reading should be done only by professionals (meaning teachers) and leave parents out and disengaged. Therefore, in all our meetings with the teachers we discussed literacy in its broader sense and emphasized the important role of parents in children's literacy learning and the importance of collaboration between parents and teachers.

We found that although the program is mainly conducted at home, it is essential that the teachers dedicate time to various activities related to the program within the classroom in order to promote children's responsibility and motivation to read. Indeed, it seems that first-grade teachers in Israel suffer from a very high workload. In addition to the fact that the teachers are responsible for the learning, (reading and math) development and mental health of 35 children in their classroom, they have to coordinate the implementation of numerous extra-curricular programs that the school principals add to their daily class activities which, despite the good intentions, create congestion and sometimes confusion. Therefore, there is a high need to be selective about the choice of extra-curricular programs and to prioritize them in addition to consulting with the teachers about their preferences. The challenges discussed above require thorough and in-depth systematic work. In addition, there were other challenges that we managed to address in the second year of implementation. These are detailed in Table 17.1.

Although in the pilot study teachers expressed concerns related to parents' readiness to commit themselves and cooperate with the program, the parents showed full cooperation and actively participated in the program. The findings show that participation in the program CRTP helped parents establish reading routines at home and made them become aware of the importance of their involvement in their children's learning and in reading aloud as a useful practice contributing to their children learning to read.

The children enjoyed the books, became independent readers and attributed their reading to both parents and teachers. Some children showed

192 Sigal Tish et al.

TABLE 17.1 Challenges and ways of coping. Created by the authors.

First year – challenges	Second year – ways of coping
The borrowing process for 35 children is long and complex. Making the program visible to keep teachers, children and parents motivated to engage in the program.	Connecting the program to the main school library system for easier digital borrowing. • Integration of the program's books into the morning-reading routine (Figure 17.3). • Organizing special activities related to reading to parents such as: 'The Reader in the Mask' – Where parents videotape the children reading the program's books wearing a mask for the other children to guess who is the reader. 'Writing like adults' – Inspired by the program's books, the children wrote their own stories with only a slight change in the characters or plot (Figure 17.4). The parents joined in the activity by taking pictures of the children which later became the illustrations of the book. In the first year the team was the initiator of these activities; however, in the second year the teachers were the initiators.
Writing in the Reading-Diary was time-consuming and inconvenient for some parents.	Creating a designated website which created a unique platform for the reading program and regulated the communication between teachers, parents and children (Figure 17.5).

FIGURE 17.3 Children's routine morning reading activity. Image created but the authors. Image created by the authors.

Children reading to their parents **193**

FIGURE 17.4 'Writing like adults' project – The King's Slippers became: Noam and Lavi's Slippers. Image created by the authors.

FIGURE 17.5 Designated website. Image created by the authors.

creativity following their participation in the program expressed in their initiative of writing their own books. In addition, participating in the program had a positive impact on the children's feelings of self-efficacy and on their motivation to read.

We found that there is a need to guide Israeli teachers to adopt a more constructivist perception of learning, to attribute to children an active role in their learning and to allow and encourage parents to participate in their children's learning.

In conclusion, early literacy learning can be described as a process of negotiated power relations between institutions and families. This program aims to strengthen the position of parents in the literacy learning of their first graders. We believe that the program supports the creation and development of a literate community that includes parents, children and teachers and may continue beyond the first year of schooling.

Notes

1 Knowledge Map – The mapping is based on large-scale applied research. It shows the recommended foci of educational investment at various ages in order to create necessary conditions for social mobility from birth to age 35, both on the individual's level and in the ecosystem – family, school, neighborhood and community.
2 MAHUT – 'The Center for information, research and development in the field of family and the education system communication'.
3 HAMMOP – The Research and Development Division of the Israeli Ministry of Education.
4 MAHUT – 'The Center for information, research and development in the field of family and the education system communication'

References

Baker, L, & Scher, D (2002). Beginning readers' motivation for reading in relation to parental beliefs and home reading experiences. *Reading Psychology, 23*(4), 239–269. https://doi.org/10.1080/713775283

Bates, CC, D'Agostino, JV, Gambrell, L, & Xu, M (2016). Reading recovery: Exploring the effects on first-graders' reading motivation and achievement. *Journal of Education for Students Placed at Risk (JESPAR), 21*(1), 47–59, DOI:10.1080/10824669.2015.1110027

Bourdieu, P (1991). *Language and Symbolic Power* (J.B. Thompson, Ed., G. Raymond & M. Adamson, Trans.). Cambridge: Polity Press in association with Basil Blackwell.

de Castell, S, & Luke, A (1986). Models of literacy in North American schools: Social and historical conditions and consequences. In. S. de Castell, A. Luke & K. Egan (Eds.), *Literacy, Society, and Schooling*, New York: Cambridge University Press.

Dickinson, DK, Griffith, J, Golinkoff, RM, & Hirsh-Pasek, K (2012). How reading books fosters language development around the world. *Child Development Research, 2012*, 1–15.

Duncan, GJ, Dowsett, CJ, Claessens, A, Magnuson, K, Huston, AC, Klebanov, P, & Japel, C (2007). School readiness and later achievement. *Developmental Psychology, 43*(6), 1428–1446.

ERI (2019). *The Knowledge Map-Advancing Social Mobility*. The Rashi Foundation, JDC-Ashalim, Jindas – The Association for Social Urban Regeneration, and the Ministry of Welfare. Retrieved from: https://socialmobility.org.il/en/%d7%a2%d7%9e%d7%95%d7%93-%d7%94%d7%91%d7%99%d7%aa-english/

Gee, JP (1990). *Social Linguistics and Literacies: Ideology in Discourses*. London: Falmer Press.

Griebel, W, & Niesel, R (2006). Co-constructing transition into kindergarten and school by children, parents and teachers. In H. Fabian & W.A. Dunlop (Eds.), *Transitions in the Early Years: Debating Continuity and Progression for Children in Early Education* (3rd ed., pp. 64–75). London: Routledge Falmer

Harris, A, & Goodall, J (2008). Do parents know they matter? Engaging all parents in learning. *Educational Research, 50*(3), 277–289, DOI:10.1080/00131880802309424

Hewison, J, & Tizard, J (1980). Parental involvement and reading attainment. *British Journal for Educational Psychology, 50*(3), 209–215.

Houen, S, Danby, S, Farrell, A, & Thorpe, K (2016). Creating spaces for children's agency: 'I Wonder ...' formulations in Teacher–Child interactions. *International Journal of Early Childhood, 48*(3), 259–276.

James, J, & James, A (2012). *Key Concepts in Childhood Studies.* London: Sage Publications.

Lankshear, C (1994). *Critical Literacy* (Occasional Paper No. 3). Belconnen, Australian Capital Territory: Australian Curriculum Studies Association.

LaRocque, M, Kleiman, I, & Darling, SM (2011). Parental involvement: The missing link in school achievement. *Preventing School Failure, 55*(3), 115–122. Taylor & Francis Group. ISSN: 1045-988X print. DOI:10.1080/10459880903472876

Luke, A (2011). Generalizing across borders. *Educational Researcher, 40*(8), 367–377.

Mentha, S, Church, A, & Page, J (2015). Teachers as brokers: Perceptions of 'Participation' and agency in early childhood. *International Journal of Children's Rights, 23*, 622–637.

Ministry of Education (2014). *Teaching plan for assimilation of the Hebrew language goals in grades 1-2.* Retrieved from: https://meyda.education.gov.il/files/olim/hatmatyeadeyhebrew.pdf

Ministry of Education (2019). *ALEF TECHILLA-Smoothing the transition from kindergarten to school.* Retrieved from: https://meyda.education.gov.il/files/yesodi/alon/alon33/kita_a.pdf

Nevo, E, & Vaknin-Nusbaum, V (2020). Enhancing motivation to read and reading abilities in first grade. *Educational Psychology, 40*(1), 22–41.

New London Group (1996). A pedagogy of multiliteracies: Designing social futures. *Harvard Educational Review, 66*(1), 60–93.

OECD (2009). *PISA 2009 Assessment Framework-Key Competencies in Reading, Mathematics and Science.* Retrieved from: https://www.oecd-ilibrary.org/education/pisa-2009-assessment-framework_9789264062658-en

OECD (2019). *Conceptual learning framework-Student agency for 2030. OECD Future of Education and Skills 2030.* Retrieved from: https://www.oecd.org/education/2030-project/teaching-and-learning/learning/student-agency/Student_Agency_for_2030_concept_note.pdf

OECD (2011). *What can parents do to help their children succeed in school? PISA IN FOCUS 2011/10.OECD Publication.* Retrieved from: https://www.oecd.org/pisa/49012097.pdf

OECD (2012). *Let's Read Them a Story! The Parent Factor in Education, PISA, OECD Publishing.* Retrieved from: http://dx.doi.org/10.1787/9789264176232-en

OECD (2000). Measuring Student Knowledge and Skills-The PISA 2000 assessment of reading, mathematical and scientific. *Education and Skill.* https://www.oecd-ilibrary.org/docserver/9789264181564-en.pdf?expires=1698733113&id=id&accname=guest&checksum=B5B660D9C70D2EBAAE1EF7E5E0D2D4C6

Sirkko, R, Kyrönlampi, T, & Puroila, AM (2019). Children's agency: Opportunities and constraints. *International Journal of Early Childhood 51*, 283–300. doi:https://doi.org/10.1007/s13158-019-00252-

Tolchinsky, L (2008). Teachers on a crossroads. *BAMICHLALA The College Voice*, vol. 20, pp. 29–39. Jerusalem: The David Yellin Academic College of Education.

Warschauer, M (1997). A sociocultural approach to literacy and its significance for CALL. In K. Murphy-Judy & R. Sanders (Eds.), *Nexus: The Convergence of*

Research & Teaching through New Information Technologies (pp. 88–97). Durham: University of North Carolina.

Weigel, DJ, Martin, S, & Bennett, K, (2006). Contributions of the home literacy environment to preschool-aged children's emerging literacy and language skills. *Early Child Development and Care*, *176*(3-4), 357–378. DOI:10.1080/03004430500063747

PART IV

More than Education and Care: Philosophical Perspectives on Early Childhood Practice

18
THE NEED FOR DIFFERENT WAYS OF THINKING

Ute Ward

Previous chapters have already given a range of ideas about what could be done differently in ECEC practice, for example, when exploring a range of workforce and training issues or when discussing pedagogical approaches. This final section is trying to gain a different perspective on some of the important issues in ECEC by using philosophical lenses. Here, even more so than in the other sections, it is evident that the themes running through the book are entangled, as are the topics addressed in the different chapters. The chapters you will find in this section are still concerned with inclusion and social justice, neoliberal pressures and preparing for future challenges. However, in line with the fourth theme of the book, sustainability and posthumanism form the core tenet of this section.

Considering the scale of the challenges we – humankind – are facing in the 21st century, we need a fundamental re-think of our values, our position in this world and our interrelationship with animals and other living beings, now often referred to as more-than-humans (for example, Murris, 2016). Over the centuries human beings have, sometimes thoughtlessly and sometimes deliberately, used and squandered the natural resources in our environment. In doing so, we have severely impacted the natural world, to the extent that the geological epoch we live in is now labelled as the Anthropocene (National Geographic Society, n.d.) to indicate that human beings are the main shapers of the world around us. However, human beings are doing more than shaping; they have wreaked havoc in the natural world, and across the globe we are now confronted with the long-term effects of our exploitative behaviour. Some of these effects are rising temperatures, melting glaciers, unprecedented floods and ferocious wildfires. Much of the underpinning reasoning for this

DOI: 10.4324/9781003471172-22

behaviour rests on 17th- and 18th-century ideas in the Western world of the superiority of scientific methods, rationality and positivism, and to some degree also of white supremacy and male dominance. Some of these ideas are perpetuated and reinforced by neoliberal thinking in the 20th and early 21st centuries, which favours individual responsibility, standards, assessment, accountability and, above all, economic profit.

In contrast, posthumanism tries to establish different discourses. Thinkers like Karen Barad and Karin Murris present a more complex worldview which embraces uncertainty, situated knowledge, experience and diverse ways of knowing (Barad, 2003; Murris, 2020). Most importantly, they no longer cast humans as supreme beings but as one life form amongst many other, more-than-human fellow beings. This entails a shift away from using natural resources exclusively for our own benefit to preserving or renewing them for all life on the planet. It invites the serious commitment to sustainability so that the generations after us will find an environment in which they and more-than-humans can survive, co-exist and prosper.

Overcoming the dominant discourse is not easy but, focusing on the field of early childhood education, Moss (2017) urges us to do just that and open the doors to different ways of thinking and to alternative stories and narratives that embrace democracy and social justice as core values. Arising out of feminist environmental humanities, there is now a call for common world pedagogies which are no longer human-centric but acknowledge the multispecies environments we live in. These give rise to ways of learning that emphasise collective-ness rather than individual child pedagogies and position human beings as part of a wider ecological system (Taylor & Pacini-Ketchabaw, 2015).

The first two chapters in this final section focus specifically on these issues. In Chapter 19 Mehmet Mart advocates for children learning outdoors while he makes the distinction between learning in and from nature. His approach is firmly embedded in posthumanist thinking, and he rejects the engagement with nature purely to observe and categorise, that is to say, objectify it. His starting point for theorising children's position in the world is Bronfenbrenner's bio-ecological framework although this does not mean that the child holds a superior position in the world or should be the centre of attention. It merely serves to help us understand the different influences on children, their development and learning.

In the following chapter, Sally Brown showcases a research project she undertook with a four-year-old boy and his family in the USA. The detailed descriptions of observed activities and interactions give a valuable insight into how the posthumanist lens can make deep learning visible. At the same time, the interconnectedness of the child with his social environment (immediate and extended families), his physical environment and the materials at his disposal is meticulously documented, and the author charts his complex thought processes and developing an understanding of the world around him.

Interestingly, he uses an iPad and watches a webinar to extend his play and learning. This is a reminder of what was discussed in the earlier chapter by Naomi Hodgson and Stefan Ramaekers (Chapter 5) on raising children in a digital age. Here it becomes clear that digital tools are just one element in the range of resources and materials used for learning. The parents in Sally Brown's research present a thoughtful approach to the use of digital tools. On the one hand, their son is allowed access to an iPad only for a restricted amount of time each day; on the other hand, digital technology enables parents and children to stay in touch with extended family members living in different countries.

In Chapter 21, Poppie Ephgrave leads us from the immediate engagement with posthumanist ideas to the philosophies of bell hooks and Paulo Freire. Her chapter considers the value of dialogue in early childhood settings and the pivotal role of experience within dialogue. Using Freire's and hooks' ideas as lenses, she reflects on the use of language in the English Early Years Foundation Stage framework (Department for Education, 2023) and on its approach to social justice. She examines and attempts to disrupt the dominant discourse in ECEC, which often unquestioningly accepts white, male ideas as the norm. Equally, she considers the situation of children whose first language is not English and the emphasis on supporting the acquisition of English while nominally valuing the child's home language. Interestingly, she emphasises that reflection on its own is not sufficient. In line with Freire's writing, she calls for praxis, by which he means action and reflection, providing a further indication of the important role of the practitioner and our potential scope to affect change in ECEC practice and policy.

The final chapter, by Liz Rouse from Australia, offers a further perspective on how a different philosophy or worldview may be employed to develop a pedagogy that is more supportive of children. She critiques the neoliberal image of children as future economic citizens and encourages us to use other indicators for children's prosperity. Returning to early educational pioneers like Fröbel, she argues that the aim of education should be the development of the self – including body, mind, feelings, aesthetics, morality, imagination and more. This leads her to propose a pedagogical approach which focuses on the spiritual and stresses relationality and connectedness, which links her comments to the other chapters in this section. As the author promotes playfulness as an element of a spiritual pedagogy, you will find further connections here to the earlier discussions of play (for example, in Chapter 19) and imagination (in Chapter 15 by Sue Nimmo), as well as parallels to Sally Brown's descriptions of entanglements in Lego play and gardening (Chapter 20).

The concepts and ideas presented in this section and the previous sections will be discussed in the concluding chapter. In addition to a summary of the main options for change, there will be a consideration of what we as individuals and professionals working with and for children can do to move from the difficult times we find ourselves in towards a better future.

References

Barad, K (2003). Posthumanist performativity: Towards an understanding of how matter comes to matter. *Signs: Journal of Women in Culture and Society*, *28*(3), 801–831. https://www.jstor.org/stable/10.1086/345321

Department for Education (2023). *Statutory Framework for the Early Years Foundation Stage*. London: Crown Copyright. Retrieved from: https://assets.publishing. service.gov.uk/government/uploads/system/uploads/attachment_data/file/1170108/EYFS_framework_from_September_2023.pdf

Moss, P (2017). Power and resistance in early childhood education: From dominant discourse to democratic experimentalism. *Journal of Pedagogy*, *8*(1), 11–32.

Murris, K (2020). Posthuman child and the diffractive teacher: Decolonizing the nature/culture binary. *Research Handbook on Childhoodnature: Assemblages of Childhood and Nature Research*, 31–55.

Murris, K (2016). *The Posthuman Child: Educational Transformation through Philosophy with Picturebooks*. London: Routledge.

National Geographic Society (n.d.). Anthropocene. In *National Geographic Encyclopedic Entry*. Retrieved from: https://education.nationalgeographic.org/resource/anthropocene/

Taylor, A, & Pacini-Ketchabaw, V (2015). Learning with children, ants and worms in the anthropocene: Towards a common world pedagogy of multispecies vulnerability. *Pedagogy, Culture and Society*.

19

LEARNING IN AND FROM NATURE

Supporting Children's Development

Mehmet Mart

Introduction

During outdoor activities, children have the freedom to shape circumstances and maintain their interest regarding their values (Mart & Waite, 2021), and learning entails the production of new ideas which enable us to comprehend the world from another perspective (Edwards, 2017). This is possible because environmental education starts with having pre-designed architectural surroundings and designs for children instead of assuming children's dispositions are sufficient to provide them with relationships between the environment and themselves (Rotas, 2019). In this case, previous research underlines the intrinsic connection between children and nature which encourages them to be active (Ward, 2018). It is important to identify children's role within the surroundings. To develop intellectually, emotionally, socially and morally, the child requires active participation in progressively more complex interactions with persons, objects and symbols in their immediate environment (Murphy, 2020). This is a focus of the bio-ecological theory of Urie Bronfenbrenner (Bronfenbrenner, 2005) which positions the child in the middle of the ecosystem. From the post-humanism perspective, nature is also seen as a place for people to be free from social regulations (Quinn, 2013), therefore incorporating post-human and/or more-than-human frameworks in early years and early childhood education is an important and timely progression (Rotas, 2019). This chapter will discuss bio-ecological and other theories focusing on the impact of environment, nature as a key, and roles in nature-related activities of children.

DOI: 10.4324/9781003471172-23

The Impact of Environment

As there is a relationship between a person and the environment (Eriksson, Ghazinour and Hammarström, 2018), learning outcomes can be different outside because it offers various experiences not available to indoor learning (O'Brien, 2009). Having such opportunities to develop relations is essential for individuals so that they can actively engage in nature-based areas to enlarge their involvement in an environment (Murphy, 2020). This engagement with nature results in healthier development compared to children learning inside (Kuo, Barnes and Jordan, 2019).

Furthermore, Bronfenbrenner underlines how the larger contexts change over time, which again are interrelated with the child, their development, and the conditions that support them, as well as the changes that happen over time in the child themself. All of these factors have their impacts on the surroundings (Sadownik, 2023). As Murphy (2020) visualised in her paper, the child is in the middle of nested spheres and is affected by their surroundings, namely, their experiences of nature at home, nature-based pedagogy in school, opportunities to engage with nature in the lived environment, heritage and history of nature in culture, and changes in access to nature over time. This is explained by Murphy (2020) in order to represent the impact of the environment on children in terms of Bronfenbrenner's bio-ecological framework. The most immediate impact is based on the experience of nature at home, followed by nature-based pedagogy in school. Bronfenbrenner placed the child at the centre of his theory of human development and intended to illustrate that the child is profoundly affected by their environment; it also emphasises the child's agency and potential influence (Sadownik, 2023). As children are active participants in society, there are likely to be various learning processes for children while interacting with their environments (Speldewinde & Campbell, 2022) as well as various perspectives on children's learning and development in addition to exploring the play-based opportunities in nature (Dockett & Perry, 2010). Therefore, Bronfenbrenner's approach can be related to children's more active participation in their environment and in their own development. For example, by climbing on fallen trees, boulder scrambling, and creek splashing, they become more aware of their capabilities and limitations (Sobel, 2016), which is essential for them to extend their development by learning in and from nature.

In addition, Almers, Askerlund, Samuelsson and Waite (2020) mention considering the impact of the natural environment during the design of outdoor grounds to improve the outcomes for children's engagement with nature, opportunities, and break options as a part of the ecosystem. At the same time, curricula may not place a distinct value on learning in or from nature for young children (Askerlund & Almers, 2016), therefore policies are required which include a combination of the natural emphasis and the reflection of research to provide a rational stance towards outdoor learning (Shepherd, 2008). In this way, the impact of the environment on children's development

Learning in and from nature **205**

and learning can be enhanced further. This is because environmental practices provide learning opportunities for children by using natural materials like wood and plants to teach instead of artificial materials (Kirova et al., 2020; Sobel, 2016). For example, Figure 19.1 indicates that children are engaging in nature to enhance their learning and development. In terms of the children pictured here, they are learning in nature to cope with various obstacles by being physically active. Nature provides these children the freedom to pursue their learning in their environment as a part of the ecosystem.

Equally, the posthuman perspective demonstrates numerous important learning opportunities from nature where learning is about inclusion, rather than based on taking a step back from nature and contemplating and categorizing it (Quinn, 2013). Compared to indoors, the outdoor environment embraces a wide range of learning opportunities and materials offering different learning tools and opportunities provided by nature (Maapalo & Østern, 2018). As part of a posthumanist approach, the important distinctions between relativity – a comparison of the feasible forms of knowledge that might occur in particular places – and the contexts in which knowledge unfolds (Snaza et al., 2014) can be fostered for learning. Thus, opportunities and contexts are

FIGURE 19.1   Children's Engagement in Nature. Photo by author.

206 Mehmet Mart

important for the learning process, and there are collaborative relations for the learning of children.

In other respects, the provided materials and opportunities vary according to cultural density. "Cultural density refers to the nature, thickness and dominance of habitus and norms of practice in places" (Waite, 2013, p. 413) which leads to the regulative heritage of each culture and its impact on practice. The children's participation and interaction with the environment are likely to be shaped by the influence of these cultural regulations (Vélez-Agosto, Soto-Crespo, Vizcarrondo-Oppenheimer and Coll, 2017) which in turn afford or limit the opportunities for children to construct their own learning. For example, when considering observational learning, the domain of attending (paying attention to other children and events) is important from a developmental perspective, and educators can note whether young children subsequently try to repeat actions they have observed others perform, which reveals whether such learning has taken place (Bronfenbrenner, 1979). Therefore, Bioecological theory emphasises examining the environments in which developing individuals spend their time and interact with others, as well as the individual's personality and the characteristics of those with whom they typically interact. It is also important to consider how individuals develop over time as well as the historical context in which they live and the mechanisms that underlie development (Rosa & Tudge, 2013).

The impact of the environment is crucial to both children's learning and development although there are various constraints around it. A limited expansion of knowledge can be explained by little prior interaction and familiarity with this natural area (Jose et al., 2017). This is because having a lack of nature-related experiences causes an inability to form the concepts related to life experiences. The management of knowledge can be described as a way of acquiring, preserving, collaborating, and implementing information through experiential learning opportunities (García-Holgado & García-Peñalvo, 2019; Yildiz, 2022). To make sense of the material discovered outside and to learn from the experience, broader ways of examining and analysing are needed (Bagelman & Tremblay, 2017). A young child's learning is greatly altered by experience richness and an environment that is more matched to her developmental needs (Sobel, 2016).

In summary, it is important to consider the impact of the environment on both development and learning opportunities in nature for children. Opportunities for children can enable them to expand their learning through the ecosystem, which might be in or from nature.

Nature as a Key to Learning

Nature provides a learning ecosystem for young children as well as offering experiences of the natural ecosystem. The natural world's ecosystem is typically thought of as an individual territorial or structural entity, like a river reservoir (Shepherd, 2008). With the affordances of nature, pinecones and pebbles take the place of the plastic mathematical instruments used in traditional preschools as the main learning resources in the forest (Sobel, 2016). However, learning from nature is not the only way to interact with it; in fact, it can miss multiple ways of thinking about and experiencing nature (Waite, Husainb, Scandone, Forsyth and Piggott, 2021). Throughout their lives, individuals get introduced to the principles, requirements, demands, and standards of new entities; conflict or crisis may emerge, in particular, during transitional periods as children learn to integrate their prior abilities and goal orientations with evolving norms (Rekers & Waters-Davies, 2021). Therefore, nature-oriented activities provide opportunities for children to experience such issues in their play as live experiences. In addition, when children learn how to adapt to their surroundings by imitating what they see, they engage in creative activities (Edwards, 2017).

While the children can engage in exploratory learning and play activities in nature, it is also a location where they can concentrate on particular tasks for an extended amount of time (O'Brien, 2009), which enables them to organise their learning process. When children participate in active learning in their local environment, they may strengthen their bonds with family and communities (Murphy, 2020). Therefore, the benefits of practising in nature appear to be growing (Kuo et al., 2019). Social relationships in practice afford support for the dismantling of barriers that children frequently encounter in play, enabling chances for creativity, experimentation and solving problems (Dockett & Perry, 2010). For example, children are able to sprint, spin, climb, and perform, so multiple opportunities for children to develop knowledge while in nature are available for exploring, and there are opportunities to include a wide range of topics in children's learning (Speldewinde & Campbell, 2022).

Nature-based opportunities involve various possibilities for children to engage with feeling uncomfortable (Wilson, 2019). Although such activities can be anticipated as risky play, these are possibilities to extend learning opportunities for children. In this regard, forests contain unsafe educational practices that are perceived as an enriching method of learning (Murphy, 2020). Also, a more natural environment can encourage learning as these spaces are peaceful and less disrupted. At the same time natural environments can help to build more comfortable interactions, and the incorporation of natural materials and independence will provide prompts for effective play opportunities for children (Kuo et al., 2019). The outdoors within these settings are not only spaces to recharge or relieve; they also serve as spaces for the educational process, therefore the necessity for these surroundings to encourage learning is key (Merewether, 2015). In this case, play for young children is defined as an activity in their surroundings in which children can showcase their learning and scaffold the educational process of those around them (Dockett & Perry, 2010).

In addition to the role of play, nature enables children to explore a rich learning opportunity (Fantasia, Oña, Wright, and Wertz, 2021) by having their playful engagements outside. Figure 19.2 is an example of what children can learn from nature. There is a bird nest for them to feel, explore, engage with, and understand. Such an opportunity is proof of the scope of learning from nature, and it is the role of the educator to harness it for the learning of children. The emphasis of post-humanism and shared-world positions is on determining the human interaction with nature rather than describing or acquiring knowledge about nature (Wilson, 2019). Shared-world positions are about the common understanding of and approaches to the natural world, reflecting a common stance with post-humanism, and are about the roles and practices in nature. They offer a way of using nature in children's learning process. Human interactions should therefore be at the core of children's learning in and from nature.

The opposite consequence is that any inquiry conducted in a non-naturalistic setting is inevitably ecologically inadequate (Bronfenbrenner, 1977). However, not everybody agrees with Bronfenbrenner, and others hold that every activity can be beneficial to learning and teaching as they are more than a game (Dockett & Perry, 2010). Also, an unstructured method in activities is similar to letting young children explore and lead their learning in the outdoors (Speldewinde & Campbell, 2022). The way to use nature as a key to learning can be considered differently in different settings. This depends on cultural aspects of learning and play (for example, the time spent in outdoors and weather perceptions) as well as social relationships, and observing activities may create notable pedagogical contexts for learning for young children (Edwards, 2017). Nature-related

FIGURE 19.2 A child explores the bird nest. Photo by author.

activities are likely to be included in many schools' mission statements and values (Rowntree Jones, Scothern, Gilbert and Anderson, 2022). However, for these to be translated into practice, the conditions of the surroundings should be considered in terms of designing educational activities as the outcomes depend on such environmental variables (Yildiz, 2022).

Although there are various opportunities in nature for learning outcomes for children, the importance given to implementing educational activities in nature might differ. A further aspect of learning from nature that is not regularly considered is the learning about and an understanding of the non-human. This includes considerations of how an individual interacts with their surroundings and is of the utmost importance in this post-human time for ensuring a future that is sustainable (van Vuuren, 2023). "Sustainability is conceived as the ability of a given ecosystem to maintain its essential functions and processes over time" (Cielęme & Daigle, 2019, p. 70). Thus, it is important to let children face natural opportunities to learn from and develop a commitment to preserving the natural world.

The Roles in Learning

According to Vygotsky, children learn by initially completing tasks with an adult before being able to do so successfully by themselves (Obee, Sandseter and Harper, 2020). In addition, as a result of children's individual curiosity and experiential work, educational outcomes accompany the learning outside (Yildiz, 2022). This is influenced by the roles given to children in their learning process, so that young children enjoy playing outside and discovering the natural world (Sobel, 2016). In this case, children can have a leading role or participating role during activities. In terms of the design of the activities, children can be given opportunities to have child-led learning opportunities as well as following the instruction of adults as part of adult-directed activities. Equally, the role of children can be alternated according to the circumstances and the learning process in different environments.

Bronfenbrenner states that "the experience of a child in daycare, in the classroom, or the informal peer group may change his pattern of activities and interaction with parents or siblings in the home, or vice versa, with consequent implications for learning and development" (Bronfenbrenner, 1977, p. 523). Regarding Bronfenbrenner's system, Sadownik states that the chronosystem includes the time component, which demonstrates how the appearance of a child's daily life may have changed over time, and how our grandparents' childhood was completely different from ours, not only in terms of access to early childhood education and care, toys, and technologies, but also in terms of the people we spent time with during our first years of life (Sadownik, 2023). As mentioned in the previous section, there are different dimensions of children's learning and development, and nature is one of the open systems for children to engage with. However, this has changed over time in terms of children's participation in nature, and there is a decrease in the number of hours children spend in nature (Beyer et al., 2015; Kadury-Slezak et al., 2023).

How education is supposed to take place in outdoor spaces depends on the perspectives of formal and informal educators. Their personal involvement in nature and attitudes towards experiential learning opportunities should emphasise knowledge, respect, and understanding of nature (Jose, Patrick and Moseley, 2017). Educational approaches to nature vary from using the immediate natural experience to manipulating it in various ways (Moore, 2013; Yildiz, 2022). Even though the education process requires active participation of children, the educators' involvement may endanger or support such learning activities. Nevertheless, naturally occurring learning experiences emerge during outdoor activities instead of merely predetermined, culturally accepted outcomes (Moore, 2013). Although the visits to nature are based on specific learning outcomes, such unplanned opportunities are highly likely to accompany the experiences. An experiential approach to teaching may function as an efficient framework for informal program creation as well as formal classroom activities related to hands-on experiences (Jose et al., 2017). Providing opportunities outside can offer additional material to indoor learning, which can serve as a substantial tool (O'Brien, 2009) to engage children in their learning. The natural setting therefore can be considered as a group of systems to support each other for children's learning and development (Bronfenbrenner, 1977).

Figure 19.3 represents a learning opportunity for children to engage with given materials. In the first instance, it might be seen as a natural place for children to learn from by themselves. However, the given materials are likely

FIGURE 19.3 An example from a nature-based school. Photo by author.

to have been placed there because of some expected learning outcomes for the children. Thus, children can learn either from or in nature considering the learning expectations. In this case, learning ecosystems can be used to provide learning environments that are flexible to meet the needs of learners as well as having opportunities for knowledge management during the learning process (García-Holgado & García-Penalvo, 2017). Therefore, most early learning environments include outside spaces which have the potential to provide several learning opportunities (Merewether, 2015).

However, physical activity levels in childcare facilities are often very low, and physical inactivity is common (Reilly, 2010). This might give additional responsibilities to adults to design surroundings considering children's inactivity and learning expectations so that individuals can learn as a result of their participation in activities (Edwards, 2017), and a visit to outdoors and green spaces encourages physical activity as well as opportunities for active learning in nature (Mygind, 2022).

The layout of the environment and the contents, such as how the setting denotes what is and is not preschool, can fix the learner's attention (Kirova, Prochner and Massing, 2020), and it is mainly the role of adults to organise or decide on learning environments. Educators frequently observe children's learning as they play (Speldewinde & Campbell, 2022), so that they can organise the learning environments for children's needs. While the landscape notion might be expanded to incorporate the interaction of natural and human forces, posthuman thinking would add important elements to how such interaction arises and concentrate on how more-than-human agency allows and impacts the way landscape emerges (Fredengren, 2015). Thus, there is a collaboration between the expectations from nature and the posthuman approach to use the possibilities for children. In other respects, adult or educator-led activities, are educator-guided activities in which adults and children can extend learning or discovery together (Edwards, 2017) but this leads children to be inactive in their learning process. In addition, early childhood research mainly demonstrates that play-based learning in itself is not sufficient, and there is a role for teachers in children's play, but the learning needs to be child-driven (Edwards, 2017). When the educator promotes child-driven learning and utilises the most efficient environment resources, or enhances them with other materials, the children can gain a clear understanding of subjects in nature (Speldewinde & Campbell, 2022).

Conclusions

Learning outside offers multiple experiences including activity in daylight, a variety of changing environmental conditions, and the opportunity to climb trees, build products from trees, and collect from the forest (Rowntree Jones et al., 2022), which are all closely related with various early childhood learning theories. Although each theory or approach focuses on different sides of learning, there are three main aspects to be explored in terms of learning in or from nature, namely the topics addressed in this chapter: the impact of the environment, nature as a key to learning and the roles in outdoor learning. Developmental, post-humanist and experiential perspectives share a joint approach to the use of nature in various ways to enrich learning outcomes of children. Nature can be described as a key to delivering the expected outcomes for learning in the given ecosystem, so the stakeholders can consider the opportunities of nature to learn in or learn from.

In conclusion, partitioners may consider ways of harnessing nature to enhance the learning of children focusing on impacts of the environment, opportunities in nature and different roles when learning in nature. It is necessary to design outdoor educational activities for children to have wider learning experiences. In addition to practitioners' considerations, decision-makers should develop strategies to extend the learning of children in and from nature by making additions to curricula and policies across all countries, because the benefits mentioned above are valid for all children. As both practitioners and decision-makers consider the learning opportunities of nature, the role of children in their own learning will be paramount and should form the key value in all stakeholders' approaches to pedagogy.

References

Almers, E., Askerlund, P., Samuelsson, T., & Waite, S. (2020). Children's preferences for schoolyard features and understanding of ecosystem service innovations - a study in five Swedish preschools. *Journal of Adventure Education and Outdoor Learning*, 1–17. https://doi.org/10.1080/14729679.2020.1773879

Askerlund, P., & Almers, E. (2016). Forest gardens–new opportunities for urban children to understand and develop relationships with other organisms. *Urban Forestry & Urban Greening*, *20*, 187–197. https://doi.org/10.1016/j.ufug.2016.08.007

Bagelman, C., & Tremblay, C. (2017). Where Pedagogy and Social Innovation Meet: Assessing the Impact of Experiential Education in the Third Sector. In R. Osman & D. J. Hornsby (Eds.), *Transforming Teaching and Learning in Higher Education: Towards a Socially Just Pedagogy in a Global* (pp. 191–217). Palgrave Macmillan. https://doi.org/10.1007/978-3-319-46176-2

Beyer, K., Bizub, J., Szabo, A., Heller, B., Kistner, A., Shawgo, E., & Zetts, C. (2015). Development and validation of the attitudes toward outdoor play scales for children. *Social Science & Medicine*, *133*, 253–260. https://doi.org/10.1016/j.socscimed.2014.10.03333

Bronfenbrenner, U. (1977). Toward an experimental ecology of human development. *American Psychologist*, *32*(7), 513–531.

Bronfenbrenner, U. (1979). *The Ecology of Human Development: Experiments by Nature and Design*. Harvard University Press.

Bronfenbrenner, U. (2005). *Making Human Beings Human: Bioecological Perspectives on Human Development*. SAGE Publications.

Cielęme, O., & Daigle, C. (2019). Posthuman sustainability: An ethos for our anthropocenic future. *Theory, Culture and Society, 36*(7–8), 67–87. https://doi.org/10.1177/0263276419873710

Dockett, S., & Perry, B. (2010). What Makes Mathematics Play? In L. Sparrow, B. Kissane, & C. Hurst (Eds.), *Shaping the Future of Mathematics Education: Proceedings of the 33rd Annual Conference of the Mathematics Education Research Group of Australasia* (pp. 715–718). MERGA.

Edwards, S. (2017). Play-based learning and intentional teaching: Forever different? *Australasian Journal of Early Childhood, 42*(2), 4–11. https://doi.org/10.23965/AJEC.42.2.01

Eriksson, M., Ghazinour, M., & Hammarström, A. (2018). Different uses of Bronfenbrenner's ecological theory in public mental health research: What is their value for guiding public mental health policy and practice? *Social Theory & Health, 16*, 414–433. https://doi.org/10.1057/s41285

Fantasia, V., Oña, L.S., Wright, C., & Wertz, A.E. (2021). Learning blossoms: Caregiver-infant interactions in an outdoor garden setting. *Infant Behavior and Development, 64*. https://doi.org/10.1016/J.INFBEH.2021.101601

Fredengren, C. (2015). Nature: Cultures-heritage, sustainability and feminist posthumanism. *Current Swedish Archaeology, 23*(1), 109–130.

García-Holgado, A., & García-Penalvo, F. J. (2017). Preliminary validation of the metamodel for developing learning ecosystems. In J. M. Dodero, M. S. Ibarra Sáiz, & I. Ruiz Rube (Eds.), *Fifth International Conference on Technological Ecosystems for Enhancing Multiculturality: Vol. Part F132203* (pp. 1–9). Association for Computing Machinery. https://doi.org/10.1145/3144826.3145439

García-Holgado, A., & García-Peñalvo, F. J. (2019). Validation of the learning ecosystem metamodel using transformation rules. *Future Generation Computer Systems, 91*, 300–310. https://doi.org/10.1016/j.future.2018.09.011

Jose, S., Patrick, P.G., & Moseley, C. (2017). Experiential learning theory: the importance of outdoor classrooms in environmental education. *International Journal of Science Education, Part B: Communication and Public Engagement, 7*(3), 269–284. https://doi.org/10.1080/21548455.2016.1272144

Kadury-Slezak, M., Tal, C., Faruchi, S., Levy, I., Tal, P., & Tish, S. (2023). Parents' perceptions of their children's outdoor activities before and during COVID-19 crisis. *Journal of Childhood, Education & Society, 4*(3), 354–372. https://doi.org/10.37291/2717638X.202343276

Kirova, A., Prochner, L., & Massing, C. (2020). *Learning to Teach Young Children.* Bloomsbury.

Kuo, M., Barnes, M., & Jordan, C. (2019). Do experiences with nature promote learning? Converging evidence of a cause-and-effect relationship. *Frontiers in Psychology, 10*(305), 1–9. https://doi.org/10.3389/fpsyg.2019.00305

Maapalo, P., & Østern, T.P. (2018). The agency of wood: Multisensory interviews with art and crafts teachers in a post-humanistic and new-materialistic perspective. *Education Inquiry, 9*(4), 380–396. https://doi.org/10.1080/20004508.2018.1424492

Mart, M., & Waite, S. (2021). Degrees of freedom: Reflections on perceived barriers to outdoor learning practice for early education in England and Turkey. *Early Years,* 1–19. https://doi.org/10.1080/09575146.2021.2012131

Merewether, J. (2015). Young children's perspectives of outdoor learning spaces: What matters? *Australasian Journal of Early Childhood, 40*(1), 99–108. https://doi.org/10.1177/183693911504000113

Moore, D.T. (2013). *Engaged Learning in the Academy: Challenges and Possibilities*. Palgrave Macmillan. https://doi.org/10.1057/9781137025197

Murphy, M.C. (2020). Bronfenbrenner's bio-ecological model: A theoretical framework to explore the forest school approach? *Journal of Outdoor and Environmental Education, 23*(2), 191–205. https://doi.org/10.1007/s42322-020-00056-5

Mygind, E. (2022). Udeskole-Pupils' physical activity and gender perspectives. In R. Jucker & J. von Au (Eds.), *High-Quality Outdoor Learning: Evidence-based Education Outside the Classroom for Children, Teachers and Society* (pp. 135–152). Springer. https://doi.org/10.1007/978-3-031-04108-2_7

Obee, P., Sandseter, E.B.H., & Harper, N.J. (2020). Children's use of environmental features affording risky play in early childhood education and care. *Early Child Development and Care*, 1–19. https://doi.org/10.1080/03004430.2020.1726904

O'Brien, L. (2009). Learning outdoors: The Forest School approach. *Education 3-13, 37*(1), 45–60. https://doi.org/10.1080/03004270802291798

Quinn, J. (2013). Theorising learning and nature: Post-human possibilities and problems. *Gender and Education, 25*(6), 738–753.

Reilly, J.J. (2010). Low levels of objectively measured physical activity in preschoolers in child care. *Medicine and Science in Sports and Exercise, 42*(3), 502–507. https://doi.org/10.1249/MSS.0b013e3181cea100

Rekers, A., & Waters-Davies, J. (2021). 'All of the Wild': Cultural formation in Wales through outdoor play at forest school. In L.T. Grindheim, H.V. Sørensen, & A. Rekers (Eds.), *Outdoor Learning and Play: Pedagogical Practices and Children's Cultural Formation* (pp. 145–159). Springer. https://doi.org/10.1007/978-3-030-72595-2_9

Rosa, E.M., & Tudge, J. (2013). Urie Bronfenbrenner's theory of human development: Its evolution from ecology to bioecology. *Journal of Family Theory and Review, 5*, 243–258. https://edisciplinas.usp.br/pluginfile.php/3476636/mod_resource/content/0/Rosa_et_al-2013-Journal_of_Family_Theory__Review.pdf

Rotas, N. (2019). Outdoor play and learning (OPAL): Activating "Loose Parts" in undisciplined childhood environments. *International Journal of Early Childhood Environmental Education, 7*(1), 73–85. https://ezp.lib.cam.ac.uk/login?url=https://search.ebscohost.com/login.aspx?direct=true&db=eric&AN=EJ1233621&site=ehost-live&scope=site

Rowntree Jones, C., Scothern, C., Gilbert, H., & Anderson, S. (2022). Creating a forest for learning: How the National Forest in the UK has developed and outdoor-based learning project. In R. Jucker & J. von Au (Eds.), *High-Quality Outdoor Learning: Evidence-based Education Outside the Classroom for Children, Teachers and Society* (pp. 367–386). Springer. https://doi.org/10.1007/978-3-031-04108-2_21

Sadownik, A.R. (2023). Bronfenbrenner: Ecology of human development in ecology of collaboration. In A.R. Sadownik & A. Višnjić Jevtić (Eds.), *(RE)theorising More-than-parental Involvement in Early Childhood Education and Care* (pp. 83–95). Springer. https://doi.org/10.1007/978-3-031-38762-3_4

Shepherd, G. (2008). The ecosystem approach: Learning from experience. In *Ecosystem Management Series* (Issue 5). IUCN (International Union for Conservation of Nature and Natural Resources). https://www.iucn.org/ecosystems

Snaza, N., Appelbaum, P., Bayne, S., Carlson, D., Morris, M., Rotas, N., Sandlin, J., Wallin, J., & Weaver, J.A. (2014). Toward a posthuman education. *Journal of*

Curriculum Theorizing, 30(2), 39–55. https://digitalcommons.georgiasouthern.edu/curriculum-facpubshttps://digitalcommons.georgiasouthern.edu/curriculum-facpubs/47

Sobel, D. (2016). *Nature Preschools and Forest Kindergartens: The Handbook for Outdoor Learning.* Redleaf Press.

Speldewinde, C., & Campbell, C. (2022). Mathematics learning in the early years through nature play. *International Journal of Early Years Education.* https://doi.org/10.1080/09669760.2022.2122026

van Vuuren, E.J. (2023). Early childhood in the era of post-humanism: Lending an ear to nature. *Journal of Curriculum Studies Research, 5*(1), 171–180. https://doi.org/10.46303/jcsr.2023.13

Vélez-Agosto, N.M., Soto-Crespo, J.G., Vizcarrondo-Oppenheimer, M., & Coll, C.G. (2017). Bronfenbrenner's bioecological theory revision: Moving culture from the macro into the micro. *Perspectives on Psychological Science, 12*(5), 900–910. https://journals.sagepub.com/doi/pdf/10.1177/1745691617704397

Waite, S. (2013). 'Knowing your place in the world': How place and culture support and obstruct educational aims. *Cambridge Journal of Education, 43*(4), 413–433.

Waite, S., Husainb, F., Scandone, B., Forsyth, E., & Piggott, H. (2021). Moving towards nature exploring progressive pathways to engage children and young people from disadvantaged backgrounds in nature-based activities. In M. Baker, N. Carr, & E. Stewart (Eds.), *Leisure Activities in the Outdoors: Learning, Developing and Challenging* (pp. 130–144). CABI. https://doi.org/10.1079/9781789248203.0011

Ward, K. (2018). What's in a dream? Natural elements, risk and loose parts in children's dream playspace drawings. *Australasian Journal of Early Childhood, 43*(1), 34–42. https://doi.org/10.23965/AJEC.43.1.04

Wilson, R. (2019). What is Nature? *The International Journal of Early Childhood Environmental Education, 7*(1), 26–39. https://www.childrenandnature.org

Yildiz, K. (2022). Experiential learning from the perspective of outdoor education leaders. *Journal of Hospitality, Leisure, Sport & Tourism Education, 30,* 1–13. https://doi.org/10.1016/j.jhlste.2021.100343

20

A POSTHUMAN PERSPECTIVE

Learning Entanglements Among a Child, Family Members, and the Material World

Sally Brown

Introduction

This chapter focuses on how human and nonhuman resources facilitate literacy learning across various contexts to disrupt the mind/body dichotomy by closely examining the material-discursive practices of Khoi, a four-year-old child, his family, and the more-than-human world. The longitudinal study explores his intra-active experiences surrounding Legos and gardening showcasing learning transformations over time. It provides a posthuman view of early literacy learning that opens the window into other ways of thinking about how young children are constantly being and becoming through intra-actions in their worlds. The chapter concludes with shifts in thinking regarding how early educators can utilize posthuman perspectives to improve pedagogical approaches to literacy learning that look toward fluid, indeterminant curricula that unfold nomadically at the hands of children and their material worlds.

Posthumanism in Early Literacy Learning

Posthumanism shifts views about literacy from a human-centric position to an equal emphasis on the interwoven nature of the more-than-human or materialities along with the human(s). Using this philosophical lens pushes the rethinking of children's play encounters and unsettles ways that pervade traditional thoughts and instructional practices about learning that currently exist (Nxumalo & Rubin, 2019). Rather than a predetermined knowledge-making process, the learning context is flipped to create and recognize embodied, playful forms of nomadic literacies. In other words, valuing the unstable, experimental, and cognitive aspects of meaning-making is important.

DOI: 10.4324/97810034/1172-24

A Posthuman Perspective **217**

Ultimately, this changes what gets counted as knowledge and opens avenues for diversity (MacDonald et al., 2020).

Murris (2021) reminds us that humans are part of the world and not separate from it. "Each thing, action, and idea" (p. 21) matters. This idea pushes thinking against the grain of mundaneness to create new understandings of theory and practice. Everyday intra-actions with the material world involve touching and being with things in playful ways (Kuby & Christ, 2020). There does not need to be a predetermined plan for what children make of literacy experiences or the idea that their productions will always be finished. Instead, recognition must be given to the social nature of literacy learning to embrace the flux of literacies unfolding through complex human and nonhuman entanglements. The practices of knowing and being cannot be separated (Toohey, Smythe, Dagenais and Forte, 2020). The bodymindmatter connections, each having agentic forces, are a move beyond the domination of the discursive aspects of traditional schooling and learning. Regarding the child as a competent meaning-maker entangled with humans and nonhuman foregrounds different ways of being, doing, and thinking (Murris, 2016).

Figure 20.1 illustrates the key aspects of posthumanism related to thinking about early literacy learning opportunities for children. Assemblages are configurations of people, objects, and practices embedded within cultural practices and historical trajectories (Lenters & McDermott, 2020). According to Deleuze and Guattari (1987), assemblages of desire are forces that create new productions and position a permanent state of becoming. So, early educators should be guided by children's interests, desires, and curiosity. This is where new realities are created. Exploring how and what is produced offers insight into children's desirings (Kuby & Rucker, 2016). Intra-activity involves entangled humans and nonhumans (Figure 20.1). Taguchi (2010) refers to this as

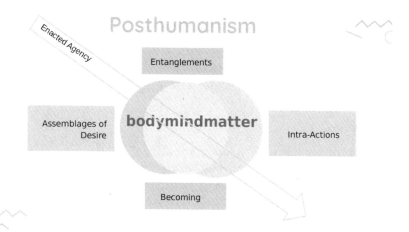

FIGURE 20.1   Complexities of the Child's Posthuman World. Image by the author.

218 Sally Brown

the material turn where materials play an equal role in constructing discourse and reality. In other paradigms, agency is attributed exclusively to humans. Enacted agency, from a posthuman perspective, reconfigures ideas about agency and who possesses it. Both the human and nonhuman are coming into being as agentive acts result in reconfiguring material-discursive practices (Barad, 2007). The available materials have the agency to impact the intra-activity and impact outcomes and trajectories. Understanding the literacy work of young children requires close attention to intra-activity across time and space.

The World of the Child

Young children communicate, play, and learn across modes within the more-than-human world (Murris, 2016). Sensory experiences and movement, affective relationships with materials and material-discursive intra-actions are entangled as children create their own forms of meaning in unexpected ways. Post-qualitative research involving young children's play using a posthumanism lens provides insight into the power of children's thinking about difference. Boldt and Leander (2017) examined the desiring flows of a six-year-old's Lego play. They highlighted how movement across time, both chronos (nowness) and aion (time simultaneously moving into the past and future), afforded the child to "break the scene" and move the narrated Lego performance forward and backward. The play continued to move because of desire across the humans and nonhumans as energy intensified.

Assemblages are enacted as children play, experiment, and explore using their bodies, identities, and discourses resulting in improvisational literacy learning. In one case stick entanglements, "acted as a catalyst for action, igniting children's imagination, and was enmeshed with complex play scenarios and storylines" (Harwood & Collier, 2017, p. 349), highlighting the need for touch and sensory experiences in early learning. The use of technology can also stimulate literacy engagements with virtual, vicarious, and physical touch opening spaces for becoming or the unexpected (Flewitt, Kucirkova, & Messer, 2014). Children are adaptable and flexible with their desirings.

The Humans

The focal child in this study is four-year-old Khoi (all names are pseudonyms). This chapter focuses on his activities between the ages of three and four when he lived in California and South Carolina, USA. He lived with his mother, father, and two younger sisters. Khoi is a biracial child with a European-American mother, Dana, and a bilingual Vietnamese-American father, Hoang. He has been exposed to a variety of languages, including Vietnamese (spoken by his father and extended family members) and Spanish at the home daycare he attended in California. At the time of the study, he attended a Montessori daycare. Both of his parents are college-educated and work in engineering and entrepreneurial IT. Khoi's parents intentionally planned material engagements for Khoi, including home-oriented activities and outside events. Technology was a part of the family's literacy practices regarding Khoi's iPad use and for sharing and communicating with extended family members.

The Material World

During this time, Khoi's material world traversed two home environments and two different daycare settings. He lived in a small apartment in California and a neighborhood home with a yard in South Carolina. Both living spaces were rich in materials commonly found in homes with young children. These included letter magnets on the refrigerator, loads of paper-based picture books, Legos, paint, drawing materials, toys, etc. Khoi had access to these materials at his request and could access many of them on his own. In addition, the parents offered digital learning opportunities through iPad apps on a limited basis. Plus, the family regularly used the iPhone to FaceTime extended family members. Outdoor experiences consisted of visits to local parks, visits to family members, which included airline travel, playing t-ball and soccer with peers, riding a scooter, drawing with chalk on the driveway, etc.

Methodological Analyses

Methodologically speaking, posthumanism helps researchers move from reflection and looking for patterns to reading data diffractively resulting in a "co-constructive process between two or more organisms" (Murris, 2016, p. 27). Since this study did not employ the traditional qualitative research methods, there was a broader inquiry to look for diffractions or differences in the data. This was guided by what is not known about how a young child makes meaning through material-discursive intra-actions, with particular materialities of play in mind. The parents supplied short video clips, photographs, and artifacts of Khoi's work as he engaged with his world. A nexus analysis (Wohlwend, 2020) was applied to video clips, images, and work samples that captured embodied literacies and entanglements. The nexus analysis focused on how Khoi was making meaning as he participated in the physical, social, and cultural environment, which was represented as a web format with physical action in the center. This included focusing on multiple semiotic systems such as gestures, visuals, and embodied learning. Probing questions about key practices included (a) who, with whom, and for what purposes, (b) which discourses mattered, (c) which actions were expected, and (d) what was the mediated action (Wohlwend, 2020).

220 Sally Brown

A further diffractive analysis followed Khoi's moves that differed from traditional notions of literacy learning. The intention was to gain insights into performative subjectivities and enactments. Diffractions are differences where newness is created and extended across time and space. This type of analysis supports plugging theory into data in a way that considers bodies, texts, relationships, data, and language that produce questions, thus moving in different directions to produce knowledge on the move (Mazzei, 2014). The result includes the unexpected, which shows different ways of being and becoming. Then, ethnographic interviews (Spradley, 2016) were conducted with the parents and child. Khoi provided insight into the process of making and unmaking things during play. His parents explained their educational goals for Khoi and how they used environmental materials and experiences to enhance his learning.

Findings

The findings demonstrate the importance of the affordances of material resources as Khoi's intra-actions unfolded. Khoi's literacy learning was entangled with humans (i.e., mother, father, sibling, extended family members) and nonhuman materials like Google, Legos, garden-related items, and books. His play was an overlapping entanglement of the human and nonhuman resources that actively influenced each other. The available materials had the agency to impact the intra-activity by reconfiguring the material-discursive practices (Barad, 2007).

Entanglements

Two entanglements are featured in this section, including building and learning with and through Legos and gardening. These intra-actions transcended time and spaces and were infused with technology and intergenerational elements (see Table 20.1). Each came together in embodied ways to extend Khoi's play and literacy learning. The events added new material layers of engagement with the world that afforded him multimodal experiences and

TABLE 20.1 Overview of Entanglements

Diffractive Entanglements	Geographies of Space	Technology	Humans - Intergenerational
Building Legos	Multiple Homes; Legoland; Daycare	FaceTime; Digital Photos; Laptop computer	Parents, Grandfather
Gardening	Gardens; Corn Field; Kitchen; Couch	iPad App	Father, Grandfather

A Posthuman Perspective **221**

unique ways of making meaning traversing across geographies of place showing the situatedness of material culture (Kervin, Comber, & Baroutsis, 2019).

Legos and Drawing

Legos were a material thread that traversed Khoi's intra-actions with the world, including humans. There were rich language learning opportunities through conversations with adults as well as reading Lego booklets. Intra-actions began with Duplos, larger blocks for younger children, and progressed to boxes of Lego blocks for free play, then involved Lego kits. The kits had specific directions that pushed for more organized building objects like a truck or spaceship. However, the parents did not enforce particular ways of being with the Legos. Instead, Khoi was free to make choices through nomadic or undirected explorations (Sherbine, 2020). Each step was part of Khoi's journey to becoming a master builder, an ever-evolving process (Kuby & Vaughn, 2015).

In terms of literacy development, Khoi extended his expressive and receptive language while touching and moving Lego pieces. Here, Khoi crafted a fire storyline with his mother, built new vocabulary, and developed communication skills. Both mother and child snapped Legos together while sitting on a rug.

Khoi: Oh, look! I made a fire truck [Snapped on the last red piece.]
Dana: Hey, maybe I'll sit over here and work on this fire for a while. Where's the shovel?
          [Mother reached for shovel and placed it in her Lego character's hand.] There's my shovel.
Khoi: [Pushed his firetruck next to his mother's character.] I'm trying to get your shovel out of your camp.

Khoi initiated the entanglement where his newly created firetruck served as a vehicle for a spontaneous oral narrative guided by his mother's inserted dialogue. As Khoi's truck intra-action was extended through the additional scene, a second fire set in play by Dana. She added to the narrative in a way to extend it and teach Khoi the word shovel. This was solidified by his uptake of the word shovel and his physical movements closer to the secondary scene. Khoi took the opportunity to touch the Lego character and grab the shovel. The intra-action continued with the two of them fighting fires. This instance allowed Khoi to practice his language skills in a meaningful context and for Dana's language to serve as a model for her son.

As time continued, Khoi's family enrolled him in an online Lego webinar sponsored by the Tucson Literacy Festival. Table 20.2 shows Khoi bent over a table, taking a close view of an iPad screen where he was listening to and watching a video-led workshop by a Lego expert and author of a children's

222 Sally Brown

TABLE 20.2 Khoi's Lego Intra-Actions. Images by the author.

(a) Lego Webinar	(b) Moveable Lego man

FIGURE 20.2 Lego Webinar.	**FIGURE 20.3** Moveable Lego Man.

nonfiction book about Legos. The image shows his intense interest through his body language, where he leans on the table to get as close to the screen as possible.

The laptop and Internet access offered additional depth to his Lego play. The author provided guided tips on creating a moveable Lego man, which Khoi built with his father directly after the workshop (Table 20.2b). Khoi used the Lego man as the focus of his play and developed a coherent and cohesive narrative around the man while embedding him with other Legos. The intervening technology and the rich textures of the Legos pushed Khoi's play to a deeper level. According to his father, "Every day he'll build something different and take it apart. Every morning he has something in mind to build. He hunts for the pieces beginning at 7 a.m."

Later, as Khoi continued his interest in building Legos, he focused on large 18-wheeler trucks and the many wheels needed to construct them. The surfaces and textures of the Legos were all part of the embodied learning experiences. Figure 20.4 is a drawing that Khoi created to show a 3-dimensional view of his truck, accompanied by a rich oral description showcasing his ability to construct a meaningful, logical narrative based on material experiences.

Khoi was not satisfied after just drawing a side view of the truck. He continued to attend to details by creating close-up views of the various parts for his audience, knowing that his mother and grandfather frequently displayed his work. According to Khoi,

> This is my 18-wheeler, but I didn't make 18 wheels. Only two sets. I guess I don't want to make all of them. We'll pretend it has 18 wheels. That's the back right there with the red lights. The bottom of the engine is right here. Black lights are on the front with the grill. It's carrying cow milk. Like real cow milk …See, here, this line is the handle to the door.

A Posthuman Perspective **223**

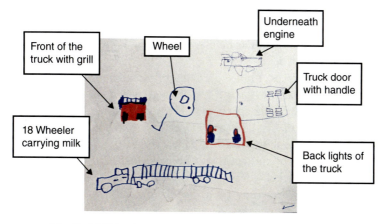

FIGURE 20.4 Khoi's 18-Wheeler Drawing. Image and annotation by the author.

He used his available language resources to communicate the intended outcomes of the drawing. While this may seem ordinary, other meanings can be found only by forging beyond a simple look at the drawing. While not visible on the black and white drawing, the backlights of the truck were colored red with a marker indicating they were turned on, which made the truck ready to transport the milk. Khoi knew this was an essential component from his Lego building experiences. As he intra-acted with the paper and markers, Khoi was a designer by choosing what to include and what not to include, how to shape the objects, and where to place them. His work was not random but principled in that it demonstrated his competence to create an imagined world (Mavers, 2011).

This experience shows us the ways in which Khoi took up prior learning experiences (building, reading directions from Lego booklets, listening to an expert, and working with family members) to lead up to this sophisticated drawing that features extended views of the truck as Khoi worked through how to represent a three-dimensional object on a flat piece of paper using markers. While drawing, he did not have the Lego truck in front of him. Instead, he drew from memory and prior experiences. Further, his development of language was expanded through the talk embedded in the Lego experiences. By mixing materials available in the environment, Khoi represented the depth of his knowledge about trucks using material-discursive tools. These moments of inventiveness and experimentation embedded within literacy illustrate transformation over time (MacDonald, et al., 2020).

Gardening

At three, Khoi unexpectedly became obsessed with the word cornucopia. He loved how it sounded as he continually repeated it and developed a deep understanding of its meaning through conversations and experiences. This laid

224 Sally Brown

the foundation for an interest in gardening, fruits, and vegetables that pushed beyond linguistics (Kuby & Rucker, 2016). Khoi's engagement with physical elements of the natural world as he played led to unique ways of constructing knowledge.

Table 20.3 showcases Khoi's gardening intra-actions and desires with humans and nonhumans. Khoi and his sister grew a small garden in pots on the porch of their California apartment. He used a flashlight to gain a closer look at the changing plants. This experience kept him continually engaged as he was able to open the sliding glass to gain access to the fruits and vegetables. Khoi could just be in the moment with no particular linear path dictating his learning (Kuby & Rucker, 2016). Daily, Khoi and his father observed the plants while physically touching them and talking about their names and the ever-occurring changes. Because Khoi was able to intra-act with the plants, more-than-human objects, his interest and curiosity were extended. He had opportunities to ask questions and develop hypotheses while learning these new vocabulary words and concepts. The family even incorporated Vietnamese plants in order to teach him about an extended world that went well beyond the borders of California.

The family frequently included Khoi in cooking activities around fresh vegetables to appreciate the natural world (Table 20.3b). To inspire healthy eating habits, the family utilized the fruits and vegetables grown on their porch and purchased others from the grocery store. Khoi played an important role in the process as he assisted in picking, cleaning, and eating the plants.

Khoi also had experience in South Carolina with an extended yard garden and visiting a corn field (Table 20.3c, d). He spent time planting outside, where he used a spade to dig in the dirt, followed by the insertion of seeds. The visit to a cornfield allowed Khoi to get lost in a sea of corn stalks, where he discovered ears of corn. He examined the different sizes to pick the right ones, which later became part of dinner. These experiences transferred to his play with farm equipment as he developed storylines around growing vegetables and using trucks to transport the produce to stores. Insight into early literacy skills was evident through his dialogue as he engaged in gardening play. As Khoi stacked the corn and eggs on his truck, he mumbled to himself:

> Get on here eggs. Plus, you too corn. Everybody is ready now for the grocery store. The truck is ready to take you. Vroom. Vroom. [Moved truck across the floor.] You have to go to the store. People ready to eat. They need food, and you are going to be their food. [Talking to the objects.] Get going. [Unloaded the food off the truck.]

Here, Khoi demonstrated his understanding of the sequencing of events, an early literacy skill serving as a foundation for reading comprehension. Although

TABLE 20.3 Gardening Experiences. All images by the author.

(a) Examining vegetables with a flashlight	(b) Washing and cooking brussels sprouts	(c) Planting seeds – outside garden	(d) Picking corn in the cornfield	(e) Playing farmer with toys	(f) iPad gardening

226 Sally Brown

he does not use specific words like first, next, or then, a sequence of events illustrated the garden/farm-to-store production cycle. He did not learn this from reading a book, but rather from life experiences that afforded him the opportunity to build his own meaning in a personally meaningful way.

Another diffraction or difference in Khoi's learning occurred as he discovered a gardening activity on his iPad. It was magical and unexpected as he experienced gardening in a new, joyful way (Davies, 2014). Each day, Khoi was allowed to engage with his iPad for 30 minutes. Routinely, Khoi went outside to the garden with his father to check the plant growth. However, upon discovering this game, Khoi decided to do his gardening inside while seated on the couch (Table 20.3f). The game allowed him to select a specific crop, plant seeds, add water, see the growth progression, and harvest the crop by picking it from the field. According to Khoi,

> Yeah. I didn't go outside today. I did my gardening inside. Want to see. [Opened iPad app.] See I can make my carrots grow by adding water. [Clicked a watering can. Instantly, the carrots became larger.] It's like going outside but I don't have to get hot. [Laughed.] It even keeps score. Tells you if you did a good job.

In this case, Khoi selected a digital gardening experience over a physical one. He suggested his preference was related to the heat associated with physical outside gardening in South Carolina. This was unexpected but a learning experience that built upon his previous gardening knowledge and invited a new way of being a gardener.

Khoi was learning how to care for a garden in a new way. The iPad afforded him the opportunity to experiment with tactile and visual forms of literacy as he figured out how to navigate the garden app without any traditional forms of reading. He clicked and moved back and forth between screens until he understood how to use the program. The clicking and tapping added touch to this learning experience, thus entangling his mind and body (Flewitt et al., 2014). All of this occurred independently, drawing from his problem-solving skills and ability to reason about the sequencing of growing vegetables to selling them. Sounds were an integral part of intra-actions. For example, visually, water was seen falling from the can on the rows of crops in synch with water sounds, making it very realistic for Khoi.

Khoi was attentive to the score displayed at the bottom of the screen. He realized the score changed based on how well he cared for his plants. When they needed watering, the score would go down. After they were freshly watered, the score went up. Khoi was also aware of when to "harvest his crop," his exact words. He stated, "You can see when it is time to harvest. That means they are ready to pick. You can't let your crop just sit there." Khoi's gestures, words, sounds, and movements on the iPad showed just how entangled the material and discursive world are for children (Hackett & Somerville, 2017). He invented a new way to accomplish his goals and interests. His manipulation of the material-discursive world will also change as he continues being and becoming.

Early Childhood Learning Spaces

This series of entanglements, Lego play and gardening, demonstrate the need not to separate human learning from materials but to view it as assemblages where play and literacy learning are part of embodied actions, identities, discourses, and the more-than-human world. Khoi used all of these modes to communicate, tell stories, and learn through play in improvisational ways. The intra-actions involved many actors, including his immediate and extended family members and non-human elements like plants and Legos, which took him beyond human centrism to a more inclusive sense of belonging in the world (Harwood & Collier, 2017). Khoi developed a reflective and questioning approach to learning that involved material-discursive intra-actions. Matter is important to children as it affords catalysts for action with unknown destinations.

Problematizing concepts like best practices in early education can forge new boundaries. Moments in time are opportunities to affect and be affected by materials highlighting the importance of the whole child and the notion of an emergent curriculum (Murris, 2016). Opening spaces for the emergence of new pedagogies that recognize the embodied literacies of human and nonhuman entanglements are needed. There should no longer be a divide between theory and practice. MacDonald et al. (2020) challenge us to "re-imagine ways to assemble, unassembled, re-assemble, and commune in both diverse and uniform ways" (p. 154). Educators need to see object-embedded assemblages as spaces where knowledge is being made in a constant state of becoming. This involves rejecting scripted curricula blind to how children's bodies are entangled with the material world (Alaimo, 2008). Material encounters are full of promise. Without this, we run the risk of missing the continual growth that is embodied in various ways of knowing.

A Bright Unfolding Future

In many cases, schools have an end goal for young students. There is a finite state to accomplish, like finishing kindergarten to move to first grade. Becoming is an undefined movement that includes nonhumans. It's a continual process affected by being/doing/knowing in concert with the material world. Early educators can offer entangled learning opportunities that value the objects, spaces, and multimodal ways intra-actions progress (Hackett & Rautio, 2019). It must involve watching and listening for the differences in

228 Sally Brown

how young learners build knowledge. In other words, educators may need to adjust their gaze to see the rich possibilities (Sherbine, 2020). Davies (2014) refers to a concept called emergent listening involving a suspension of judgments. Do not limit learning to traditional, fixed forms of knowledge. Instead, be open to the various artifacts students create as they are in a state of becoming literate beings. Be able to see and hear how ideas come to life. When scripts and expected outcomes do not confine educators, they have the possibility to value the explorations of children and notice their sophisticated ideas (Kuby & Vaughn, 2015).

Childhood learning journeys should not be predetermined, but unfolding intersections of play and imagination. Medina, Perry and Wohlwend (2022) frame literacy learning this way, "The acts of doing and being with the complexities of how we enact and embody moment-to-moment relationships with other people, things, and places generate new knowledge and practices that relate to positions beyond the sedimented or dominant conventions or discourses of any given situation" (p. 14). Educators have the power to unpack existing toolboxes, investigate the tools, and invent new ones to see bright possibilities for the future (Taguchi, 2010).

References

Alaimo, S (2008). Trans-corporeal feminisms and the ethical space of nature. *Material Feminisms*, *25*(2), 237–264.

Barad, K (2007). *Meeting the Universe Halfway: Quantum Physics and the Entanglement of Matter and Meaning.* Duke University Press.

Boldt, GM, & Leander, K (2017). Becoming through 'the break': A post-human account of a child's play. *Journal of Early Childhood Literacy*, *17*(3), 409–425.

Davies, B (2014). *Listening to Children: Being and Becoming.* Routledge.

Deleuze, G, & Guattari, F (1987). *A Thousand Plateaus: Capitalism and Schizophrenia*, trans. B. Massumi. London: Continuum, vol. 2004, p. 322.

Flewitt, R, Kucirkova, N, & Messer, D (2014). Touching the virtual, touching the real: iPads and enabling literacy for students experiencing disability. *Australian Journal of Language and Literacy*, *37*(2), 107–116.

Hackett, A, & Rautio, P (2019). Answering the world: Young children's running and rolling as more-than-human multimodal meaning making. *International Journal of Qualitative Studies in Education*, *32*(8), 1019–1031.

Hackett, A, & Somerville, M (2017). Posthuman literacies: Young children moving in time, place and more-than-human worlds. *Journal of Early Childhood Literacy*, *17*(3), 374–391.

Harwood, D, & Collier, D (2017). The matter of the stick: Storying/(re) storying children's literacies in the forest. *Journal of Early Childhood Literacy*, *17*(3), 336–352.

Kervin, L, Comber, B, & Baroutsis, A (2019). Sociomaterial dimensions of early literacy learning spaces: Moving through classrooms with teacher and children. In H. Hughes, J. Franz, & J. Willis (Eds.), *School Spaces for Student Wellbeing and Learning: Insights from Research and Practice* (pp. 21–38). Springer.

Kuby, C, & Christ, RC (2020). *Speculative Pedagogies of Qualitative Inquiry*. Routledge.

Kuby, C, & Rucker, T (2016). *Go be a writer!: Expanding the curricular boundaries of literacy learning with children*. Teachers College Press.

Kuby, C, & Vaughn, M (2015). Young children's identities becoming: Exploring agency in the creation of multimodal literacies. *Journal of Early Childhood Literacy, 15*(4), 433–472.

Lenters, K, & McDermott, M (2020). Introducing affect, embodiment, and place in critical literacy. In K. Lenters and M. McDermott (Eds.), *Affect, Embodiment, and Place in Critical Literacy* (pp. 1–18). Routledge.

MacDonald, M, Hill, C, & Sinclair, N (2020). The problem and potential of representation: Being and becoming. In K. Toohey, S. Smythe, D. Dagenais, & M. Forte (Eds.), *Transforming Language and Literacy Education: New Materialism, Posthumanism, and onto Ethics* (pp. 153–174). Routledge.

Mavers, D (2011). *Children's Writing and Drawing as Design: The Remarkable in the Unremarkable*. Routledge.

Mazzei, LA (2014). Beyond an Easy Sense: A Diffractive Analysis. *Qualitative Inquiry, 20*(6), 742–746.

Medina, CL, Perry, M, & Wohlwend, K (2022). *Playful Methods: Engaging the Unexpected in Literacy Research*. Taylor & Francis.

Murris, K (2021). Introduction: Making kin: Postqualitative, new materialist and critical posthumanist research. In *Navigating the Postqualitative, New Materialist and Critical Posthumanist Terrain across Disciplines* (pp. 1–21). Routledge.

Murris, K (2016). *The Posthuman Child: Educational Transformation through Philosophy with Picturebooks*. Routledge.

Nxumalo, F, & Rubin, JC (2019). Encountering waste landscapes: More-than-human place literacies in early childhood education. In C. Kuby, K. Spector, & J. Thiel (Eds.), *Posthumanism and literacy education* (pp. 201–213). Routledge.

Sherbine, K (2020). Track Star+ thing power: Be(com)ing in the literacy workshop. *Journal of Early Childhood Literacy, 20*(4), 613–630.

Spradley, JP (2016). *The Ethnographic Interview*. Waveland Press.

Taguchi, HL (2010). Rethinking pedagogical practices in early childhood education: A multidimensional approach to learning and inclusion. *Contemporary Perspectives on Early Childhood Education*, 14–32.

Toohey, K, Smythe, S, Dagenais, D, & Forte, M (Eds.) (2020). *Transforming Language and Literacy Education: New Materialism, Posthumanism, and onto Ethics*. Routledge.

Wohlwend, K, (2020). *Literacies that Move and Matter: Nexus Analysis for Contemporary Childhoods*. Routledge.

21

THE NEED FOR DIALOGUE

bell hooks, Paulo Freire, and the English Early
Years Sector

Poppie Ephgrave

Introduction

This chapter explores the concept of dialogue in relation to social justice and
social change within the context of the early years education sector in England.
The two key texts this chapter draws upon are Paulo Freire's *Pedagogy of the
Oppressed* (1970) and bell hooks' *Teaching to Transgress* (1994)[1]. In the
Pedagogy of the Oppressed Paulo Freire defines oppression as a dehumanising
act; both the oppressors and those being oppressed are stripped of their
humanity during the process. Freire states the way to transform oppression is
through the humanising act of dialogue. However, for dialogue to be meaningful it must contain the two elements of action and reflection; this is called
praxis, and dialogue without these properties results in verbalism and activism.
Freire defines these practices (verbalism and activism) as not being humanising
and states that true dialogue (praxis) is the way that we achieve significance as
human beings. It is important to note that Freire explains everybody has the
right to engage in dialogue; we were not born to be silent. Dialogue to Freire
is the way we can reverse oppression and enact social change.

bell hooks is heavily influenced by Freire, describing him as her mentor and
guide. hooks draws upon Freire's definition of dialogue throughout her discussions to explore the critical pedagogy of 'education of freedom'. hooks
approaches dialogue as a liberatory tool and uses it to challenge social justice
issues, as well as to help heal her own experiences of oppression. hooks achieves
this through analysing her experiences in the classroom as both a student and
a professional. Through her essays, hooks creates a framework for dialogue
that we can draw upon as educators. These frameworks include the concept of
'engaged pedagogy', which forms the basis of her recommendations.

DOI: 10.4324/9781003471172-25

In this chapter we will explore the concept of dialogue through hooks' and Freire's definitions, and I emphasise that dialogue is not to be restricted to particular contexts such as the written or spoken word; dialogue is a universal phrase for human interaction. The works of Freire and hooks will be used as a tool throughout this chapter to analyse and critique the English early years sector. By drawing upon further literature, I will assess the value their teachings can have when applied to early years practice, whilst offering recommendations for settings and policymakers. These suggestions have been considered within the context of enacting social change, ensuring social justice, and providing children with secure foundations for the future. The chapter starts with an exploration of the importance of language in dialogue and then moves on to considering the value of experience.

The Importance of Language Within Dialogue

hooks discusses the use of language in a powerful way through analysing her experience of reading Adrienne Rich's poem, The Burning of Paper Instead of Children (1989). In this poem Rich (1989) speaks against domination, racism, and class oppression. hooks explores her feelings in relation to a statement from the poem:

'this is the oppressor's language, yet I need it to talk to you'
(Rich, 1989)

She imagines how Africans who were brought to the United States against their will felt about having to learn English resulting in the loss of their language and having to witness their words become meaningless with foreign voices no longer allowed to be spoken. hooks' main discourse throughout her analysis is the way language is explicitly linked to the domination of the oppressed. She explains how the English language was used to enforce the colonisation of the Africans who were displaced or moved to the United States of America. This resulted in language attrition, meaning they lost their native language due to their spoken word being rendered meaningless (Smidt, 2022). Through this hooks explains how we need to ensure that other languages are not lost in contemporary culture, especially because during discussions of diversity and multiculturalism the concept of language is often absent. hooks therefore calls for the celebration of diverse voices, language, and speech, particularly those that disrupt the dominance of standard English. hooks explains we can achieve this through presenting written and spoken word in the classroom that is not always accessible to all students. hooks states we need to change how we think about language and its uses; everyone is worthy of being heard, not just those who speak standard English.

232 Poppie Ephgrave

hooks speaks directly about the language we use in terms of our dialect whereas Freire deliberates the structures and properties surrounding dialogue. He considers the use of language within multiple dimensions such as manipulation, the use of the true word (praxis) and how we should have faith in people's dialogue whilst also not being naïve. A key reflection of Freire's on the importance of language is his discussion surrounding revolutionary leadership. Within this he draws upon the selected works of Mao-Tse-Tung (1967 in Freire, 1970) and their enquiry into the importance of leaders adhering to the needs of the masses. It states that 'cultural workers' must link themselves to the masses and follow their needs and wishes. I believe Freire's insertion of this into his discussion has a place when applied to frameworks and structures for society but not when we are looking at minority and oppressed groups of people. When we apply Freire's points on adhering to the masses by using the dominant language, this would result in many native languages not being used and would have consequences of underrepresentation. This differs from hooks discussions of language in which she explains we should not always use the dominant discourse in educational settings. hooks does not follow this notion of adhering to the masses when she calls for enabling students and teachers to represent minority voices. Therefore, we need to consider how we achieve a balance between the two arguments in our early years classrooms.

Freire attempts to find this balance when he considers language in a more explicit fashion (Child, 2014). We can draw parallels to hooks' considerations on the power that language can hold and its role in oppression and colonisation. Here Freire states that you cannot discuss language without thinking of ideology and power (Child, 2014). He also asks the question of who is the one to say that a particular accent or way of thinking is more cultivated. Freire accepts that teachers need to teach the more dominant discourse and that all people have a right to learn the dominant pattern (Child, 2014). But educators must be specific in the way they teach this, and Freire discusses the key features to teaching the dominant language emphasising that it is necessary for the teacher to explain and make clear that all ways of thinking and everybody's voice are as beautiful as the dominant dialect. The teacher must defend everybody's right to speak the way they do.

In his article 'aboriginalising methodology: considering the canoe', Peter Cole (2002) shows us an example of how academic practice can be presented in non-traditional ways. He constructs his writing around his Aboriginal language, his native way of thinking and grammar, for example:

> ama sqit nilhsten skwatsits tsexox welcome to the sound of running water ideo morphic ortho graphies.

> *(Cole, 2002. pp. 447)*

In doing so, he shows how we can successfully put hooks' arguments on including native languages into educational practice. Cole's thoughts correspond directly to hooks by discussing many similar areas such as how the English language was forced upon his nation when attending residential schools in the US. He also explains how in some places his language was deemed un-official (Cole, 2002). He talks about his experience of allowing himself to be un-consciously colonised by the use of the English language. However, when analysing this in relation to Freire's viewpoint in Child (2014), we can see further evidence of how his view of the oppressed having to learn the dominant language can become problematic. It is evident that it can create feelings of further oppression when people are required to use a forced language in educational settings, which demonstrates further the need for early childhood settings to create a balance and include discussions, activities, and provocations around the concepts of language and differing languages for children to explore.

During my time as a baby room leader, I had a child join my setting who was struggling to settle into nursery and presented themselves as being very quiet and withdrawn. After having a discussion with their parents, they shared with us the information that the child spoke Spanish at home as well as English. The child had developed a strong bank of words in her home language. Following this information, we produced some flash cards with Spanish words for the staff to use with the child. After a few weeks the child became fully engaged and would bring staff members animal toys using the Spanish words to tell us what they had found. They also enjoyed pointing out items in the book in Spanish. It enabled us as staff members to understand what the child's needs were as they began to use the words Agua (water) and Leche (milk) in the setting. This shows us how we can use children's different experiences to enable them to grow in confidence and facilitate them in being understood in the way they wish. It also further highlights the importance of parent partnerships and enabling parents to feel they can share information surrounding home languages within settings.

However, when we apply hooks' pedagogy of enabling students to use their home languages to the English Early Years Foundation Stage Statutory Framework (Department for Education, 2023), an issue arises, namely, the language the Framework uses itself. The Framework states

> for children whose home language is not English, providers must take reasonable steps to provide opportunities for children to develop and use their home language in play and learning, supporting their language development at home.
>
> *(Department for Education, 2023. Pp. 17)*

234 Poppie Ephgrave

However, what constitutes a *reasonable* step? Fumoto, Hargreaves and Maxwell already explored this issue in 2007. They stated that although it was reassuring to see mention of children with English as an additional language in early years guidance, it did not yet seek to provide practitioners with the underpinning knowledge they required. For example, many practitioners did not understand why it was important for parents to continue encouraging the development of the child's native language at home and believed bilingualism was something they would grow out of (Fumoto et al., 2007). Whilst Fumoto et al.'s analysis was written some time ago, we are still experiencing the same ambiguity and uncertainty in today's updated Framework. Therefore, the Statutory Framework has to provide further guidance to practitioners. There is a clear need for further training and support for those working with children who have English as an additional language (Fumoto et al., 2007). I would suggest that policymakers begin by applying hooks' pedagogy and start having regular discussions surrounding the use of foreign languages in early years settings.

As stated by Pirrie, Fang and O'Brien (2021), there is an educational imperative to care for language, taking responsibility for our words and their meaning. We also need to be alert to our own language, acknowledging that we cannot fully know what our words will mean to others. This applies to both our Early Years Statutory Frameworks and our individual interactions with children, families and staff. It shows us the significance early years settings and educators can have through enabling all key players to use their home language within the sector. It also highlights the flaw in our current framework that privileges children who already have a comprehensive understanding of standard English as it explicitly states that children need to learn English to be able to truly benefit from the opportunities available to them when they begin Year 1 in primary school (Department for Education, 2023). What message is this telling children and parents in our care about their sense of being and belonging that, if they do not learn English by the age of 5, they are not going to be able to access these opportunities?

As Freire explores, many political and educational plans have failed because their authors designed them according to their own personal views of reality. When considering the limited ethnic diversity within the current English government, who created this Framework, it is evident why there are significant flaws and a lack of consideration for the true needs of children with additional languages. Whilst there is no official data on the number of members of parliament from minority backgrounds, it is estimated that following the 2019 general election, 10% of members of the House of Commons were from minority ethnic backgrounds. This is significantly lower than the population average (Uberoi & Carthew, 2023). Therefore, to improve the Early Years Statutory Framework guidance for practitioners on supporting children with English as an additional language, we need to follow Freire's suggestions and start by engaging dialogically with people who access early years settings with additional languages on both a policy and practice level. Following the work of hooks and Freire, this is the only way to truly liberate the people within the sector. Following Freire's notion of libertarian education, we can enact social change by understanding where our practice needs to be modified in order to benefit the oppressed, by understanding their needs. Policymakers can then improve frameworks, educate practitioners, and put into action (praxis) the changes required. Altering the Framework creates a level of accountability to settings. However, practitioners and early years settings can individually raise their standards of 'reasonable steps' and engage in dialogue with the families currently at our settings with immediate effect. This is key because there are still many dominant discourses that consolidate power and privilege (Gereluk, 2012) that influence our everyday lives, such as the supremacy of standard English within the Early Years Statutory Framework.

Additionally, we can draw upon ideas from both hooks and Freire to improve the early years sector for people who have English as an additional language. We can implement Freire's discussions on the role of the teacher in engaging in dialogue surrounding language and hooks' recommendations of using multiple languages in educational settings. It is important to encourage people to take a step back and realise we do not always have to understand the entire narrative. There is value in reflection and silence. We can also include works such as Peter Cole's (2002) to educate early years practitioners and encourage them to ask questions similar to Carroll and O'Connor (2012). This is with the aim of improving the experiences of children within the early years foundation stage, to enable them to build secure foundations for their future.

The Value of Experience Within Dialogue

Freire places significant importance on the inclusion of experience within education, and he discusses this through his critique of the banking concept. The banking concept understands knowledge as a gift that is bestowed upon students with the teaching being positioned as all-knowing and wholly necessary. Freire explains that dialogue for education cannot simply be reduced to one person depositing ideas into another. It is not our role as human beings to talk to people solely about our view of the world or to impose our view upon them. We are to engage in a back-and-forth dialogue about their view as well as our own. Freire explains that the banking concept is used by dominant elites to encourage further passivity in the oppressed. hooks also critiques the banking concept in her essays stating that with so many teachers using this standpoint, it becomes so difficult to create a learning community that embraces multiculturalism. The two authors are united in their views of the banking concept, and both offer similar critiques and solutions for moving forward from an education of depositing.

236 Poppie Ephgrave

Freire explains that the banking concept mirrors oppressive society as a whole and encourages people to accept what is bestowed upon them. There is no room or inspiration for critical thinking, particularly in adult education. He explains that educators can overcome this by rejecting the banking concept and creating an environment where the teachers and students are mutual learners. This causes a shift in the students' experiences as they are no longer passive listeners; they are co-investigators engaging in a consistent dialogue with the teacher. Now the role of the teacher is to provide the material to the students for their consideration and move the learning forward for all. Freire explains how this can lead to increased engagement due to the students being able to relate to the content and feel less alienated from what they are learning. Rejecting the banking concept and enabling education as the practice of freedom allows for authentic reflection, providing people with a consciousness to the world around them. In Freire's view this is essential for social change and justice.

hooks discusses education as the practice of freedom within the context of the classroom, stating that this is a way of teaching that anyone can learn. If we believe our work is not merely to share information but to share the intellectual and spiritual growth of our students, we will be providing the conditions that are essential for deep and meaningful learning to take place. hooks explores this further by discussing how the educational system she was taught in failed to address her social reality causing her to lose interest and feel uncomfortable within this setting. This highlights how important it is for us to include the students' experiences within our practice to encourage critical awareness and engagement in their education. This allows the students to develop their own internal monologue of thought and analysis that should be encouraged and shared in the classroom. However, hooks highlights that as educators, we need to be extra vigilant in our work to ensure that neglected discourses are enabled to enter the classroom discussions when internal monologues are being shared. hooks gives the example of many white males that have entered her classroom insistent that their experiences and voice are worth being heard. She reflects upon this stating that it is due to the politics of race and gender within a white supremacy context, that grants them this authority without them having to desire for it. It is our job as early years educators to challenge this narrative from the start of a child's educational journey.

Freire discusses the notion of the thematic universe, which is essentially the reality that people perceive themselves to be living in. Freire states that this is where we must go to find the content of education, and to get there, we must engage in dialogue. We can see how hooks explores the thematic universe in her pedagogy, similar to Freire in the way she discusses how she will adapt her practice depending on what is brought up in the classroom. hooks explains that one day she might ask her students to ponder what they want to know and what their end goal might be. Or sometimes the dialogue of experience can halt them from reaching the goals they had set out to achieve. hooks explains that it is okay to not achieve the goals as all learning is valuable. Something that hooks and Freire both explore regularly throughout their discussions surrounding dialogue is how it is a fluid and changing experience. Dialogue surrounding experiences is often the ignitor to change and fluidity in dialogue and social justice issues. I believe it is the experience of the people that is the most important aspect to analyse in relation to learning and development. If we do not hear the experiences of others, we may not be able to help them advance from them or deepen our own understanding of the world we live in. This further highlights the importance of including experiences related to the child's reality in the early years classroom.

Chetty (2016) shows us the value of including children's experiences in the classroom through his discussion of children's story writing in the school context. Although this does not correspond directly to early childhood education, we can apply this to how we teach in the early childhood sector. Chetty (2016) explains that in his classroom children of colour would write stories featuring traditional English names, although this did not reflect their home experience. He encourages teachers to give these children permission to write about their own experiences and for us to reflect on what resources we have in the classroom. In the Ted talk, Chimamanda Ngozi Adichie (2019) also stresses the importance of having literature that represents children's experiences in connection with how we can never have too much representative literature. She explores the notion that we need to ensure we are consciously picking stories that represent the children we are reading to and that we share a wide variety of perspectives. Practitioners need to challenge stereotypes themselves and show an awareness to how impressionable children are through literature (Adichie, 2019). Adichie's talk (2019) truly resonated with me as I came from a private setting fortunate enough to have a lot of representative books. However, it really encouraged me to reflect on whether I myself and other practitioners are truly mindful of what we are reading to the children and on the need to be more attentive in how we pick the stories off the bookshelf. It led me to conclude that to enhance the children's experiences and cultural capital we need to improve our own first. When applying this to hooks and Freire, we can see how important it is to engage in dialogue with the children and families we work with regarding their experiences so that we can ensure we have the resources and discussions available to enable the children and families to feel valued and enhance the child's learning and development further.

When analysing the importance of experience in dialogue in relation to early childhood education in England, I think there are already some areas of Freire's and hooks' practice that the sector tries to embrace. Experience is a strong focal point through much of early childhood literature surrounding the importance of the unique child and the value children's personal experiences hold within their learning (Department for Education, 2021; Gouldsboro, 2017). We also consider the unique child through theorists such as Bronfenbrenner (1979). His work regarding children at the centre of their environments and his highlighting of the importance of this within both family settings and wider contexts is now a large contributing theory that underpins many early childhood education practices (Bronfenbrenner, 1979; Hayes, O'Toole and Halpenny, 2017). We have also seen a large shift in common practice to child-initiated learning and in-the-moment planning. This allows the children to draw upon their own experiences and interests to determine what they would like to learn, play with and access throughout the nursery day (Ephgrave, 2018). When the theory is applied correctly, the practitioners engage in dialogue with the children to enhance their learning and development, talking to them about what they are experiencing and asking the children questions to deepen their knowledge of the world around them.

However, in my experience, when this is being implemented into settings, there is a lot of ambiguity surrounding the role of the practitioner. It can sometimes revert to discussions about the 'power' of the teacher. Fisher (2016) discusses how child-led learning as a concept puts the child in control of their learning. Describing the role of the child in this way instantly creates a sense of lack of control for the teacher. In contrast, drawing upon hooks' and Freire's pedagogy of the teacher also being involved in the learning experience and stepping away from the banking concept can enhance the understanding and value of child-led learning. We are very privileged in the English early years sector in comparison to the National Curriculum to have a framework that allows settings some scope to develop and implement their own curriculum. Although this comes with its challenges when working under regulatory bodies such as Ofsted (Office for Standards in Education). Recently, we have seen an upsurge of stories in the press and on social media that highlight the stress, anxiety and health impacts from Ofsted inspections on early childhood practitioners (Albin-Clark & Archer, 2023). The criticisms highlight that the intense scrutiny and weighting of Ofsted gradings has significantly resulted in a diminished sense of agency for early childhood educators (Osgood, 2010). However, I believe that as a sector we need to take advantage of the flexible statutory framework, and, through claiming back our agency, we can create a shift in practice to include the child's voice and experiences further. I also believe if we implement this from a young age, it will aid children in critical thinking strategies and allow them to experience the benefits of an education of freedom, setting secure foundations for life.

Conclusion

In conjunction with hooks and Freire, we can see that it is our role as early years educators to open the dialogue, looking at the language we use and the experiences we, the children, the families, and the staff members bring to the table, to enable critical thinkers. This will aid us in creating a more just society to improve the lives of everybody.

The Need for Dialogue **239**

As explored by hooks and Freire, education should be for freedom and can play a vital role in the improvements of our society. Eagleton (1992) in hooks explains that children make the best theorists since they have not been educated into accepting the routines of society as 'natural'. Children are therefore not afraid to ask the most embarrassing and fundamental questions. As a practitioner it is our role to foster this way of thinking and encourage the questioning to continue.

By applying Freire's and hooks' pedagogies surrounding experience and language we can enable a dialogue in early childhood between all contributing parties to move forward, discuss and break the limiting boundaries of oppressive societies. Opening the dialogue is the purpose of education and without the inclusion of other languages and different experiences within this dialogue, how can we expect to move forward and advance towards a just society? We need to continue to open the dialogue and act upon it to advance our practice as individuals and in our settings by sharing our experiences with others. We can achieve this by creating a learning community that is empowered to enact change for the benefit of social justice within the early years sector and potentially in wider society.

Note

1 Throughout the chapter when discussing hooks and Freire I will be referring to the below texts unless specified otherwise.
hooks = hooks, b. (1994) *Teaching to Transgress. Education as the Practice of Freedom.* Abingdon. Routledge.
Freire = Freire, P. (1970) *Pedagogy of the Oppressed.* London. Penguin Classics.

References

Adichie, CN (2019). *Chimamanda Ngozi Adichie: The danger of a single story.* YouTube. Retrieved from: https://www.youtube.com/watch?v=D9Ihs241zeg
Albin-Clark, J & Archer, N (2023). Resisting intensified accountability: is now the time for inspection reform? *Early Education.* Retrieved from: Resisting intensified accountability: is now the time for inspection reform? - Early Education (early-education.org.uk)
Bronfenbrenner, U (1979). *The Ecology of Human Development: Experiments by Nature and Design.* Cambridge, MA. Harvard University Press.
Carroll, T. & O'Connor, A. (2012) EYFS: English as an Additional Language – Second best? *Nursery World.* Retrieved from: https://www.nurseryworld.co.uk/features/article/eyfs-english-as-an-additional-language-second-best
Chetty, D (2016). 'You can't say that! Stories have to be about white people' In Shukla, N. (Ed.), *The Good Immigrant.* London: Unbound. pp. 70–76.
Child, E (2014.) *Paulo Freire: On Language and Power.* YouTube. Retrieved from: https://www.youtube.com/watch?v=DTwY2nGONs8
Cole, P (2002). aboriginalizing methodology: considering the canoe. *Qualitative Studies in Education, 15*(4), 447–459. Retrieved from: http://knowledgepublic.pbworks.com/f/Cole-AboriginalizingMethodology.pdf

Department for Education (2023). *Early years foundation stage statutory framework. For group and school-based providers.* Retrieved from: https://assets.publishing. service.gov.uk/media/659d3e68aaae22001356dc46/Early_years_foundation_ stage_statutory_framework_for_group_and_school-based_providers.pdf

Eagleton, T (1992). Literary theory: An introduction, 2nd ed. In Hooks, B. (Ed.), (1994) *Teaching to Transgress. Education as the Practice of Freedom.* Abingdon: Routledge.

Ephgrave, A (2018). *Planning in the Moment with Young Children. A Practical Guide for Early Years Practitioners and Parents.* Abingdon: Routledge. Retrieved from: https://ebookcentral.proquest.com/lib/herts/reader.action?docID=52577 07&ppg=7

Fisher, J (2016). *Interacting or Interfering? Improving Interaction in the Early Years.* Maidenhead: McGraw-Hill Education.

Freire, P (1970). *Pedagogy of the Oppressed.* London: Penguin Classics.

Fumoto, H, Hargreaves, DJ, & Maxwell, S (2007). Teachers' perceptions of their relationships with children who speak English as an additional language in early childhood settings. *Journal of Early Childhood Research*, 5(2), 135–153. Retrieved from: https://journals.sagepub.com/doi/epdf/10.1177/1476718X07076680

Gereluk, D (2012). Education for social justice. In Provenzo, E.F. & Renaud, J.P. (Eds.), *Encyclopaedia of the Social and Cultural Foundations of Education.* London: SAGE Publications. pp. 728–732.

Gouldsboro, JM (2017). *Promoting British Values in the Early Years: How to Foster a Sense of Belonging.* Abingdon: Routledge. Retrieved from: https://ebookcentral. proquest.com/lib/herts/reader.action?docID=4891086&ppg=5

Hayes, N, O'Toole, L & Halpenny, AM (2017). *Introducing Bronfenbrenner: A Guide for Practitioners and Students in Early Years Education.* Abingdon: Routledge. Retrieved from: https://ebookcentral.proquest.com/lib/herts/detail.action?docID=4825055

Hooks, B (1994). *Teaching to Transgress. Education as the Practice of Freedom.* Abingdon: Routledge.

Mao-Tse-Tung (1967). *Vol. III. The united front in cultural work.* In Freire, P.(Ed.) (1970) *Pedagogy of the Oppressed.* London: Penguin Classics.

Osgood, J (2010). Reconstructing professionalism in ECEC: The case for the 'critically reflective emotional professional. *Early Years*, 30(2), 119–133.

Pirrie, A, Fang, N, & O'Brien, E (2021). *Dancing in the Dark. A Survivor's Guide to the University.* Scotland: Tilosophy press.

Rich, A (1989). *The Burning of Paper not Children.* Retrieved from: http:// poemaseningles.blogspot.com/2004/09/adrienne-rich-burning-of-paper-instead. html

Smidt, MS (2022). *Language Attrition.* University of Essex. Retrieved from: https:// languageattrition.org

Uberoi, E & Carthew, H (2023). *Research Briefing. Ethnic Diversity in Politics and Public Life.* UK Parliament House of Commons Library. Retrieved from: https:// commonslibrary.parliament.uk/research-briefings/sn01156/

22

NURTURING THE SPIRITUAL IN CHILDREN – ENACTING A SPIRITUAL PEDAGOGY TO DEVELOP CHILDREN'S SENSE OF SELF

Elizabeth Rouse

Introduction

Contemporary early childhood education is framed by a policy context which suggests that educators have the responsibility to prepare children as competent contributors to a productive society. UNESCO (2023) states that early childhood education and care (ECEC) "can lay the foundation for good health and nutrition, learning and educational success, social-emotional learning, and economic productivity throughout life". ECEC is seen as a cost-effective form of human capital development (Heckman, 2012; Penn, 2010), and early years education is often justified for its potential to afford a society future economic benefit (Murray, 2023) and competitiveness (Penn, 2010). Investing in young children's education is viewed as essential for "greater labour market participation and earnings, better physical health and fewer healthcare costs, and lower involvement in criminal activity throughout the life course of individuals who participate in high-quality ECEC" (OECD, 2021, p. 21). Contemporary images of ECEC settings are now of places where children's outcomes are "mainly concerned with the future development, educational attainment and employability of the child, in a context of increasing competition and change" (Dahlberg & Moss, 2005, p. 4).

'What it means to learn' is being viewed through a lens of attainment, whereby learning is measured by the extent to which children are successful in attaining the skills and knowledge they need to contribute as successful future economic citizens. This discourse around the aim and purpose of ECEC has resulted in a global movement trending towards the implementation of push-down curricula which focus on outcomes comparable to those identified in curricula designed for older children (Sims, 2017). Contemporary ECEC

DOI: 10.4324/9781003471172-26

242 Elizabeth Rouse

policy and curriculum approaches are being shaped by international organisations such as the OECD, the World Bank and UNESCO. ECEC is all too often viewed as a "means to train children for school" (Moss, 2010, p. 9) where there is an emphasis "on competition, more formal teaching of 'the basics', rigidly defined outcomes and oppressive testing and assessment regimes" (Best, 2016, p. 273). To meet this global and international productivity agenda, increasing time is now spent focusing on literacy and math instruction, and taking or preparing for tests in ECEC (Miller & Almon, 2009), so that children on entering compulsory schooling can be competent in achieving standardised literacy and numeracy benchmarks. Sims argues that "learning outcomes not easily matched to those identified in the [curriculum] framework[s] are not valued, perhaps ignored and perhaps not addressed" (Sims, 2017, p. 4).

In this contemporary discourse where children are positioned as future economic citizens, what it means to be and children's sense of self, are framed by the extent to which they are assessed as having the potential to contribute to a future productive society. What is missing from the rhetoric of success from this human capital perspective is a more holistic understanding of childhood through a standpoint of children as beings. The image today's children have of themselves as competent and successful humans is based not on who they are (of being), but who they will become. In this context what children will become is not based on ethical, moral or social values regarding what it means to be a citizen. Children are now held responsible for attaining the measures of academic success that are deemed necessary to prevent becoming "illiterate and innumerate persons, who are a drag on productivity and a source of social and economic problems" (Heckman and Masterov, 2007, p. 452). Nitecki and Wasmuth (2021, p. 6) suggest that this image of the child positions them as "a saviour of the future" where they are regarded as objects, to be manipulated as pawns in a bigger economic paradigm.

In contrast, Jackson (2009, cited in Moss, 2010, p. 13) views prosperity not through an economic lens, but through the argument that "prosperity consists in our ability to flourish as human beings". There is an alternate paradigm regarding what it means to be human, where the focus is on the becoming of the self. What it means to be human should not be measured by economic prosperity, but rather by an individual's sense of self, one's sense of their own being and the empathy and compassion they have for others. Biesta (2015) argues for an alternate viewpoint regarding the aim and purpose of education as introducing children to the ways of doing and ways of being that are part of the existing traditions. His belief is that education should be about the ways it impacts on the personhood of the child, and what it means to 'be'.

This chapter will argue that rather than engaging with and perpetuating the view that to be human is to be productive in economic ways, and that the role of early childhood educators is to "train children for school" (Moss, 2010,

p. 9), a more important role of early childhood education and care is to reframe children's sense of what it means to be human. Froebel suggests that it is important to educate the whole child,

> to facilitate the development of its body, mind, feelings, aesthetic aware-ness, morality and potential for imaginative and creative activity, to encour-age the ('inner') engagement with the ('outer') world through 'self-action', to experience what it is to know joy and sadness, to love and to be loved – to become a person as fully and as meaningfully as is possible.
>
> *(Best, 2016, p. 281)*

Froebel saw all things in nature (animal, vegetable, and mineral) as being con-nected and understood the interrelationship between human and non-human, where there is a unity in all things. He viewed the purpose of education as instilling in children an appreciation of natural forms and harmonies (Provenzo, 2009). Noddings (2013) explains humans are naturally in relation with others and our very individuality is defined within this set of relations, suggesting that as human beings we are all interconnected, interdependent relational beings (London, 2016; Noddings, 2013; Zhang & Wu, 2016). Froebel believed that people need to be educated to think for themselves, and not to rely on the thinking of others to tell them how they should think (Bruce, 2015). To "be" a free thinker in this context is to know oneself, and one's place in the world. Selfhood involves a commitment to others as well as being "true to oneself" (Bruner, 2004, p. 11).

The phenomenon of self – what it means to be

Bruner (2004) argued that selfhood is a way of "framing one's consciousness, one's position, one's identity, one's commitment with respect to another" (Bruner, 1990, p. 101). He saw education as playing a crucial role in the for-mation of self. For Bruner, the single most universal human experience is the phenomenon of self. *Self* is an individual's reflexive stance of her or his own particular identity (Jenkins, 2014). Bruner believed that self-making is humans' principle means for establishing our uniqueness. One's sense of self, and how one sees oneself in the world, is shaped by the culture and experiences that surround a person and is formed by their connection and interactions with the world. These experiences shape the way children perceive themselves – their sense of identity.

Identity as defined by Eaude (2020, p. 17) is "a construct which encapsu-lates all elements of who a person is, and feels that she or he is …and is loosely associated with concepts like personality, character and self". It is about who one is involving qualities and dispositions, such as resilience, empathy and compassion (Eaude, 2016). Identity centres around an understanding of

244 Elizabeth Rouse

"who am I", "where do I fit in" and "why am I here" (Eaude, 2020, p. 18). Champagne (2009, p. 2) argues that identity is "experienced, supported and developed … by relationships and experiences". Learning should be about understanding one's sense of self, of being, and of what it means to be human. The essence of what it means to "be" is in danger of being eroded and transformed when children are positioned as units of economic potential, where children's value and worth are measured by the extent to which they fulfil human capital expectations. In contrast, Froebel believed the child to have a natural predisposition to see "the truth", and thus to make the connections between the contrasts necessary for understanding (Best, 2016, p. 277). Froebel connected this with an understanding of spiritual education.

The importance of nurturing the spiritual in young children

Spirituality is included in many early childhood curricula and frameworks globally (Rouse and Hyde forthcoming). Nurturing the spiritual child is shaped by relations and connectivity– supporting young children to engage in ethical relations with self, others and the world. The spirit is, for Froebel, *not* some unsubstantial 'part' of us, but is more like the essence or *whole* of us, of that which is "inner" (Best, 2016, p. 281).

The Early Years Framework for Australia defines the spiritual as "a range of human experiences including a sense of awe and wonder, or peacefulness, and an exploration of being and knowing" (Australian Government Department of Education, 2022, p. 68). Spirituality includes interwoven notions of spirit, soul, inner being, and heart - all of which comprise the 'who' one is as a person (Greenfield, 2018). Spirituality is "an aspect of humanity common to all persons throughout every stage of their life and is located in the potential of every child to relate to and make sense of questions of ultimate significance" (Goodliff, 2013, p. 28). Furthermore, Bone, Cullen and Loveridge (2007) suggest that spirituality has the power to introduce mystery and wonder into otherwise mundane events and may support feeling whole or complete. Spirituality deals with meaning, purpose and direction in life (Baker, 2003).

Children's spirituality, while "inherently mysterious…is often – and most obviously for young children – manifested, and enhanced, within everyday experience" (Eaude 2009, 191). Across the literature words such as "awe", "wonder", "joy", "happiness" (Grajczonek, 2012; Mata-McMahon, Haslip & Schein, 2019; Robinson, 2022) are used to describe children engaging with the spiritual. In keeping with this understanding, Hay and Nye (2006) suggest that children have an ability called spiritual sensing, which is guiding them to embrace wonder, awe and imagination to experience life's mysteries. In addition, Eaude (2020) argues that spiritual development involves the search for identity, meaning and purpose. Early years educators are in a prime position to nurture this aspect of a child's spiritual awakening and development, and to do so requires an understanding of what it means to *"be"*. "Children's spiritual development is touched, influenced and shaped not only by themselves, but also by those with whom they interact as well as by the world around them" (Stockinger, 2019, p.307). When learning is viewed through a spiritual lens, the focus shifts from *learning for attainment* to *learning about self*.

A pedagogy for nurturing the spiritual

When children are seen through a human capital lens, there is a danger of thinking of children professionally (van Manen, 2015), rather than thinking of children holistically through a lens that focuses on what it means to be human. A human capital view of childhood leads to thinking about children in an abstract way – as categories based on common characteristics that allow children to be grouped – and in education this grouping is largely based on levels of academic attainment or success. The uniqueness of each child is overlooked, and children are 'measured' in preconceived ways, often based on external measurements of what success should look like, and the relationship experienced is predicated on the category children have been grouped into.

Teaching involves the adult in a pedagogical relationship with children (van Manen, 1990) and teachers "act deliberately, thoughtfully and purposefully to support children's learning" (Australian Government Department of Education, 2022, p. 22). The pedagogical relationship is an intentional relation, one in which the intent of the teacher is "always determined in a double direction: by caring for a child as he or she is and by caring for the child for what she may become" (van Manen, 2015, 119). Noddings (2013) argues that relationships are ontologically basic to humanity and suggests that identity is defined by the set of relationships individuals have with other humans. Relationality is fundamental for all of us (Noddings, 2013), leading to a feeling of acceptance, empathy, compassion and respect for all beings (de Souza and Watson, 2016; Eaude, 2016; Zhang and Wu, 2016) and Spiritual development is shaped by relations and connectivity– supporting young children to engage in ethical relations with self, others and the world – to see and understand the unity in all things. Relationality and connectedness are essential to being human and are key components of spirituality (de Souza and Halafoff, 2017, Rowlings, 2008). Therefore, Noddings (2013, p. 30) argues that education must involve an ethical relationship between the teacher and the child that involves the teacher being in "feeling with the other", where one sees the concern, delight or interest in the eyes of the child. She argues for the establishment of caring relationships rooted in receptivity, relatedness and responsiveness which she sees as the foundation of pedagogy.

Mata-McMahon et al. (2019) go further and argue that children's spirituality is the 'life force' that propels learning. Nurturing the spiritual child involves teachers thinking of pedagogy in terms of spirituality. More importantly it involves educators enacting pedagogies that show the child the importance of who they are in the here and now, their place in the world and their responsibility to this world. van Manen (2015) discusses pedagogy in terms of understanding the inner life of a child, knowing how he or she experiences things, how they look at the world, how they act and most importantly how each child is a unique person. He presents pedagogy as an intensely experienced relation between the adult and the child. From an ontological perspective, who they will become should not premise on a child's capacity for an economic contribution to a society's prosperity, but on their capacity to be human. To flourish as a human being is to connect with human qualities such as love, kindness, forgiveness, and generosity (Thomas and Lockwood, 2009). Through engaging with these qualities children can develop empathy towards humans and non-humans and can begin to act altruistically towards others. A spiritual pedagogy recognises that children are not just citizens of the future, but are citizens of the here and now, who live in, and participate in, a world where freedom, tolerance, debate and social justice are valued (Sims, 2017). It supports the creation of a space where children are enabled to think for themselves, and not to rely on the thinking of others to tell them how they should think (Bruce, 2015). Holistic pedagogical approaches which encompass a nurturing of the spiritual child, support children to develop capacities to feel, think, and imagine themselves relationally (Blaikie, Daigle and Vasseur, 2020), and together form parts of a child's spiritual development.

The concept of pedagogical relation should be critical and fundamental in educational thought (van Manen, 2015). van Manen suggests that all children want to be regarded – to be valued, seen, known, as well as cared for and watched over. To be "recognised" from a pedagogical perspective involves interpersonal encounters that are intertwined between the relation one has with one's self, and the relation to other. He reminds teachers that "children are not there for us – we are there for them … they come to us bearing a gift: the gift of experiencing the possible … they experience life as possibility" (van Manen, 2015, p.35). van Manen further argues that pedagogy requires a sensitive understanding of the nature of childhood, and the kinds of lives children are living. In adding to this, Noddings (2003) argues that humans have a fundamental desire for happiness, and this should be an aim of education. Consequently, teaching should respond to every human's need to feel happiness. "Happy people are rarely violent or intentionally cruel, either to other human beings or to non-human animals" (Noddings, 2003, p. 2). She draws from Aristotle's notion of "*eudaimonia*" which she translates as human flourishing and in turn calls happiness (Noddings, 2003).

Educators working with young children need to develop a consciousness regarding how their actions and responses to children, through a dialogic and bi-directional connection with the child, foster a positive sense of who they are. Nohl (1967, cited in van Manen, 2015, p. 119) spoke about this in terms of it being a pedagogical relation – an intensely experienced relationship emerging between the adult and the child. The pedagogical relation is more than just a bi-directional experience between the teacher and the child, it is something that encapsulates and surrounds people where they are enabled to experience their singularity and uniqueness. This is akin to what Buber (2008) describes as the *I-Thou* relation; one in which each is truly present with the other in the here and now. Teachers therefore have to engage in more than a professional relationship with children; they have to see the whole child, and through the pedagogical relation, foster in children a sense of their own being, of who they are and of the connection with self that supports them to flourish as human beings.

For educators this means they need to intentionally plan responsive engagements with children that enable them to flourish and develop a positive sense of who they are, and their connection with what it means to be human. As mentioned above, this requires educators engaging in ethical relationships with children involving "feeling with the other" (Noddings, 2013, p. 30), so that the educator can see the delight and joy through the eyes of the child, and in turn, support the child to engage with their own sense of purpose.

Playfulness as spiritual pedagogy

To be spiritual is to be playful, to celebrate joy and happiness. For educators, to be playful (and engage in playfulness) is to engage with children in practices that endeavour to find the child's inner glee – their sense of wonder and joy. Educators need to celebrate and share delight in and with the child experiencing the awe and wonderment that is found through being curious, spontaneous and in the moment. Children need opportunities to wonder as this introduces a sense of mystery into children's lives where they are consumed by a moment in time. It is connected to the emotions of joy, love and awe (Mata-McMahon et al., 2019) and "begins as a wave of surprise" (Piersol 2014, cited in Robinson, 2022, p. 158) leading to feelings of amazement and curiosity.

A spiritual pedagogy is about celebrating what it means to be, and nurtures the child's inner peace. Peace is a state of being. To have inner peace, is to have a tranquil, calm and harmonious state of mind and heart, which can work to eliminate anxieties, fears and worries, and can help remove negative thoughts, stress, lack of satisfaction and unhappiness. It is about being at peace with one's self, and the relationship one has with one's sense of being. To be at peace is to feel relaxed, calm and safe, to be happy and be able to connect with what brings one a sense of presence being in the moment.

Playfulness is being present with the child and connecting with the child on a deeper plane, but also enabling children to be fully present in the here and now. Nurturing spirituality through playfulness requires educators engaging in an ethical relationship with the child that involves being present with the child to see the delight and joy through their eyes, and in turn, support the child to engage with their own sense of purpose. Being playful, to experience awe and wonder enables children to experience through their senses, the physical world – to connect with something other than themselves, and to understand the relationship they have with both human and non-human entities.

For Froebel, play is "the purest, most spiritual activity of man at this stage, and, at the same time, typical of human life as a whole – of the inner natural life in man and all things. (Froebel 1887, 55, cited in Best, 2016, p. 280). Through play children are enabled to become transfixed in the moment. Play provides a context for children to explore and reveal who they are, as they play alone or with others engaging in spaces of mystery and imagination. Imaginative and pretend play provides opportunities for children to draw on their unique inner selves and inner worlds to express their understanding and awareness of their connections to more than self. Imagination is an essential human capacity where humans create spaces which are beyond time and place (Goodliff, 2013). When children engage in exploration through the creative and expressive arts (such as painting, drawing, music, dance) they express their feelings, thinking and knowing about who they are, fostering a sense of self in ways that support them to make meaning of their world, and what it means to be. Through this creative expression of self, children can explore the mystery and wonder that surrounds them, and it could be argued connect with a more spiritual self as they transcend from an external thinking of themselves as they exist and become conscious of their personal identity.

Creating a space where the spiritual can be nurtured requires teachers to purposefully and carefully provide aesthetically beautiful and stimulating environments, which enable children to engage in relational consciousness with self, other and the non-human world, and in which children can have opportunities to be contemplative. In these spaces children can learn to appreciate what might otherwise be seen as ordinary or mundane, and children's everyday play and experiences thus become spaces of many possibilities. When children are present in the space and fully and intrinsically engaged in the play, they are enjoying the spiritual moment (Mata-McMahon et al., 2019).

Concluding thoughts

This chapter has highlighted the need for educators to re-examine the aim and purpose of early childhood education to see beyond a lens of childhood wherein which children are afforded value based on their capacity to meet the demands expected of them as "saviour[s] of the future" (Nitecki and Wasmuth, 2021, p. 6). As educators we have an ethical and moral responsibility to see not just the academic child, but the human child; the child who is celebrated for who they are in the here and now. van Manen (2015) reminds us that all children want to be regarded – to be valued, seen, known, as well as cared for and watched over. Therefore, it is one of the most important roles for educators to see the inner child, their self and their sense of being. Thinking of pedagogy through a spiritual lens provides a frame whereby educators can consciously and purposefully plan for and nurture the whole child. It is only then that children can develop a relational consciousness of their own place in a world which is beyond the human, understanding how both the human and non-human world are interconnected. To live and exist in the world requires a valuing of both self and others, and to be in feeling with the other (Noddings, 2013). Young children have the capability to develop empathy and act altruistically towards others.

A pedagogy which is framed by an understanding of the spiritual supports young children to engage in ethical caring in a post-human world, where one is not measured by academic achievement, but by notions of spirit, soul, inner being, and heart. Educators need to intentionally plan for playful and contemplative environments whereby children can experience joy, wonder, curiosity, and mystery. This supports children to transcend from an external thinking of themselves and their existence, to develop an inner consciousness of their personal identity. Play and being playful is "the purest, most spiritual activity of man" (Froebel 1887, p. 55, cited in Best, 2016, p. 280). When early years educators reposition their pedagogy to encompass their inner playfulness, then they will be present with the child and connecting with the child on a deeper plane. Through this, children are enabled to be fully present in the here and now, where they develop a sense of their own being, of "who they are" (Eaude, 2020), and of the I-self connection that supports them to flourish as human beings.

References

Australian Government Department of Education (2022). *Belonging, Being and Becoming: The Early Years Learning Framework for Australia (V2.0)*. Australian Government Department of Education for the Ministerial Council. https://www.acecqa.gov.au/sites/default/files/2023-01/EYLF-2022-V2.0.pdf

Baker, DC (2003). Studies of the inner life: The impact of spirituality on quality of life. *Quality of Life Research 12*(Suppl. 1), 51–57.

Best, R (2016). Exploring the spiritual in the pedagogy of Friedrich Froebel. *International Journal of Children's spirituality*, 21(3–4), 272–282. http://dx.doi.org/10.1080/1364436X.2016.1231664

Biesta, G (2015). Teaching, teacher education, and the humanities: Reconsidering education as a *Geisteswissenschaft*. *Educational Theory*, 65, 665–679.

Blaikie, F, Daigle, C, & Vasseur, L (2020). *New Pathways for Teaching and Learning: The Posthumanist Approach*. Ottawa, Canada: Canadian Commission for UNESCO.

Bone, J, Cullen, J, & Loveridge, J (2007). Everyday spirituality: An aspect of the holistic curriculum in action. *Contemporary Issues in Early Childhood*, 8(4), 344–354. http://dx.doi.org/10.2304/ciec.2007.8.4.344

250 Elizabeth Rouse

Bruce, T (2015). Friedrich Froebel. In T. David, K. Goouch, & S. Powell (Eds.), *The Routledge International Handbook of Philosophies and Theories of Early Childhood Education and Care.* https://www.routledgehandbooks.com/doi/10.4324/9781315678979.ch3

Bruner, J (1990). *Acts of Meaning.* Harvard University Press.

Bruner, J (2004). The narrative creation of self. In L.E. Angus & J. McLeod (Eds.), *The Handbook of Narrative and Psychotherapy: Practice, Theory and Research* (pp. 9–21). Sage Publications.

Buber, M (2008). *I and Thou.* Howard Books.

Champagne, E (2009). Together on the journey of plurality. *International Journal of Children's Spirituality, 14*(1), 1–3. DOI:10.1080/13644360802658677

Dahlberg, G, & Moss, P (2005). *Ethics and Politics in Early Childhood Education.* Routledge Falmer.

De Souza, M, & Halafoff, A (2017). Spiritual wellbeing in education. In M. De Souza & A. Halafoff (Eds.), *Re-enchanting education and spiritual wellbeing* (pp. 7–22). Routledge.

De Souza, M, & Watson, J (2016). Understandings and applications of contemporaryspirituality: Analysing the voices. In M. de Souza, J. Bone & J. Watson (Eds.), *Spirituality across Disciplines: Research and Practice* (pp. 331–348). Springer.

Eaude, T (2009). Happiness, emotional well-being and mental health – what has children's spirituality to offer? *International Journal of Children's Spirituality, 14*(3), 185–196.

Eaude, T (2016). *New Perspectives on Young Children's Moral Education – Developing Character through a Virtue Ethic Approach.* Bloomsbury Academic.

Eaude, T (2020). *Identity, Culture and Belonging: Educating Young Children for a Changing World.* Bloomsbury Academic.

Goodliff, G (2013). Spirituality expressed in creative learning: Young children's imagining play as space for mediating their spirituality. *Early Child Development and Care, 183*(8), 1054–1107. DOI:10.1080/03004430.2013.792253

Grajczonek, J (2012). Interrogating the spiritual as constructed in belonging, being and becoming: The early years learning framework for Australia. *Australasian Journal of Early Childhood, 37*(1), 152–160. DOI:10.1177/183693911203700118

Greenfield, CF (2018). Investigation into New Zealand early childhood teachers' perspectives on spirituality and Wairau in teaching. *International Journal of Children's Spirituality, 23*(3), 275–290, DOI:10.1080/1364436X.2018.1460333

Hay, D, & Nye, R (2006). *The Spirit of the Child* (2nd edition). Jessica Kingsley.

Heckman, JJ (2012). *Invest in Early Childhood Development: Reduce Deficits, Strengthen the Economy.* https://heckmanequation.org/wp-content/uploads/2013/07/F_HeckmanDeficitPieceCUSTOM-Generic_052714-3-1.pdf

Heckman, JJ, & Masterov, DV (2007). *Review of Agricultural Economics, 29*(3), 446–493. DOI:10.1111/j.1467-9353.2007.00359

Jenkins, R (2014). *Social Identity.* Taylor & Francis Group.

London, R (2016). Spirituality and education: A framework. In M. de Souza, J. Bone & J. Watson (Eds.), *Spirituality across Disciplines: Research and Practice* (pp. 95–106). Springer International Publishing.

Mata-McMahon, J, Haslip, M, & Schein, DL (2019). Early childhood educators' perceptions of nurturing spirituality in secular settings. *Early Child Development and Care, 189*(14), 2233–2251, DOI:10.1080/03004430.2018.1445734

Miller, E, & Almon, J (2009). *Crisis in the Kindergarten: Why Children Need to Play in School.* Alliance for Childhood. Retrieved from: https://files.eric.ed.gov/fulltext/ED504839.pdf

Moss, P (2010). We cannot continue as we are: The educator in an education for survival. *Contemporary Issues in Early Childhood, 11*(1), 8–19. http://dx.doi.org/10.2304/ciec.2010.11.1.8

Murray, J (2023). What is the purpose of education? A context for early childhood education. *International Journal of Early Years Education, 31*(3), 571–578. DOI: 10.1080/09669760.2023.2238399

Nitecki, E, & Wasmuth, H (2021). The child as "other": The duality of the other and a pedagogy of care. In Z. Kinkead Clark & K.A. Escayg (Eds.), *Reconceptualizing Quality in Early Childhood Education, Care and Development: Understanding the Child and Community* (pp. 3–23). Palgrave MacMillan.

Noddings, N (2013). *Caring: A Relational Approach to Ethics and Moral Education* (2nd ed, updated). University of California Press.

Noddings, N (2003). *Happiness and Education.* Cambridge University Press.

OECD (2021), *Starting Strong VI: Supporting Meaningful Interactions in Early Childhood Education and Care,* Starting Strong, OECD Publishing, Paris, https://doi.org/10.1787/f47a06ae-en

Penn, H (2010). Shaping the future: how human capital arguments about investment in early childhood are being (mis)used in poor countries. In N. Yelland (Ed.), *Contemporary Perspectives on Early Childhood Education* (pp. 49–65). McGraw-Hill Education.

Provenzo, EF (2009). Friedrich Froebel's gifts: Connecting the spiritual and aesthetic to the real world of play and learning. *American Journal of Play.* http://www.journalofplay.org/sites/www.journalofplay.org/files/pdf-articles/2-1-article-friedrich-froebels-gifts.pdf

Robinson, C (2022). The potential of 'wonder' to engage children's spirituality: It's so much more than pondering. *International Journal of Children's Spirituality,* DOI: 10.1080/1364436X.2022.2080646

Rowlings, L (2008). Linking spirituality, school communities, grief and well-being. *International Journal of Children's Spirituality, 13*(3), 241–251.

Sims, M (2017). Neoliberalism and early childhood. *Cogent Education.* https://doi.org/10.1080/2331186X.2017.1365411

Stockinger, H (2019). Developing spirituality – an equal right of every child? *International Journal of Children's Spirituality, 24*(3), 307–319. DOI:10.1080/1364436X.2019.1646218

Thomas, P & Lockwood, V (2009). *Nurturing the Spiritual Child: Compassion, Connection and a Sense of Self.* Early Childhood Australia.

UNESCO (2023). *What You Need to Know about Early Childhood Care and Education.* Retrieved from: https://www.unesco.org/en/early-childhood-education/need-know?TSPD_101_R0=080713870fab2000886afd60c5f29eb8d2909f614e83c189ccd2c11e43dec953bfd736ce2407284008b3c0871b143000f81b18698bced73cd87a2b42556dd8706aab09ac903e8e137638b8eb460e44ff77265f98c355c82b129c8bb94cbe755d

van Manen, M (1990). *Researching Lived Experience: Human Science for an Action Sensitive Pedagogy.* New York: State University of New York Press.

van Manen, M (2015). *Pedagogical Tact: Knowing What to do When You Don't Know What to do.* Routledge.

Zhang, K, & Wu, DI (2016). Towards a holistic teacher education: Spirituality and special education teacher training. In M. de Souza, J. Bone & J. Watson (Eds.), *Spirituality across Disciplines: Research and Practice* (pp. 35–150). Springer International Publishing.

23
TOWARDS A BETTER FUTURE

Ute Ward

All the chapters in this book have, in their individual ways, addressed one or more of the four themes highlighted in the introduction chapter while also responding to the core questions of the book: What is the current state in which we find the early childhood education and care (ECEC) sector? And what can we learn from recent events, crises and developments to work towards a better future and to be prepared for further challenges when they come? Collectively the chapters raise many issues that need addressing but also show-case positive initiatives and actions that are already part of practice in some countries and could provide solutions for others further afield. To summarise the suggestions and ideas from the different chapters, it will be helpful to look at each theme individually before exploring how we can work towards a vision for the future.

Overcoming crises and preparing for future challenges

Chapter 16 by Mabel Giraldo directly addresses how we can prepare more effectively for natural or man-made disasters, while other chapters respond to crises like the pandemic (Chapter 7 on professional development for Croatian EC teachers), inequality (Chapter 10 on the London Early Years Foundation), digitalisation (Chapter 3 on live streaming) and the fear of Artificial Intelligence (AI) (Chapters 4 and 5). We find ECEC in the stranglehold of prescribed curricula and narrow learning outcomes, with limited funding and an under-paid and undervalued workforce, poor provision in disadvantaged neighbour-hoods, and unequal access to high quality support for children's learning and development. Against such a backdrop, dealing with COVID-19 and the ensuing lockdowns was immensely challenging. In many countries, local and

DOI: 10.4324/9781003471172-27

national governments have examined and reflected on their responses and are now trying to prepare more effectively for future health emergencies. Alongside such large-scale planning, we also need to ask what preparedness means in early childhood settings, kindergartens and nurseries.

Based on the comments in the chapters addressing digitalisation and workforce development, it is apparent that many practitioners lacked IT skills and struggled to provide appropriate online support for children's development and learning during lockdown. The European Framework for Digital Competence of Educators offers a valuable tool to help settings and governments to address this (Redecker and Punie, 2017). However, the need for training goes beyond basic technical skills, and practitioners would benefit from exploring what an online early childhood pedagogy should entail. It would be crucial to avoid reinforcing the schoolification that is already prevalent under neoliberal government guidance, and, alongside the support for children, there should be a greater emphasis on the support for parents. Some parents have reported that they greatly appreciated being able to talk to practitioners during the pandemic as this gave them reassurance and confidence in their own abilities. This points to the role changes many practitioners experienced during the pandemic: In addition to becoming developers of online learning material, they also became moral support, adviser and confidante for some parents (for example, Tish, Levy, Tal and Peleg, 2023). Consequently, part of preparedness for future challenges demands more extensive training (either pre- or in-service) on different pedagogical approaches and delivery methods, and on the work with parents. The latter is often merely an add-on, and few colleges and universities offer extensive modules on how to engage with parents. However, this deserves much greater attention, and the support for parents' learning and well-being should become an established strand in early childhood studies.

The COVID-19 pandemic lends itself as a recent example of a crisis, but the comments here apply equally to other disasters that affect whole communities. In addition to planning and preparing for the immediate emergency, attention should also be given to the long-term effects of such events. This raises the question of what type and level of care traumatised or displaced children need. Using the pandemic and the United Kingdom as examples, the recovery envisaged by the government focuses on how educators and teachers could help children make up for lost time in their literacy and numeracy learning and in preparing for standardised tests. However, children's emotional well-being, their experiences of confinement in the home and their fears about further infections are barely discussed or considered in the discourses of recovery. A single action or scheme also seems woefully inadequate, and preparedness to overcome traumatic events requires far more and not simply action after the event. To help children live through and overcome adversity, two prerequisites ought to be in place: Firstly, we need to understand children as active agents in their own lives. Many chapters have drawn a corresponding image of children, for example, in Chapter 17 or in Chapter 20, which demonstrate children's competence and capabilities. Secondly, the early childhood years need a much greater emphasis on children's emotional well-being, not as an afterthought in the curriculum guidance or as a way of facilitating literacy and numeracy learning but as the core tenet of all education and care. Only when children develop a strong sense of self and are able to participate in and be respected by the community around them can they develop the resilience and the capacity to overcome future challenges. At national level this would require a dramatic shift in early childhood guidance and curriculum frameworks. At setting level much change could be brought about by enhancing the ethos in the staff team, by grounding the interactions between children and practitioners in relational pedagogy, and by resisting the overemphasis on assessment and predetermined learning outcomes.

Inclusion of all children and their families for greater social justice

The inclusion issues mentioned in the various chapters are manifold, and we can see that limited access to or exclusion from learning, settings, community or society are present in a wide range of different circumstances. For example, Sharon Skehill in Chapter 13 presents research in relation to leadership for inclusion; in Chapter 16 Mabel Giraldo tackles disaster planning, which often ignores children with special educational needs or disabilities; and Silvia Blanch Gelabert and Gemma París-Romia (Chapter 14) consider inclusion of all children in the nursery room itself. At the same time, there are indications that ECEC practitioners themselves experience a lack of inclusion, evident in the absence of guidance for settings during the pandemic, in their low status and poor pay, or in the discriminatory practice of barring access to teachers' professional training and development programmes in Croatia (see Chapter 7). These are different ways of excluding or discriminating against individual members within a society. More widely many countries are at present also trying to maybe not exclude completely but at least limit considerably the number of migrants and refugees crossing their borders in the hope of a safer life and better economic conditions than those they are exposed to in their home countries. What is perceived as otherness can therefore be directed towards fellow citizens as well as newcomers and may be based, for example, on economic situation, religion, ethnicity, nationality, ability or lifestyle choices. Lack of inclusion and othering invariably lead to high inequality and reduced social justice, which hamper children's development and well-being.

Looking across the many chapters in this book, the attitudes, skills and knowledge of practitioners are a recurring feature when improvements to practice are being discussed. For example, Lewis Stockwell and Michael Young's chapter on the pedagogic creed module in higher education directly aims to help future practitioners to become self-aware and begin to formulate their values in the work with young children. We know that self-efficacy beliefs and self-awareness are indicators for higher quality in the support for children's learning and development (for example, Raymond and Gabriel, 2023). The formation of values and beliefs is intricately linked to how we understand ourselves in relation to others around us. Positioning theory argues that even before we enter into interactions with others, we will already have allocated positions to them and, importantly, to ourselves as well. This process of positioning, the allocation of fluid parts or roles, arises out of personal experiences and narratives, and reflects our beliefs, values and emotions (Harré and Langenhove, 2010). It is often done subconsciously and requires our reflections and self-awareness to surface them. Positioning is not static, and as we interact with others, we may find that they challenge the positionings we had attributed to them. At the same time, we may find that the way we had positioned ourselves does not help us to effectively communicate with others.

What positioning theory emphasises is that our thought processes shape our behaviour and interactions. Consequently, if we want to change how we relate to and are with others, we need to start with shifting our thinking. Engaging in reflective practice, formulating our values, examining our belief systems and trying to understand the consequences of our positionings are therefore the first steps to increased inclusion and equitable access to early childhood learning and development. The mentoring framework suggested in Chapter 8 by Marg Rogers and her colleagues could provide a useful tool to facilitate individual reflection and changes to practice. In addition to individuals examining their thought processes and attitudes, it is also necessary to carry these considerations into teams. For managers and team leaders, there are two aspects to consider. Firstly, there is a need to formulate as a team what the core values and beliefs are that underpin a setting's work. Often mission or value statements are distant phrases which do not bear much weight in day-to-day practice. However, turning intentions and values into lived experience is crucial to ensure consistency of approach and to increase social justice in the nursery community. Secondly, staff members need to be given the time and space to engage in individual reflection and team discussions. In many settings there is still an expectation that training, reflection and team meetings are not part of working hours, and, instead, practitioners are expected to give up family/personal time to take part. This undervalues the importance of developing individual competencies and attitudes as well as setting ethos and pedagogy.

Early childhood practice beyond neoliberal regulatory pressure

Neoliberalism as the guiding concept for governments in their political, economic and social decisions is widespread, especially in westernised developed countries. Its impact on education, and early childhood education and care in particular, is far-reaching: For years the marketisation of the sector has progressed with more and more private providers operating on a for-profit basis. Childcare has become a commodity which is sold to parents with presumed quality based on narrow curricula and predetermined outcomes. For practitioners, neoliberalism means increased accountability and performativity, as well as low pay and inadequate investment in their professional development. Considerations of neoliberal agendas form the backdrop to many of the chapters which are presented here. For example, it is a strong feature in Chapter 10, which highlights social enterprises as one way of tackling the growing inequality in neoliberal contexts. The commodification of ECEC is also an element that Brooke Richardson and Joanne Lehrer investigate in Chapter 3 as part of their exploration of live-streaming in Canadian nurseries.

Peter Moss, together with many other eminent academics and researchers, urges ECEC practitioners to resist and stand up to neoliberal pressures in our sector (Moss, 2017; Vandenbroeck, Lehrer & Mitchell, 2023). They urge practitioners to narrate their lived experiences and develop discourses that provide alternatives to the dominant neoliberal discourse. These ideas of resistance are reflected in many of the chapters above, for example, in the approaches taken at LEYF (Chapter 10) or in the spiritual pedagogy advocated by Liz Rouse (Chapter 22). As already outlined above, one of the foundations of these alternative perspectives is an image of the child, not as an empty vessel to be filled with predetermined knowledge but as a competent agent in their own learning and development.

What is implied here is the need for an understanding of what it means to be an ECEC practitioner that reaches beyond the boundaries of a nursery or kindergarten. Government action (or inaction) has a dramatic impact on young children and ECEC provision, and we need to be mindful of their plans, priorities and intentions. As we can see from many of the chapters in this book, there are already examples of resistance and of finding alternative ways of being and working with young children. As a form of resistance to the dominant neoliberal discourse, these are political actions. The view beyond the boundaries of our early childhood setting also implies having to see and care about, for and with the families and communities the children live in. This may take the form of material support, for example, many schools in England have been providing food parcels and clothing to families facing financial hardship. In addition to knowing individual families, we also have to get to know the local communities, their concerns and their strengths. This will broaden our understanding of children's lived experiences outside their ECEC setting. If we are committed to caring for the holistic child, we cannot ignore the world beyond the nursery gate. Quite the opposite, we should take a role in community matters and advocate for children and their families at local and national level. This could mean engaging with local planning applications to help shape the environment children live in (which Mehmet Mart outlines as crucial in

Chapter 19) or getting involved in consultations for new curriculum guidance, ensuring that parents' voices are heard alongside those of other community members and stakeholder (as in Chapter 11).

The political stance envisaged here is not a party political one (although it would be useful to have more understanding of and knowledge about children and families in political parties and in national governments). What is required more than anything, and by more people, is what Kamenarac (2023) calls 'minor politics', small actions we can take in local matters and in our immediate context. Others describe this as local activism, which will strengthen democratic engagement (for example, Roberts-Holmes & Moss, 2021; Chomsky, 2021). The common theme is the willingness to stand up for what is right, serves the best interest of children and supports families in their communities. Over time small actions will add up to greater changes and eventually lead to a paradigm shift away from neoliberalism. Importantly our actions and engagement should reach beyond the field of education and address family support, medical and mental health services (which are under threat in many communities), adult learning, benefits and employment advice, community services, transport links and much more. As Bronfenbrenner's bio-ecological theory indicates, for the child to flourish, we need to think about and reach across the boundaries of his model's spheres of influence (Bronfenbrenner, 2005).

Creating sustainable practice in a posthuman, post-Anthropocene world

The fourth theme running through the book relates to much wider issues than just early childhood education; it is concerned with the position of humans in the world as a whole and our prospects for long-term survival on our planet. The impact human beings have had and are having is devastating. Immediate action is required to lessen and, if possible, reverse the damage we are doing for our own well-being and that of more-than-human beings (see United Nations Framework Convention on Climate Change, 2023). Some of the chapters in this book encourage us to pay more attention to our entanglements with materials and more-than-humans, which play a central role in children's learning and development (for example, Chapter 20 by Sally Brown or Chapter 19 by Mehment Mart). Economic and environmental sustainability also feature in Section 3 on workforce and management. As mentioned above, the matters raised here clearly go beyond the boundaries of individual ECEC settings, and they interlink with the call for self-awareness and reflection outlined in the first part of this chapter. What these issues point to is our responsibility as citizens. As citizens in our local communities and nations, we have a responsibility to model and uphold respect for all forms of life, social justice, equity of access to education and other values as outlined in the Universal Declaration of Human Rights (United Nations, 1948). However, we are also

Towards a better future **259**

global citizens, benefitting from natural and man-made resources from well beyond our national boundaries (just think of the food that crosses oceans every day to feed us or the minerals and rare metals required to manufacture our mobile phones). Consequently, we have a responsibility that reaches across national borders, especially bearing in mind the historic role many European countries played in the exploitation of African, Australian, Asian and South American peoples and societies. At the same time, it is very obvious now that the impact of industrialisation and excessive use of natural resources contributes to global warming, that is to say, the warming of the climate around the world, not just in our respective home countries.

Addressing such global threats requires action at many levels. For us as individuals, it may mean traveling less to reduce our carbon footprint, diligently separating recyclables or repairing equipment rather than buying new. At national level, our governments need to press ahead with policies promoting renewable energy and reducing the use of cars. As ECEC practitioners and teachers, we also have a responsibility towards young children and their futures. In the first instance, this means modelling responsible behaviour and ensuring environmental sustainability in our settings. However, there seems to be much more to do than just worry about the here and now, and we have to reflect on the basic question of 'What is education for?'

Education may be understood to mean the transfer of knowledge from teacher to child, from one generation to the next. However, we need to question if this prepares young children appropriately for the challenges they will encounter in their lives. As a society and as human beings, we cannot know yet what we will need to know in 20- or 30-years' time. Teaching knowledge as such is therefore not going to be very effective. We need to think about and commit to an approach to education that fosters children's confidence and their curiosity, their ability to problem-solve and be creative, their belief in themselves as competent and confident agents who matter and can make a difference in their own and their communities' lives. We also need to instil in them a sense of responsibility to other humans and to more-than-humans based in the ethics of care and the principles of social democracy. This moves us closer to educating citizens for a precarious present and for an uncertain future.

One vision or many visions?

Throughout the book you have encountered chapters from many different countries with examples of resistance to dominant practice, of ways how we could do things differently and how we could prepare more effectively for the challenges of the future. This final chapter has outlined some of the areas in which action is needed, starting with a focus on our own thoughts, attitudes and beliefs as individuals, professionals and citizens. Beyond the self, action and change is needed in settings, including work practices and pedagogies, and our sphere of influence and engagement has to reach beyond the boundaries of our nurseries and preschools to connect with and influence local communities and national governments. Lastly, there is the need to accept responsibility as global citizens and implement practices, actions and principles that sustain all human and more-than-human life.

I hope the many ideas and examples presented in this book have encouraged and motivated you to reflect on <u>your</u> approach to practice, <u>your</u> identity as a practitioner working with or for young children, and <u>your</u> vision for meaningful practice and effective support for learning and development in early childhood. The emphasis on 'your' approach, identity and vision is fundamental in this respect, because here, as in the support for children's learning and development, one size cannot fit all. To plan effective and meaningful changes and actions will only be possible if you bear in mind the cultural and societal context you live in (Lehrer et al., 2023). Histories, traditions and expectations are as varied as peoples and communities, and although these should not be followed blindly, how and what you question and want to reshape will be situated in your local context. This context will indicate what is required now, what can be addressed in a month's time or next year, and what is achievable at personal, professional and societal level. I would therefore hold that the early childhood sector does not require one new vision for the future but many visions grounded in local communities reflecting a range of different values, beliefs and attitudes with the common themes of human rights, social justice and environmental, social and economic sustainability.

Such localised action does not, and cannot, happen in isolation, and you should think about change as collective action. As Poppie Ephgrave highlights in Chapter 21, dialogue is crucial, and support for your change agenda could come from a wide range of different sources: the colleagues in your own nursery or from a network of settings in your neighbourhood; the parents and families you meet daily; community leaders in your neighbourhood; existing networks of early childhood practitioners or researchers (like the European Early Childhood Education Research Association or L' Organisation Mondiale pour L'Education Pre-Scolaire); academics, that is to say, authors, lecturers and fellow students; or informal online communities of practice; to name but a few. Sustaining your resolve and motivation for change will be easier if you reach out and develop a network of support with like-minded people. At the same time, planning what is achievable and how to implement change will benefit from different perspectives and experiences. It is not going to be easy to affect change to systems and practices that are engrained, but this should not stop you from making a start. Once you understand what is necessary and what we owe our children and our planet, it will be impossible to sit still. Peter Moss already said in 2010 that we can't carry on as we are. I would like to add, we cannot sit and wait for others to initiate the changes we need to see in early childhood education and care. We need to – and we can – bring about change ourselves!

References

Bronfenbrenner, U (2005). *Making Human Beings Human: Bioecological Perspectives on Human Development.* SAGE Publications.

Chomsky, N (2021). *The Precipice.* Great Britain: Penguin Books

Harré, R, & Van Langenhove, L (2010). 'Varieties of positioning.' In *People and Societies*, Van Langenhove, L. (ed). New York, NY: Routledge.

Kamenarac, O (2023, September 1). *EC Teacher activism, 'minor politics' and refusal of neoliberal discourses. European Early Childhood Education Research Conference*, Cascais, Portugal, August 30–September 2.

Lehrer, J, Hadley, F, Rouse, L, Van Laere, K, Blanch Gelabert, S, & Ward, U (2023). 'Conclusions: A conversation about insights related to democratic relationships with families.' In *Relationships with Families in Early Childhood Education and Care*, Lehrer, J., Hadley, F., Van Laere, K. & Rouse, L. (eds). Abingdon: Routledge, pp. 185–194.

Moss, P (2017). Power and resistance in early childhood education: From dominant discourse to democratic experimentalism. *Journal of Pedagogy, 8*(1), 11–32.

Moss, P (2010). We cannot continue as we are: The educator in an education for survival. *Contemporary Issues in Early Childhood, 11*(1), 8–19. https://doi.org/10.2304/ciec.2010.11.1.8

Raymond, S, & Gabriel, F (2023). An ecological framework for early years teacher self-efficacy development. *Teaching and Teacher Education.* 132. https://doi.org/10.1016/j.tate.2023.104252

Redecker, G, & Punie, Y (2017). *European Framework for the Digital Competence of Educators (DigCompEdu).* Luxembourg: Publications Office of the European Union. Retrieved from: https://joint-research-centre.ec.europa.eu/digcompedu_en

Roberts-Holmes, G, & Moss, P (2021). *Neoliberalism and Early Childhood Education: markets, imaginaries and governance.* Abingdon: Routledge.

Tish, S, Levy, I, Tal, P, & Peleg, A (2023). Parent-pre-school teacher relations during the COVID-19 pandemic – Promoters and undermining factors. *Pedagogical Research, 8*(1), em0149. https://doi.org/10.29333/pr/12724

United Nations Framework Convention on Climate Change (2023). *COP28UEA Declaration on Climate and Health.* Retrieved from: https://www.cop28.com/en/about-cop28

United Nations (1948). *Universal Declaration of Human Rights.* Retrieved from: https://www.un.org/en/about-us/universal-declaration-of-human-rights

Vandenbroeck, M, Lehrer, J, & Mitchell, L (2023). *The Decommodification of Early Childhood Education and Care: Resisting Neoliberalism.* London: Routledge.

INDEX

Pages in *italics* refer to figures and pages in **bold** refer to tables.

Aboriginal peoples 110, **111**, 113–114, **115**, 116
accountability 71, 77; professional 58–59, 64
activism 230, 258; citizen 55
advocates 74, **76**, 77, 80
aesthetics, relational 146
agency 218, 220, 238; children's 22, 119, 183; child's 204; for early childhood educators 20, 22, 238; enacted 218; more-than-human 211
agent 259; active 78, 254–255
agentic child 131
Aistear, the early childhood curriculum framework in Ireland 131
analysis, thematic 73
Anthropocene 199; post 258–259
Aphantasia 160
apps 39, 219; use of 27
Aristotle 89, 91, 246
art: and education 141–142; inclusion and 141–142
artificial intelligence (AI) 2, 10, 26–27, 31–36
artistic experiences 142–148, 154–155
artistic languages 147–148, 151–152, 155
artist in residence 148–154
assemblages 217–218, 227; of desire *217*
assessment 30, 35, 91–92, 112, 116, 118–119

autonomy: children's 145, 177; professional 21, 53, 80

balancer 74, **75**, 77, 80
banking concept 235–236, 238
Barad, K 200
being and becoming 87, 216, *217*, 220, 227; belonging 108
bio-ecological theory 203–204, 206, 258
Blåfugl 143, 145
bodymindmatter 217, *217*
Bourdieu, P 184
Bronfenbrenner, U 203–204, 208–209, 238
Bruner, J 243

capital, human 241–242, 244–245
changemakers 74, **76**, 77, 80
childcare 96–97, 257; Canadian 13–14, 16–17, 21–22
children: with disabilities 169–178; as future economic citizens 241–242; here and now 246, 248–249; raising 39–48, 126; as saviours 242, 248
Children Read to their Parents 182–194
child voice 131–134, 175, 236, 238
Chomsky, N 4, 55
citizen 258; future economic 241–242; global 259–260

co-creation 141, 148, 152–153
Cole, P 232–233
colonisation 231–232
commodification, of care 21
commodity 21; daycare as 17, 96
communication 133–134
community: learning 59–61, 65, 235, 239; of practice 54, 72, 78, 88, 105, 260
competence: digital 26–36, 61; pedagogical 29–30, 35; professional 29, 35, 57
consumerism 40, 71
continuous professional development (CPD) 57–58, 129–131; professional identity and 135–136
creativity 146, 148–155, 159, 161, 163, 207
critical thinking 91, *150*, 150–152, 236, 238
cultural density 206
curiosity 166
curriculum: early years 163–164; emergent 132, 227; play-based 132; *see also* play-based learning; push-down 241; spiral *100*

Dasein 130, 135, 137
Dearden, R F 90–91
Dewey, J 86–88
dialogue 230–239; Socratic 83–85
diffraction 219–220, 226
diffractive analysis 220
digital: competence 26–36, 61; migrants 39, 47; natives 39, 47; resources 30, 35; technology 26, 39–41, 45–47
digitalisation 9, 27, 36
digitality 27, 30, 32, **33**
disability inclusion xi, 173, 176
disadvantaged background, children from 95–98, 104, 106
disaster 169; impact of 169–172; management 174–177; risk reduction (DRR) 173–174
desirings 217–218
diversity 87, **111**, 114, **115**; inclusion and 118, 125–126; and multiculturalism 231
drivers 74, **75**, 77, 80
Dweck, C 104

The Early Years Foundation Stage (England) (EYFS) 98, 163, 233, 235
Early Years Framework for Australia (EYLF) 108–119

ecosystem 206–209
education: art and 141–142; of freedom 230, 238; as social responsibility 109; transformative 88, 155
educational process 207
emotional well-being 185, 254–255
empowering: educators 132; learners 30, 35–36, 132, 135
empowerment 83–84, 99, 103–104, 146, 155
engagement: family 109, 133–134; in nature *205*; parental 42; *see also* parents; professional 64–65; stakeholder 109
entanglement 216–220, *217*, 227; diffractive **220**
environment: enabling *100*; impact of 204–207, 211–212; *see also* learning
environmental practices 205
Erasmus+ 'I'm not a robot' 26, 31, **33**, 35
espais c 148–155
eudaimonia 246
The European Framework for the Digital Competence of Educators 26–36, 61
experience: within dialogue 235–238; lived 21–22, 55, 89, 127, 130, 133, 256–257

families 2–3, 20, 22, 46, 77, 97, 102, 104, **115**, 125, 133, 143, 145, 184, 237, 255, 257–258; as experts 117; involving 108–119; perspectives 117
Feminist Care Ethics (FCE) 15
feminist critical discourse analysis (FCDA) 16
Feminist Political Economy (FPE) 15
flourish 99, 131, 162, 166, 242
flourishing 90, 246
focus group 61–62
Framework for Learning and Development *136*, 136–137
Freire, P 85, 92, 101, 105, 230–239
Froebel, F 243–244, 248

gardening **220**, 223–226, **225**
Goleman, D 161, 164
Gopnik, A 126
governance structure 97, 102

Heidegger, M 130–131, 133
hooks, b 151, 230–239
human rights-based approach 172–173
Hume, D 158

264 Index

identity: democratic 86; educator 72–73; *see also* professional identity; electronic 59, 63, 66; sense of **111**, 243

imagination 153–154, 157–166, 248; and the early years curriculum 163–164; and neuroscience 159–161; pedagogy of 165–166

imaginative thinking 158–159, 161–162, 164–166

inclusion 3–4, 87, 100, 129–137, 255–256; of all children 125, 255–256; and art 141–142; coordinator 130, 135; and diversity 118; of persons with disabilities 173; *see also* disability inclusion

inclusive culture 131–132

inclusive education 133, 136, 141

inclusive practices 130, 133–134; lead 135–136

inclusivity 140, 148

inequality 64, 141, 255, 257

instrumentalisation 43

intelligence, emotional 158, 161, 164–165; *see also* artificial intelligence

Interstice, Encounters between Artists, Children and Educators 141–148

intra-action *217*, 218, 220–222, **222**, 224, 226–227

intra-activity 217–218, 220

iPad **225**, 226

I-Thou relation 247

Kant, I 158

Katz, L G 72

knowledge creator 74, **75**, 77, 80

labour: care 16, 22; domestic 64; emotional 53; social reproductive 15–16

language: Aboriginal 232–233; within dialogue 231–235; dominant 232–233; English as an additional 234–235

Lave, J 72, 105; *see also* community of practice

leaders 74, **75**–76, 80, 232; social 102–105

leadership 78, 99; for inclusion 129–137; revolutionary 232; social 102–105, *103*

learning: child-driven 211; child-led 209, 238; environment 89, 98, 132, 147, 152, 211; nature as key to 206–209; observational 206; play-based 90–91, 118–119; *see also* play-based curriculum; roles in 209–211; virtual 59–60, **62**

Lego 218, **220**, 221–223, **222**

lifeworld 31, 35; approach 28; of educators 135

literacy 182–185, 188–189, 216–218, 220, 224; digital 31, 34–35; learning 182–183, 185–186, 193, 216–218, 220, 227–228; nomadic 216; program implementation 186–188, *187*, *189*

London Early Years Foundation (LEYF) 95–106

Lundy, L 131–133

making change happen (LEYF model) *106*

managerialism 4, 70–72

van Manen, M 245–246, 248

market 15–16, 22; mixed model 95–96, 105; *see also* commodity

material-discursive: intra-actions 218–219, 227; practices 216, 218, 220; tools 223; world 227

materialities 216, 219

Mental Synthesis Theory 159–160

Mezirow, J 88–89, 91

mind/body dichotomy 216

mixed methods approach 73, 109

moral: action 89; *see also* phronesis; dispositions 89; education 99; goods 89; purposes 91; responsibility 248; values 90, 242

more-than-human 211, 216, 218, 227, 258–259; *see also* non-human

Moss, P 4, 200, 257, 260

Murris, K 200, 217–219

nature-based: pedagogy 204; school *210*

neoliberal 95–96, 125; framework 71; principles 125; regulatory gaze 256–258

neoliberalism 4, 70–73, 106, 109–200; in ECEC 72

nexus analysis 219

Noddings, N 243, 245–247

non-human/nonhuman 4, 209, 217–218, 220, 227, 243, 246, 248–249; *see also* more-than-human

normative gaze 46

oppression 230–231, 233–234
optimists 74, 76–77, 77, 80

parent-child, relationship 43, 46–47
parenting 42–44; *see also* raising children; culture 43; digital 45–46
parents: engagement with 133–134; as expert 43, 48; involvement 133, 182–184, *189*; partnership with 98, 134; relationships with 133; as representatives of culture 44–45; support for 54, 254
partnership **111**, 112, 117–118; family-educator 117; *see also* parents
pedagogical relation 246–247
pedagogical relationship 245
pedagogical work, digital competencies in 31–32
pedagogic approach xxi–xxii
pedagogic creed 83–93
pedagogy: of co-creation 141; of imagination 165–166; nature-based 204; relational 131, 133, 255; social 99–104, *100*; for social justice 96, 98–101; spiritual 241–249
peer learning methodology 142–148, *144*
peer mentoring 78–79
performativity 4, 71–72, 90, 257
phenomenology 127, 129–130; hermeneutic 129–130
philosophy of education 85–86
phronesis 89–90
Plato 158, 160
play **33**, 35, 40–41, 116, 132, 162, 207, 218, 220–222, 227, 248–249, 258; learning through 112, 147; right to play 177
play-based: curriculum 132; education 90–91; learning 9, 112, 118–119, 204, 211
playfulness 177, 247–248
politicisation 43
positioning theory 256
possibility thinking 165
posthumanism 199–200, *217*, 218; in early literacy learning 216–218; perspective 216–218, 258–259
posthuman/ist: approach 205, 211; lens 200; perspective 212; thinking 200, 211
practical wisdom 89
praxis xx–xxii, 230, 232, 235
praxeological intentions xxii–xxiii

preservationist pedagogical approach 28
professional development 57–66, 78, 103; virtual 59–61, 65; *see also* continuous professional development
professional engagement 36
professional identity 70–80; and the CPD experience 135–136
psychologisation 43

quality 21–22, 70–72, 96, 106, 133, 135–136, 142, 241; high 99, 102–103, 106, 141; webcams as markers of 18

raising children, as an intergenerational relationship 44–45; *see also* parenting
reflective practice 61, 99, 256
relationality 245
relationships 98–99, *100*, 102, **111**, 112, **115**, 117, 119, 133, 245; creative 150, 155; with families 20; with materials 218, 228; with parents 133; social 207–208
resistance 20, *28*, 77, 257, 259; to the dominant neoliberal discourse 257
responsibility: educators' ethical and moral 248; parental 48
right to play 177
robotics 27, **33**, 34, 36

schoolification 18, 126, 254
scientisation 43
self 245, 248–249; phenomenon of 243–245; sense of 241–243, 248
self-awareness 161, 164, 256, 258
self-confidence: children's 190; educators' 72
self-efficacy 60, 190, 193, 256
selfhood 243
Sendai Framework 173, 176
shared-world positions 208
Siraj-Blatchford, I 164
social change 99, 230–231, 235–236
social enterprise 96–98, 101–106
social integration 99, 165
social justice 3, 98–101, 199–200, 230–231, 237, 239, 255–256
social media; *see also* digital; digitalisation; risks related to 40–41
social purpose 96–97, 99, 103–104
spiritual: development 244–246; education 244; nurturing the 244–245; *see also* pedagogy

266 Index

spirituality **115**, 244–245, 247
surveillance 13, 16, 21; video 16
sustainability 96–97, 101–102, 106, **115**, 209, 259–260; economic 54, 102, 258; environmental 55, 102, 258–259; social 102
sustainable practice 258–259
sustained shared thinking 164

teachers 104, 134, 142–143, 185, *189*, 232, 236, 238, 245; development 57–66; ECE 59–61; role of 234, 236; Selfie for 30; training 143–147, 155; *see also* educator
teaching: experiential approach to 210; and learning 30, 35–36, 87–88, 163
thematic universe 236
theory of mind 161, 164
Torres Strait Islander people 110, **111**, 113–114, **115**, 116
transition, to primary school 134–135
Tronto, J 10, 15
trust 20, 22; building 20

United Nations Convention on the Rights of the Child (UNCRC) 131–132, 142, 173
United Nations Convention on the Rights of the Persons with Disability (CRPD) 173, 175, 177

values 92, 99, 104, **111**, 199–200, 256; and beliefs 91–92, 131, 256; moral or social 242
The Verona Charter on the Rescue of Persons with Disabilities in Case of Disaster 173
video, live stream 13–23
virtue ethics 85, 89

well-being 2–3, 99, 254, 258; children's 58, 66, 79, 101, **116**, 126, 131, 255; *see also* emotional well-being; professional 66, 70, 80
Wenger, E 72, 105; *see also* community of practice

Printed in the United States
by Baker & Taylor Publisher Services